SUPERMAN GODFALL

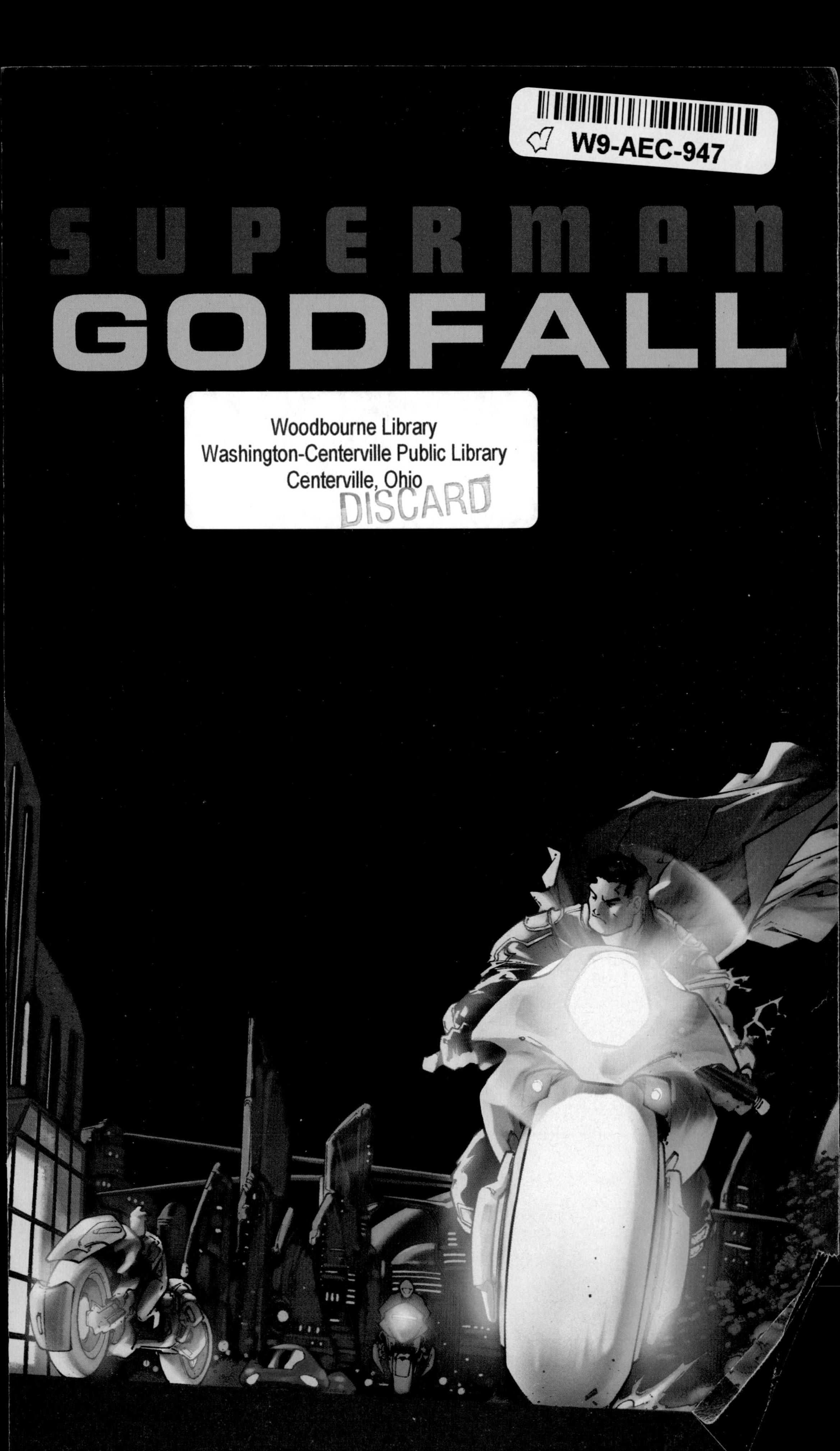

SUPE GOD

Michael Turner & Joe Kelly
WRITERS

Talent Caldwell
PENCILLER

Jason Gorder
INKER

Peter Steigerwald
with **Grafiksismik & Christina Strain**
COLORISTS

Comicraft
LETTERER

Michael Turner
ORIGINAL SERIES COVERS

SUPERMAN CREATED BY
Jerry Siegel & Joe Shuster

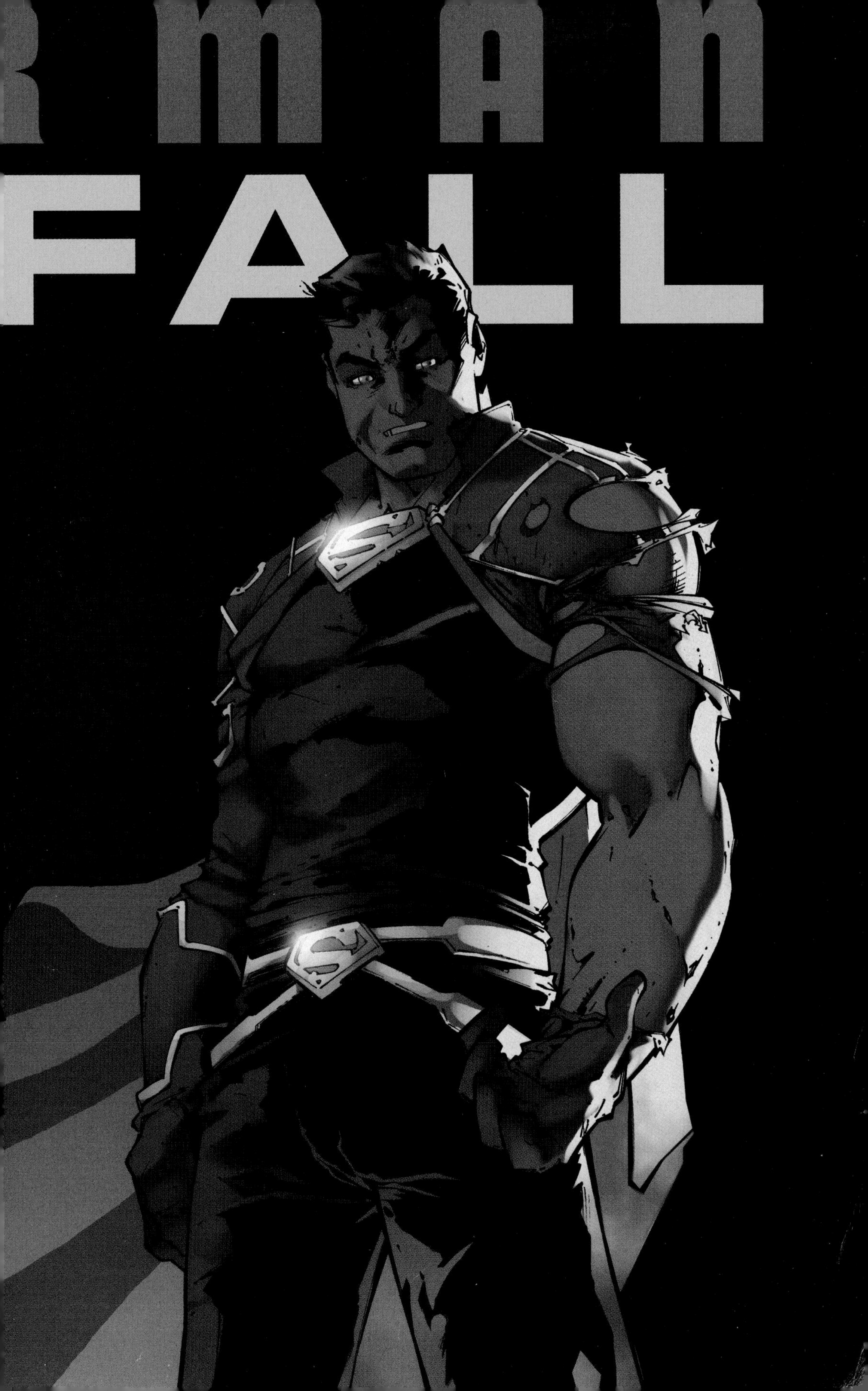
FALL

FOREWORD

Skip this foreword...

Especially if this is your first time reading *Godfall*. As they say in the digital realms, "Here there be SPOILERS." You might also consider passing this up if writers waxing on about their own work or superstar collaborators gives you the hives. Instead, go. Read the story. Rock on with your bad self...I'll be here when you change your mind. Then, for your "behind the scenes" pleasure, I'll reveal to you the three "*secret origins*" of *Godfall*...(And they say comics can't compete with DVD's—Feh!)

This is how it started:

After four years on ACTION COMICS, it was time for me to say adios to Metropolis. With #810 complete, I called Eddie to reminisce and, of course, scare up more work. "Hey, Eddie! Sure has been fun, hasn't it? Four years of Truth, Justice, and Stuff! Good times...Good times. SO, what do you want to do next?"

A pause.

"How about six issues of Superman? With the Aspen Guys."

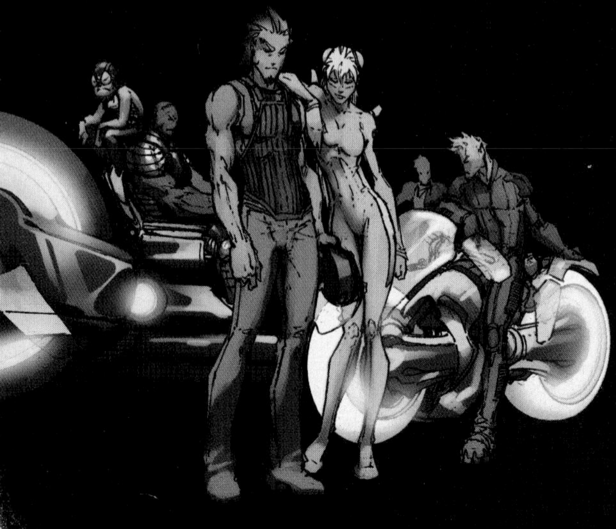

I'm not sure that you *can* go home again (did I even get a chance to *leave*?), but you can have a hell of a time visiting, especially if you're with someone who's never been there before. Enter the Aspen artisans: Mike Turner, Talent Caldwell, Jason Gorder, Peter Steigerwald, Christina Strain, and their secret weapon/baby-faced whip-cracker, Frank Mastromauro; and with them, an opportunity to explore a sleek, modern take on Superman. Twist my arm, why don't you.

This is how it started:

"I want to see Superman on a BIKE. You know, like a cool Akira motorcycle..."

When Mike Turner gets excited, it's hard not to share his enthusiasm. A giant-sized kid in a candy store, you can't help but feel the buzz when he gets that look in his eye and tears into story...but Superman on a *bike*? ("You will believe a man can ride a motorcycle!") There were elements of *Godfall* that Mike and I inherited when we signed on, but Motorcross 8000 wasn't one of them. The obvious question was...why the hell NOT?

Part of the fun of co-writing with Mike came from the fact that, until this story, there was nary a spit curl nor an "up, up, and away" in his body of work. In fact, everyone at Aspen looked at Superman with fresh eyes; excited to have the opportunity to play with the Man of Steel and respectful of the character, but untainted by preconceptions about the franchise. Why can't he ride a cool bike? Why can't Kandor be an island instead of just a city? It was a liberating and infectious vibe that ran not only through the story construction, but Talent and Jason's art style, and Peter and Christina's mind-blowing colors as well.

This is how it started:

With a short sequence that you will *not* read in the pages of Godfall, a few bits of dialogue that ended up on the editorial "cutting room floor..."

Superman's memory has returned. His world is twisted inside out and he's explaining to Basqat and the bikers what happened and how he arrived in Kandor:

"I had just barely survived the fight of my life..." In flashback, a still-smoking Superman complete with requisite torn cape lumbers into the Fortress of Solitude, exhausted, but safe. "Before I could even catch a breath, I heard the alarm. Distress signal from Kandor." (In this version, we didn't try to bind Superman's detour into Kandor to any specific event in recent continuity, but that changed later...)

"I was exhausted, pushed to the limits... but I looked down at the bottle and thought..." With a melancholy smirk, Superman shrugs, "It's only Kandor. How bad can it be?"

"It's only Kandor."

Kandor first appeared in ACTION COMICS #242, published in July of 1958; also the first appearance of Brainiac, both created by Otto Binder and Al Plastino. While Brainiac has continued to play prominently in Superman's adventures, Kandor has primarily enjoyed that kindly place of nostalgia where the Fortress's Giant Key, Krypto, and plaid Kryptonite are kept.

Naturally, that means I'm genetically programmed to love Kandor.

I never thought that Kandor was stupid. Not as a kid, not as a teenager who knew there was a guy named Gulliver and that he Traveled. An entire civilization — the LAST of its kind, kept in a GLASS BOTTLE at the whim of anyone who happens by it?! Kandor not only struck me as cool, but also a place of great danger. To enter Kandor is to sacrifice size, power, and perspective. (I don't care how strong you are, an inch high is an inch high!) Shatter the dome, and sheets of alien sky crack and rain death. Shove it hard enough, and an earthquake devastates the city. Drop it, and a world dies screaming.

Forget about Kandor... And what happens to it then?

Alien prejudice. Fascism. Zealotry. The Deification of Superman... and his fall from grace.

"It's only Kandor"? Not anymore.

JOE KELLY
APRIL 2004

Faster than a speeding bullet,

more powerful than a locomotive, able to leap the tallest buildings with a single bound… **Superman** is known to all as the world's greatest super-hero. While he has faced many challenges that have tested his heroic abilities, the Man of Steel now finds himself in a situation that has its roots in several of his past adventures…

When Superman arrived on Earth, he was just the infant **Kal-El**, rocketed from his doomed birth world of Krypton by his parents **Jor-El** and **Lara**. His spacecraft was discovered by **Jonathan** and **Martha Kent** when it crashed near their farm in Smallville, Kansas. They raised him as **Clark Kent**, and instilled in him wholesome values. As he matured, Clark discovered that Earth's yellow sun gave him strange and unique abilities like flight, heat vision and superhuman strength. Clark adopted the guise of Superman and swore to use his powers to battle for truth, justice and the American Way.

While he is human in many respects, Kal-El still holds several reminders of his alien birth world near to his heart. Many of these artifacts are kept at his **Fortress of Solitude**, a sanctuary hidden inside an interdimensional tesseract in the icy regions of Antarctica. This home away from home contains many strange and unusual items: a holographic memorial of Krypton and Kal-El's birth parents; the bottle city of **Kandor**, a miniaturized land populated by many alien races; and the Fortress's robotic caretaker **Kelex**, among others.

Although he is a protector of all mankind, Superman calls **Metropolis** home. A sprawling city teeming with skyscrapers and bustling with activity, Metropolis is known to many as the City of Tomorrow. Unfortunately, that description became even more fitting thanks to the machinations of **Brainiac 13**, a robotic version of Superman's nemesis downloaded to our reality from a distant future. At the dawn of the new millennium, B13 infected Metropolis with a nanotechnological virus that upgraded the machinery and architecture in the city to an amazing and sometimes dangerous level.

Superman was able to stop Brainiac's plans to make the world over in his mechanical image before the virus could spread outside of Metropolis, but he didn't realize the extent of B13's plans. The techno-makeover also transformed Earth into an outpost in our timestream against the entropic celestial force known as **Imperiex**. A being of unimaginable power, Imperiex's sole purpose was to destroy the universe so that it could be started again. Many worlds fell in the path of Imperiex. Earth became the final beachhead against his demolition, and Superman took the role of leader of a myriad of alien forces. When Superman was on the verge of defeating Imperiex, Brainiac 13 returned, hoping to rekindle his plans to remake the universe in his image. That hope was shattered, as Superman sent both Imperiex and B13 through an Apokoliptian boom tube back to the instant of the Big Bang, effectively spreading out both forces through the timestream.

Some time later, Superman found himself manipulated by the enigmatic **Futuresmiths**, cloaked beings who used Metropolis's tech to change the course of time. In an effort to confuse and distract the Man of Steel from their true plans, they engineered many events, including the creation of **Cir-El** – a new Supergirl who claimed to be Superman's daughter – and a robotic Superman from a farflung future who warned of an impending technological doom thanks to the Futuresmiths.

This **Robot Superman** took Kal-El into the timestream itself to witness how his actions in the present were all planned to bring about the Futuresmiths and unleash a deadly nanotech virus upon humankind. Finally, thousands of years in the future, Superman confronted the Futuresmiths, who were revealed to be merely servants of another consciousness: Brainiac 12. This iteration of the green-skinned despot used Cir-El to take hold in the present (disguised as the one thing Superman would not attack: his offspring) and ensure a world overrun by machines that would give rise to an even more powerful Brainiac 13. Locked in a struggle with Brainiac 12, Superman tumbled into the timestream, where he left his foe trapped inside a temporal anomaly, imprisoned in a sort of phantom zone. This act of heroism left Superman adrift through time, tumbling through a multitude of possible realities until he arrived on a Krypton that was never destroyed, and where Jor-El and Lara never sent him to Earth...or so it seems...

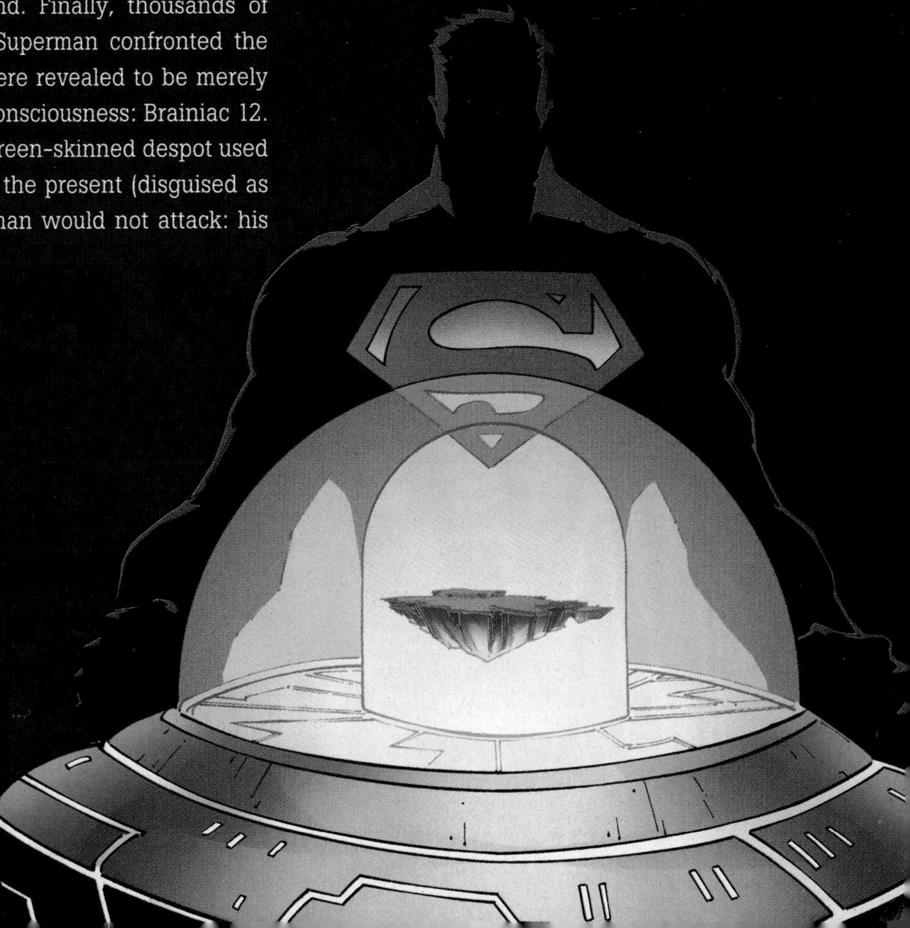

CAST OF CHARACTERS

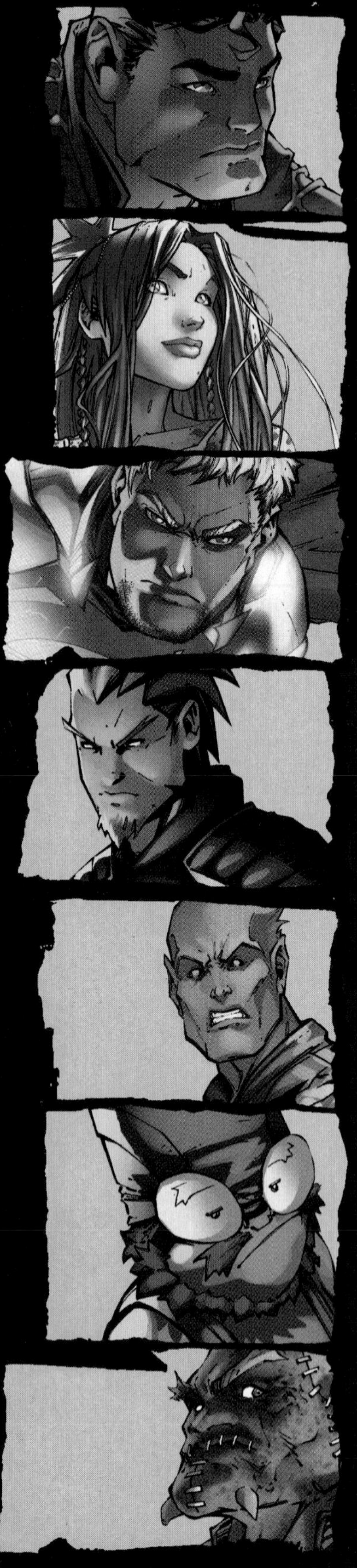

KAL-EL Life on Krypton sometimes isn't easy for Kal-El. His late father Jor-El was renowned for his many scientific achievements, the greatest of which was the Terraforge, a construct that reaches into the heart of Krypton itself to stabilize the planet and prevent its demise. With all this prestige bestowed upon the House of El, Kal often finds it hard to live up to the people's expectations in his job as Undersecretary of the Kryptonian Council. Despite his moments of self-doubt, Kal leads a mundane yet happy existence on Krypton with his wife Lyla. But he sometimes can't help thinking there's something more to his simple life...

LYLA Beautiful bride of Kal-El, Lyla works at the Terraforge helping to control the planetwide quakes that once threatened to tear Krypton apart. Her striking looks hide a deep devotion to her faith in a greater power. Kal-El and Lyla live comfortably, despite the fact that she's an alien, not the most desirable of social standings on Krypton.

PREUS As Sergeant of the Citizens Patrol Corps (CPC), Preus is sworn to protect the people of Krypton at all costs. Just about every kid on Krypton wants to join the CPC, but Preus doesn't care about the fame and glory: his single-minded passion is to uphold all of the laws of the land, including those that restrict and punish the alien population. That's the one part of his job he might take too much pride in...

BASQAT Leader of Krypton's gang of guerrilla bikers, Basqat is a man of ideals, chief among them freedom and equal rights for the alien population of Krypton. He's assembled a group of other non-Ks to fight for what he believes in, no matter the cost.

SHIRE As second-in-command to Basqat, Shire is the backbone that keeps the gang together. A skilled and agile speedbiker, Shire holds fast to his ideals, even though he might not always agree with his leader.

MAMOTH The diminutive Mamoth rides sidecar to Jigsaw, and is a scrappy, cantankerous runt. He might spout nonsense, but Mamoth will fight for his freedom with his last breath, just like the rest of the gang. An excellent mechanic, Mamoth is also in charge of keeping the gang's bikes in working order.

JIGSAW He's the mute muscle of Basqat's gang of speedbikers and best friend of Mamoth, a hulking beast of a man who takes command of whatever road he's on. Jigsaw's weapon of choice is his energy-whip, though he could just as easily take out his opponents with his bare hands.

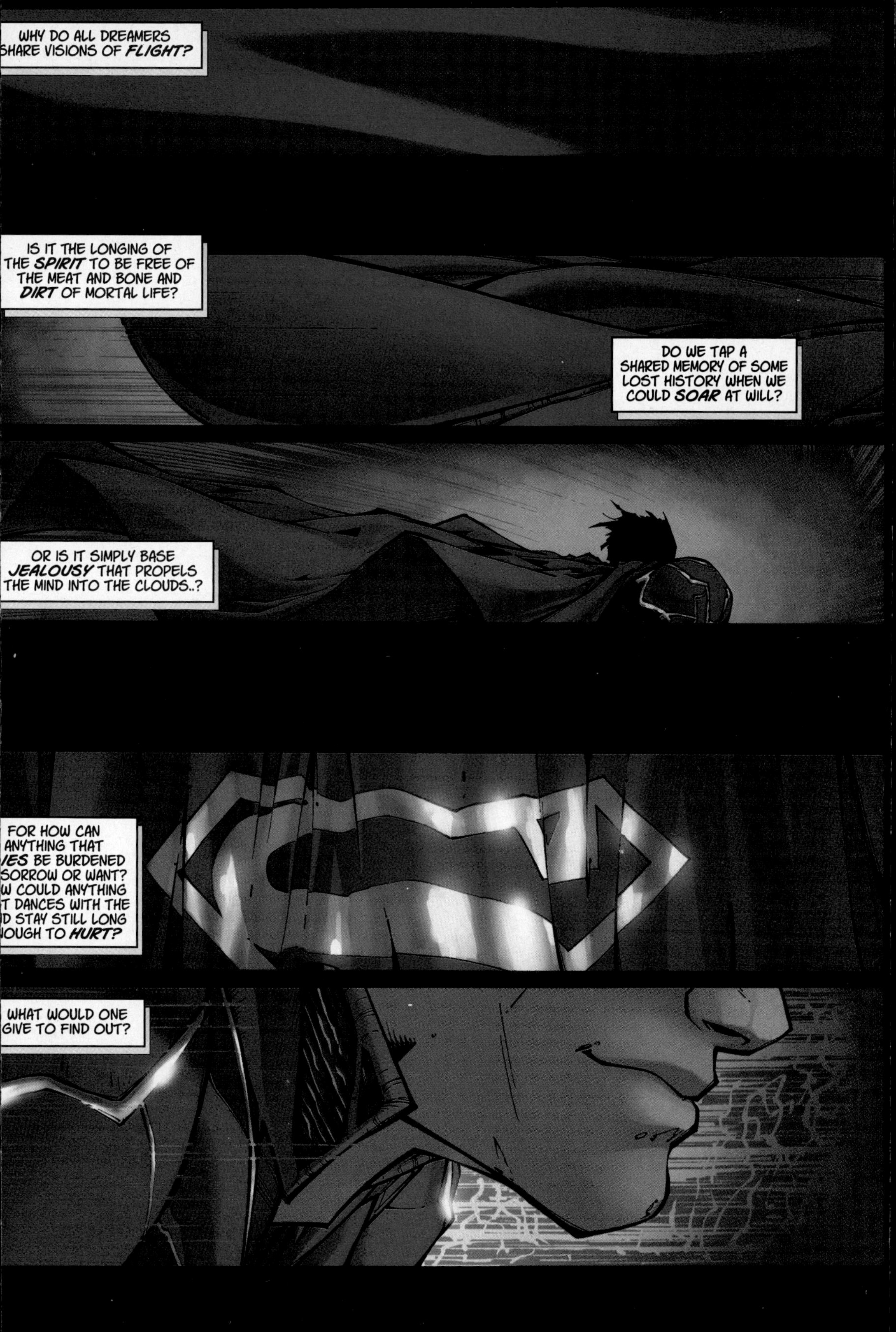
WHY DO ALL DREAMERS SHARE VISIONS OF FLIGHT?
IS IT THE LONGING OF THE SPIRIT TO BE FREE OF THE MEAT AND BONE AND DIRT OF MORTAL LIFE?
DO WE TAP A SHARED MEMORY OF SOME LOST HISTORY WHEN WE COULD SOAR AT WILL?
OR IS IT SIMPLY BASE JEALOUSY THAT PROPELS THE MIND INTO THE CLOUDS..?
FOR HOW CAN ANYTHING THAT IES BE BURDENED SORROW OR WANT? W COULD ANYTHING T DANCES WITH THE D STAY STILL LONG NOUGH TO HURT?
WHAT WOULD ONE GIVE TO FIND OUT?

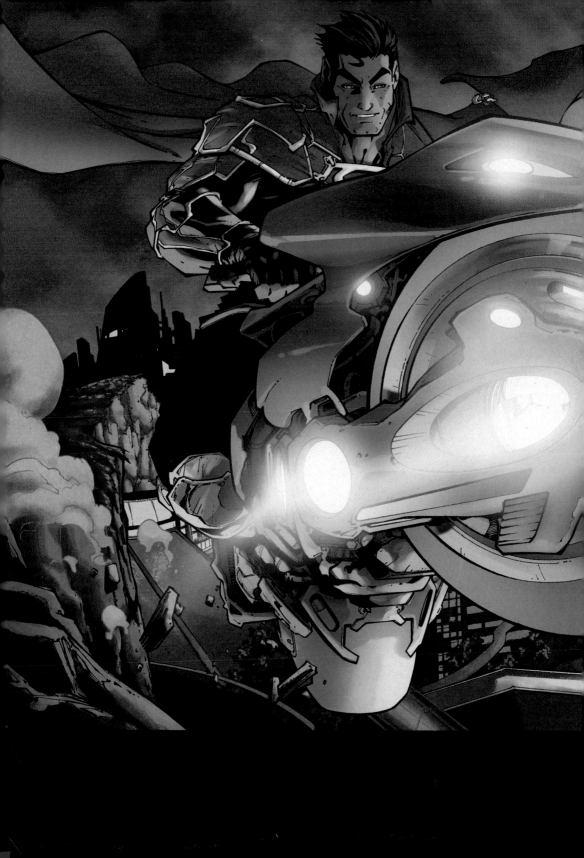

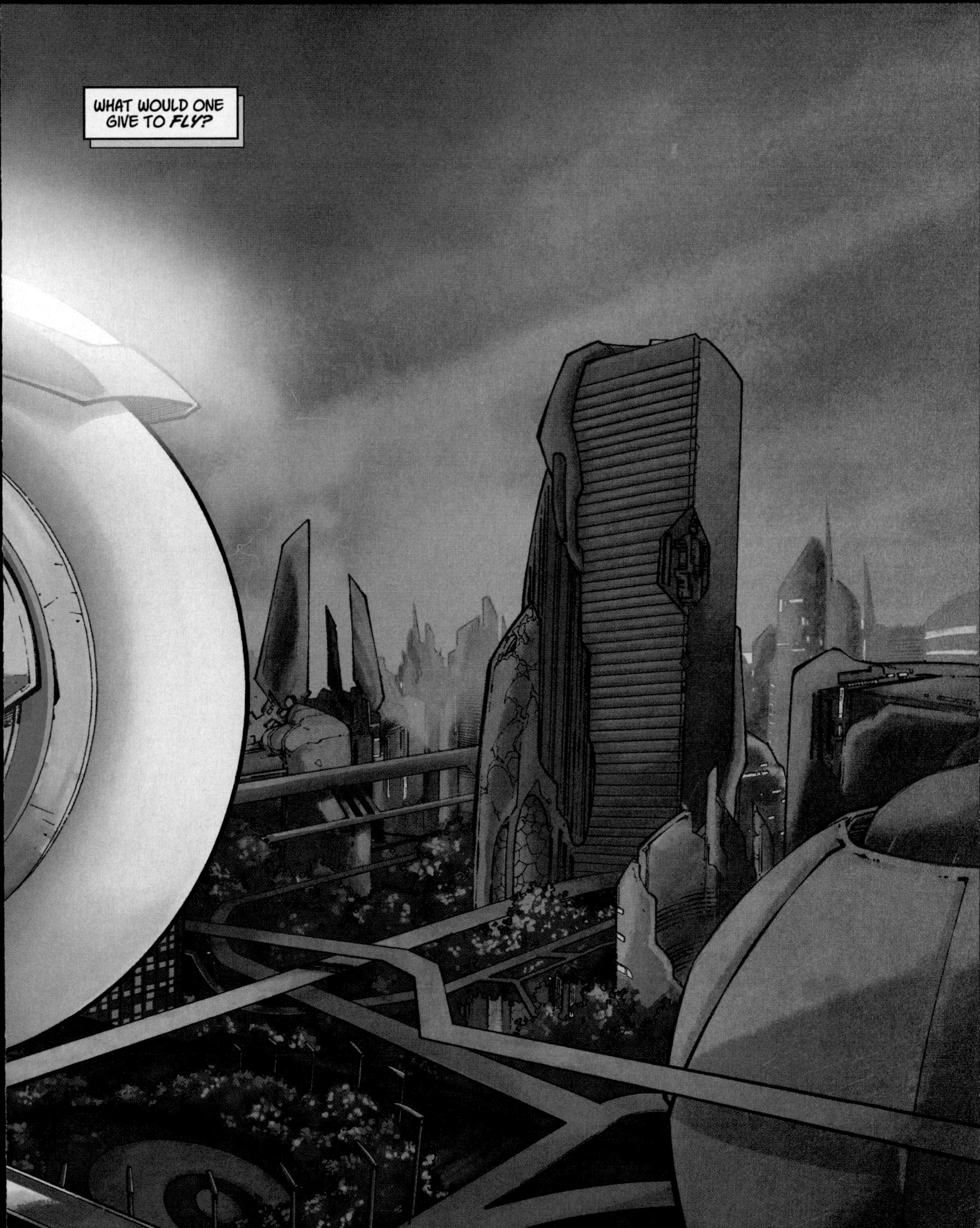
WHAT WOULD ONE GIVE TO *FLY?*

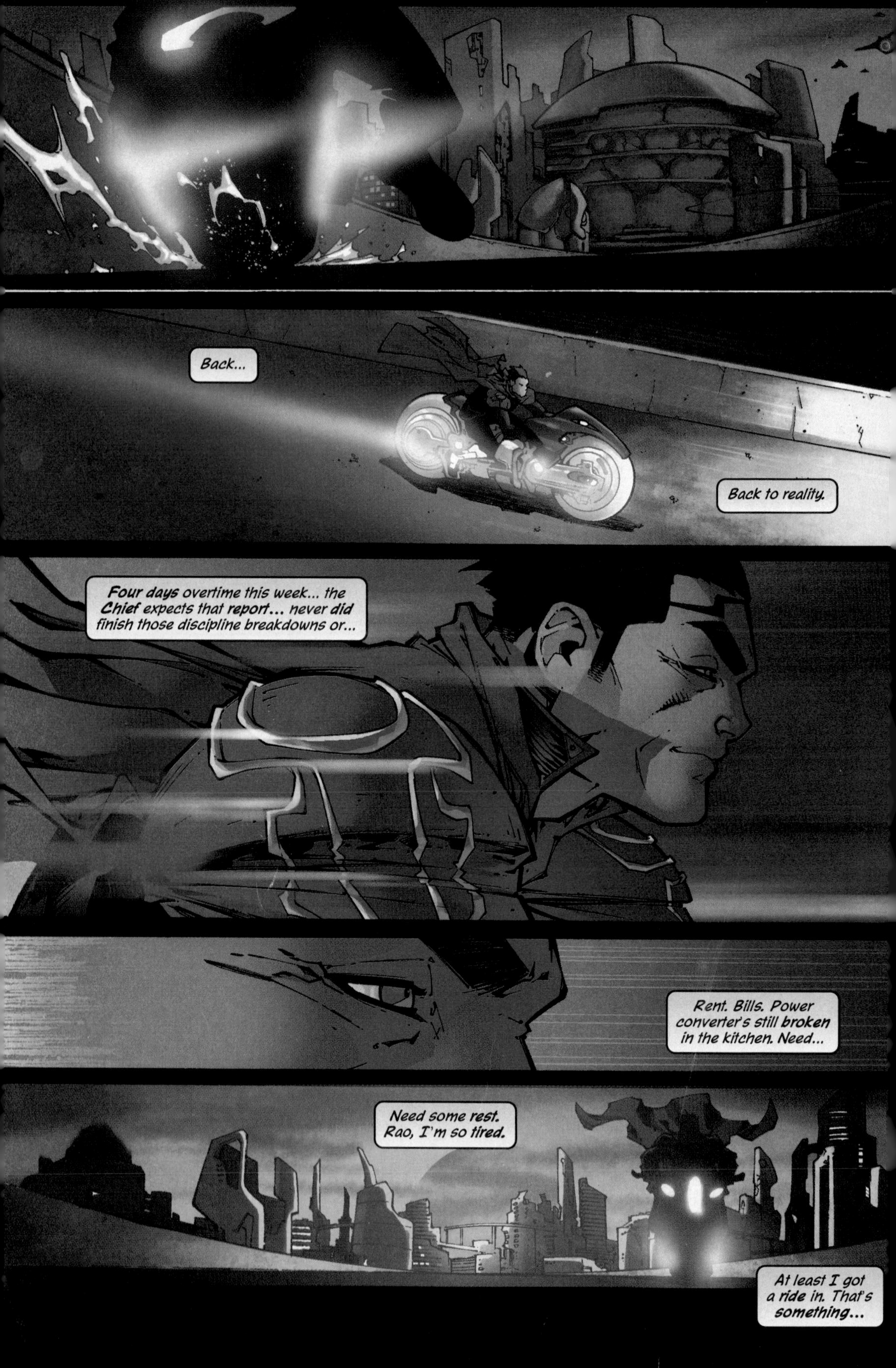

Back...
Back to reality.
Four days overtime this week... the Chief expects that report... never did finish those discipline breakdowns or...
Rent. Bills. Power converter's still broken in the kitchen. Need...
Need some rest. Rao, I'm so tired.
At least I got a ride in. That's something...

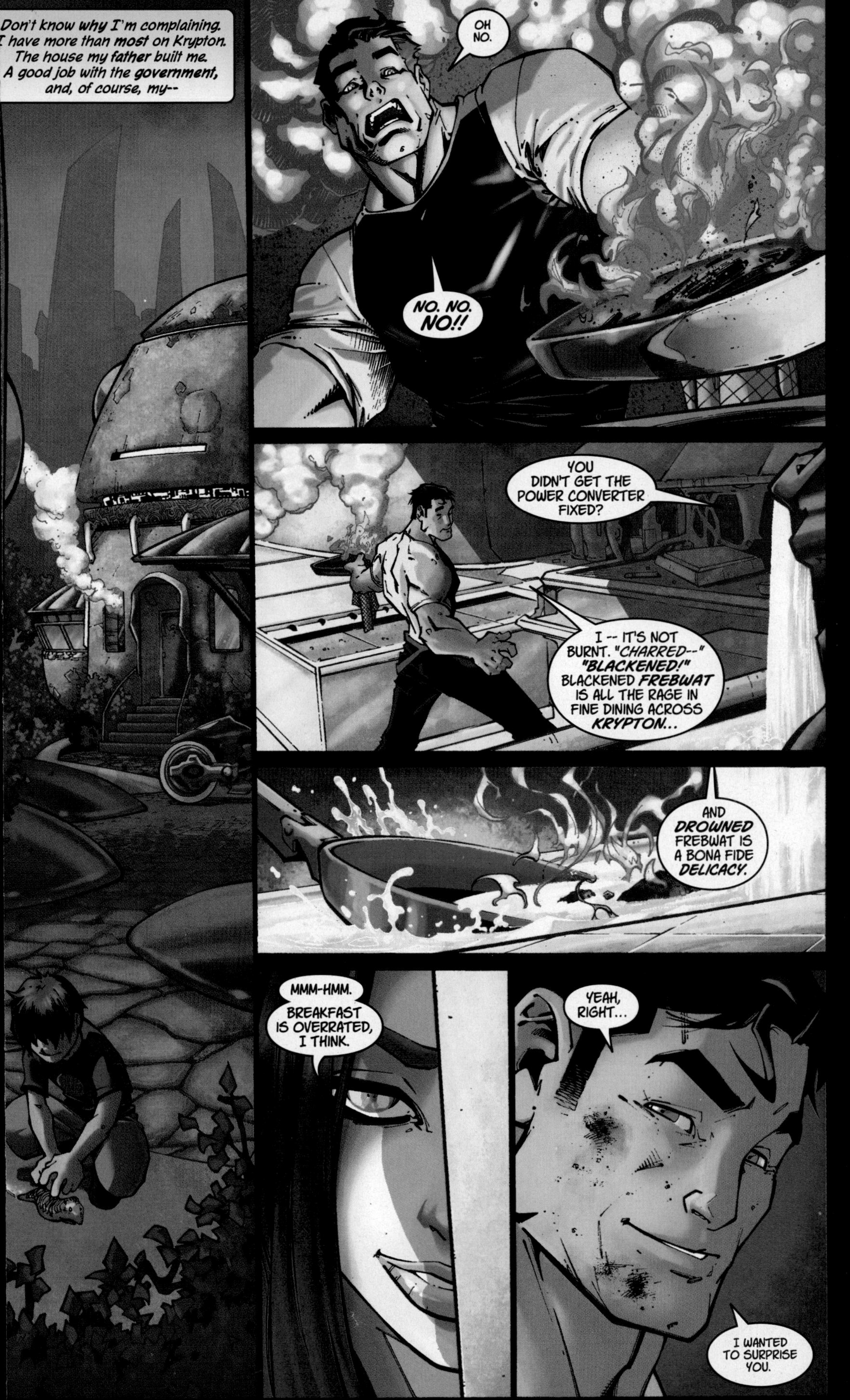

Don't know why I'm complaining. I have more than most on Krypton. The house my father built me. A good job with the government, and, of course, my--
OH NO.
NO. NO. NO!!
YOU DIDN'T GET THE POWER CONVERTER FIXED?
I -- IT'S NOT BURNT. "CHARRED--" "BLACKENED!" BLACKENED FREBWAT IS ALL THE RAGE IN FINE DINING ACROSS KRYPTON...
AND DROWNED FREBWAT IS A BONA FIDE DELICACY.
MMM-HMM. BREAKFAST IS OVERRATED, I THINK.
YEAH, RIGHT...
I WANTED TO SURPRISE YOU.

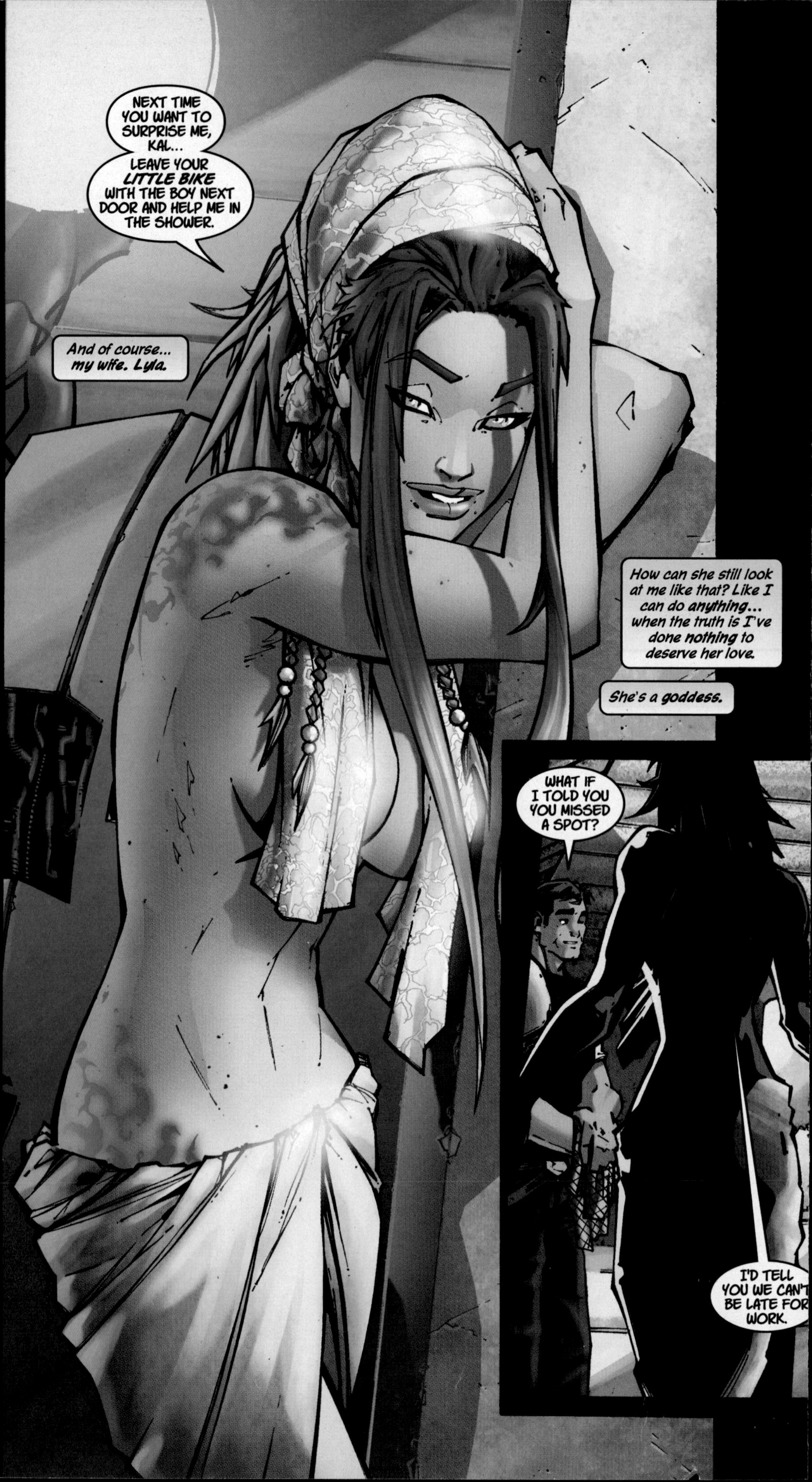

NEXT TIME YOU WANT TO SURPRISE ME, KAL...
LEAVE YOUR ***LITTLE BIKE*** WITH THE BOY NEXT DOOR AND HELP ME IN THE SHOWER.
And of course... my wife. Lyla.
*How can she still look at me like that? Like I can do **anything**... when the truth is I've done **nothing** to deserve her love.*
*She's a **goddess**.*
WHAT IF I TOLD YOU YOU MISSED A SPOT?
I'D TELL YOU WE CAN'T BE LATE FOR WORK.

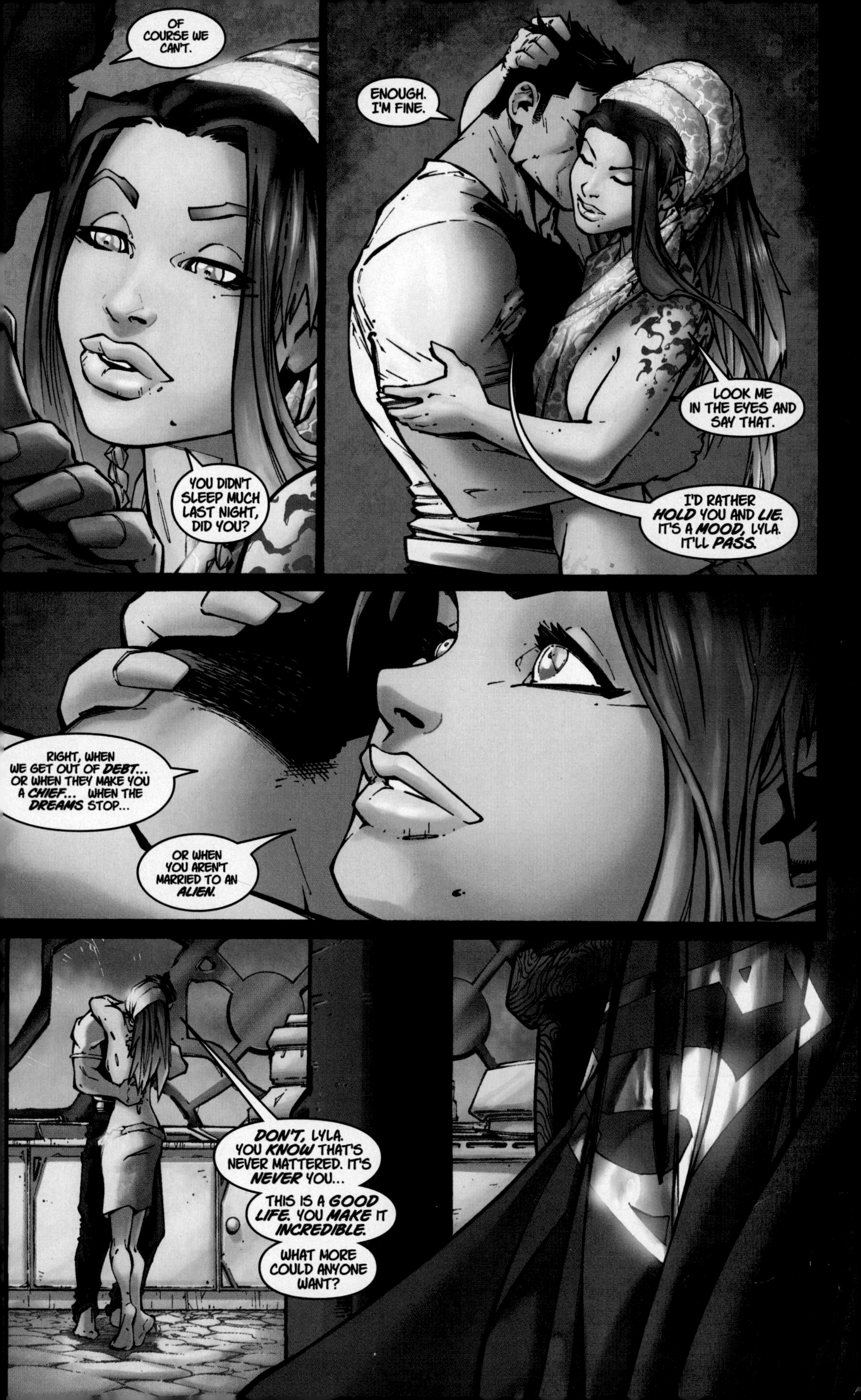
OF COURSE WE CAN'T.
YOU DIDN'T SLEEP MUCH LAST NIGHT, DID YOU?
ENOUGH. I'M FINE.
LOOK ME IN THE EYES AND SAY THAT.
I'D RATHER HOLD YOU AND LIE. IT'S A MOOD, LYLA. IT'LL PASS.
RIGHT, WHEN WE GET OUT OF DEBT... OR WHEN THEY MAKE YOU A CHIEF... WHEN THE DREAMS STOP...
OR WHEN YOU AREN'T MARRIED TO AN ALIEN.
DON'T, LYLA. YOU KNOW THAT'S NEVER MATTERED. IT'S NEVER YOU...
THIS IS A GOOD LIFE. YOU MAKE IT INCREDIBLE.
WHAT MORE COULD ANYONE WANT?

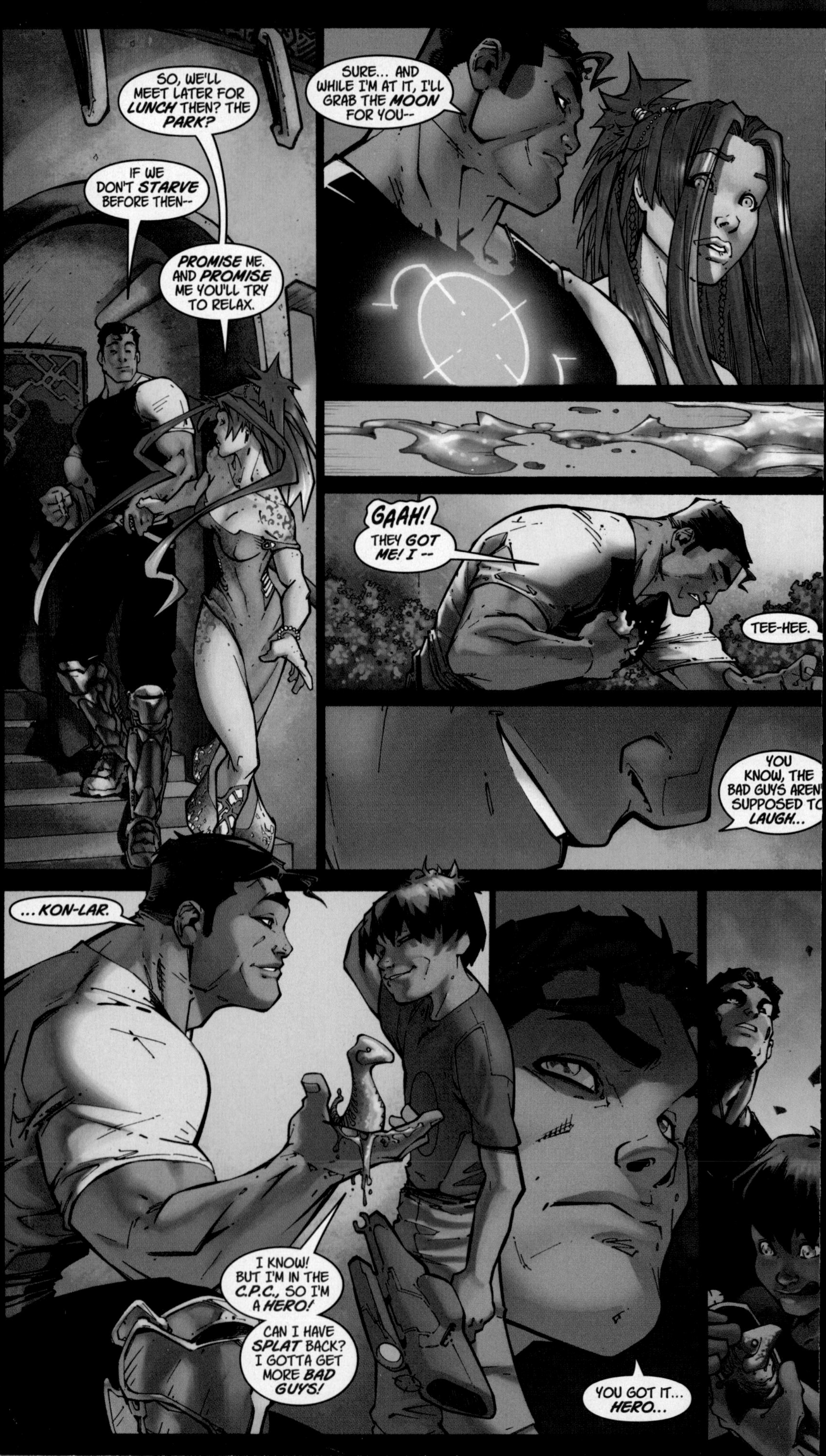
SO, WE'LL MEET LATER FOR LUNCH THEN? THE PARK?
IF WE DON'T STARVE BEFORE THEN--
PROMISE ME. AND PROMISE ME YOU'LL TRY TO RELAX.
SURE... AND WHILE I'M AT IT, I'LL GRAB THE MOON FOR YOU--
GAAH! THEY GOT ME! I --
TEE-HEE.
YOU KNOW, THE BAD GUYS AREN'T SUPPOSED TO LAUGH...
...KON-LAR.
I KNOW! BUT I'M IN THE C.P.C., SO I'M A HERO!
CAN I HAVE SPLAT BACK? I GOTTA GET MORE BAD GUYS!
YOU GOT IT... HERO...

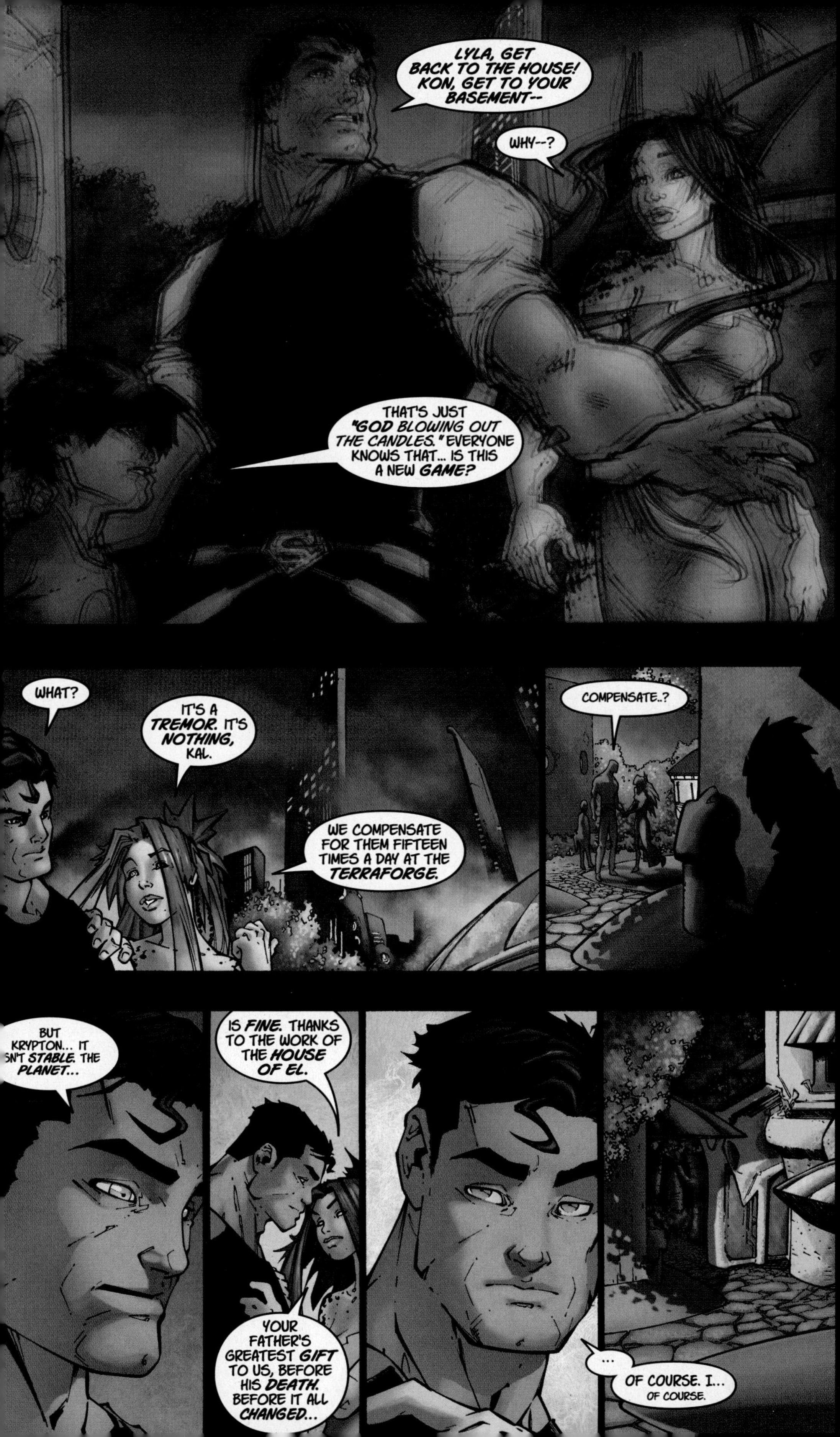
LYLA, GET BACK TO THE HOUSE! KON, GET TO YOUR BASEMENT--
WHY--?
THAT'S JUST "GOD BLOWING OUT THE CANDLES." EVERYONE KNOWS THAT... IS THIS A NEW GAME?
WHAT?
IT'S A TREMOR. IT'S NOTHING, KAL.
WE COMPENSATE FOR THEM FIFTEEN TIMES A DAY AT THE TERRAFORGE.
COMPENSATE..?
BUT KRYPTON... IT ISN'T STABLE. THE PLANET...
IS FINE. THANKS TO THE WORK OF THE HOUSE OF EL.
YOUR FATHER'S GREATEST GIFT TO US, BEFORE HIS DEATH. BEFORE IT ALL CHANGED...
...
OF COURSE. I... OF COURSE.

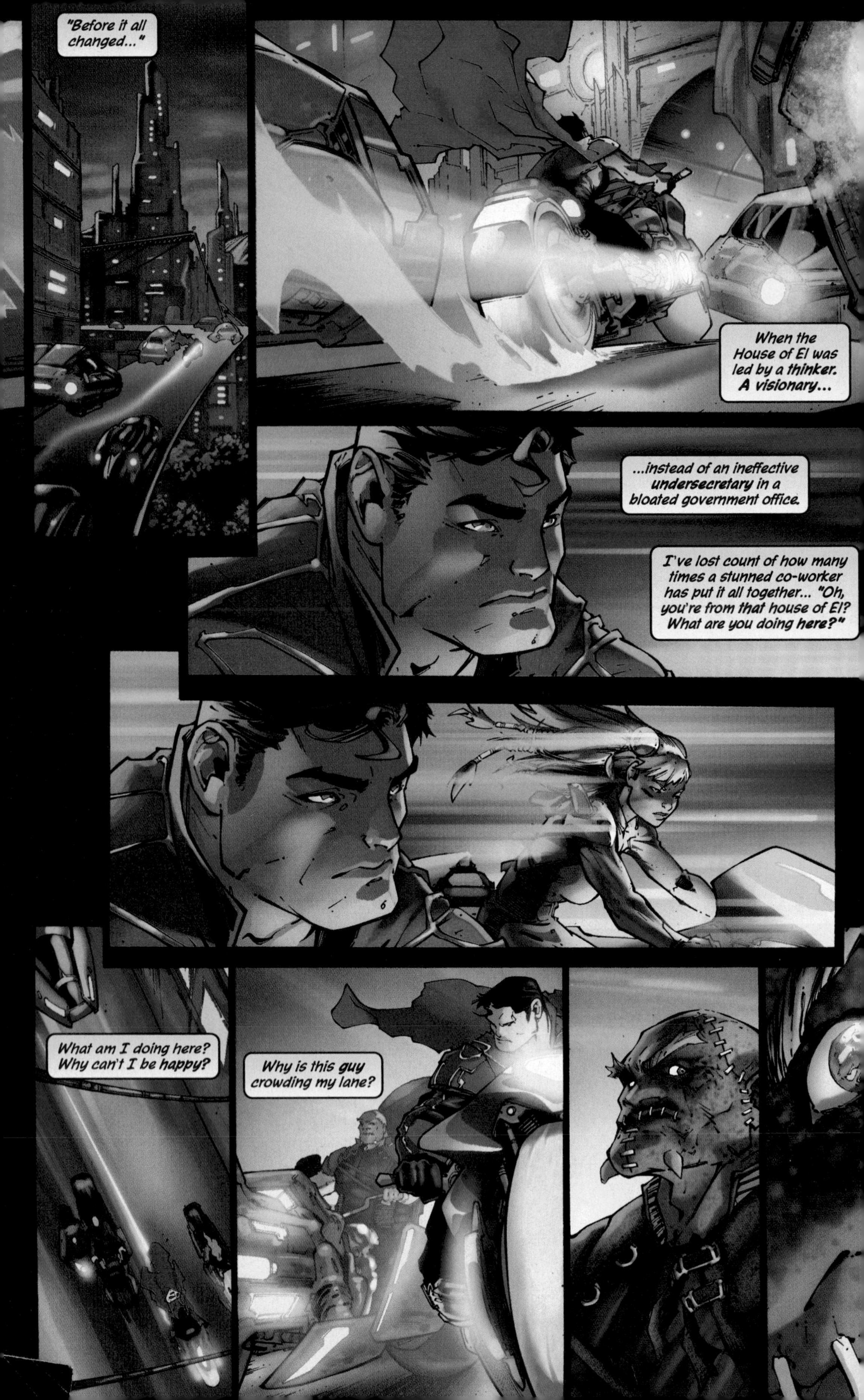
"Before it all changed..."
When the House of El was led by a thinker. A visionary...
...instead of an ineffective undersecretary in a bloated government office.
I've lost count of how many times a stunned co-worker has put it all together... "Oh, you're from that house of El? What are you doing here?"
What am I doing here? Why can't I be happy?
Why is this guy crowding my lane?

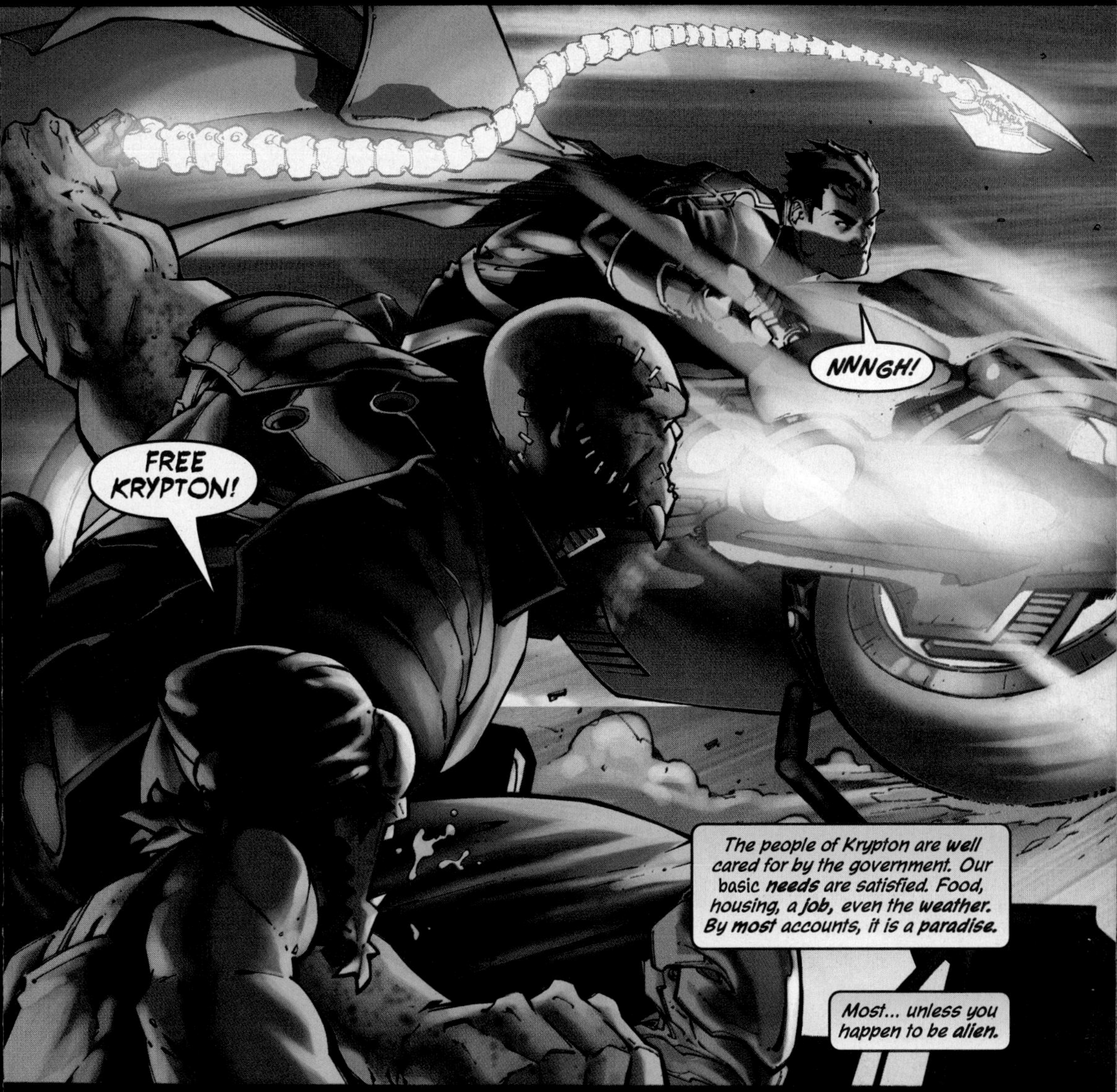
NNNGH!
FREE KRYPTON!
The people of Krypton are well cared for by the government. Our basic needs are satisfied. Food, housing, a job, even the weather. By most accounts, it is a paradise.
Most... unless you happen to be alien.

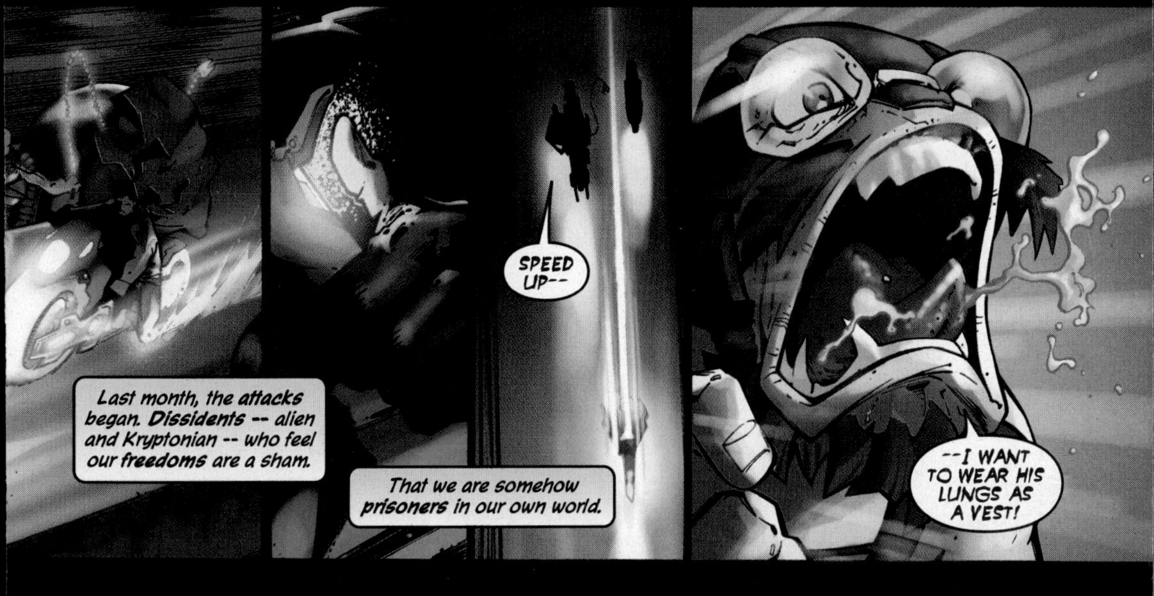
Last month, the attacks began. Dissidents -- alien and Kryptonian -- who feel our freedoms are a sham.
SPEED UP--
That we are somehow prisoners in our own world.
--I WANT TO WEAR HIS LUNGS AS A VEST!

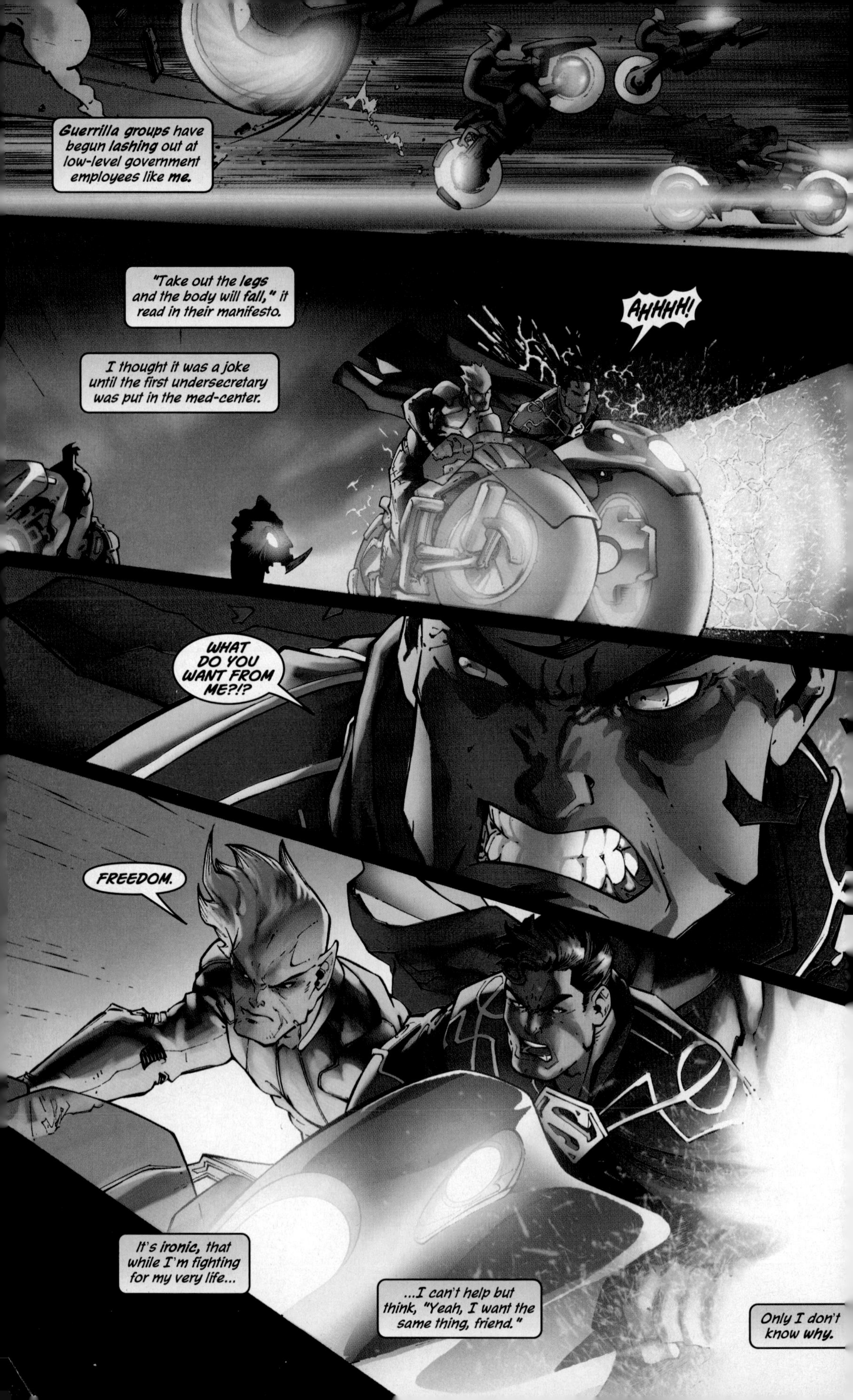
Guerrilla groups have begun lashing out at low-level government employees like me.
"Take out the legs and the body will fall," it read in their manifesto.
AHHHH!
I thought it was a joke until the first undersecretary was put in the med-center.
WHAT DO YOU WANT FROM ME?!?
FREEDOM.
It's ironic, that while I'm fighting for my very life...
...I can't help but think, "Yeah, I want the same thing, friend."
Only I don't know why.

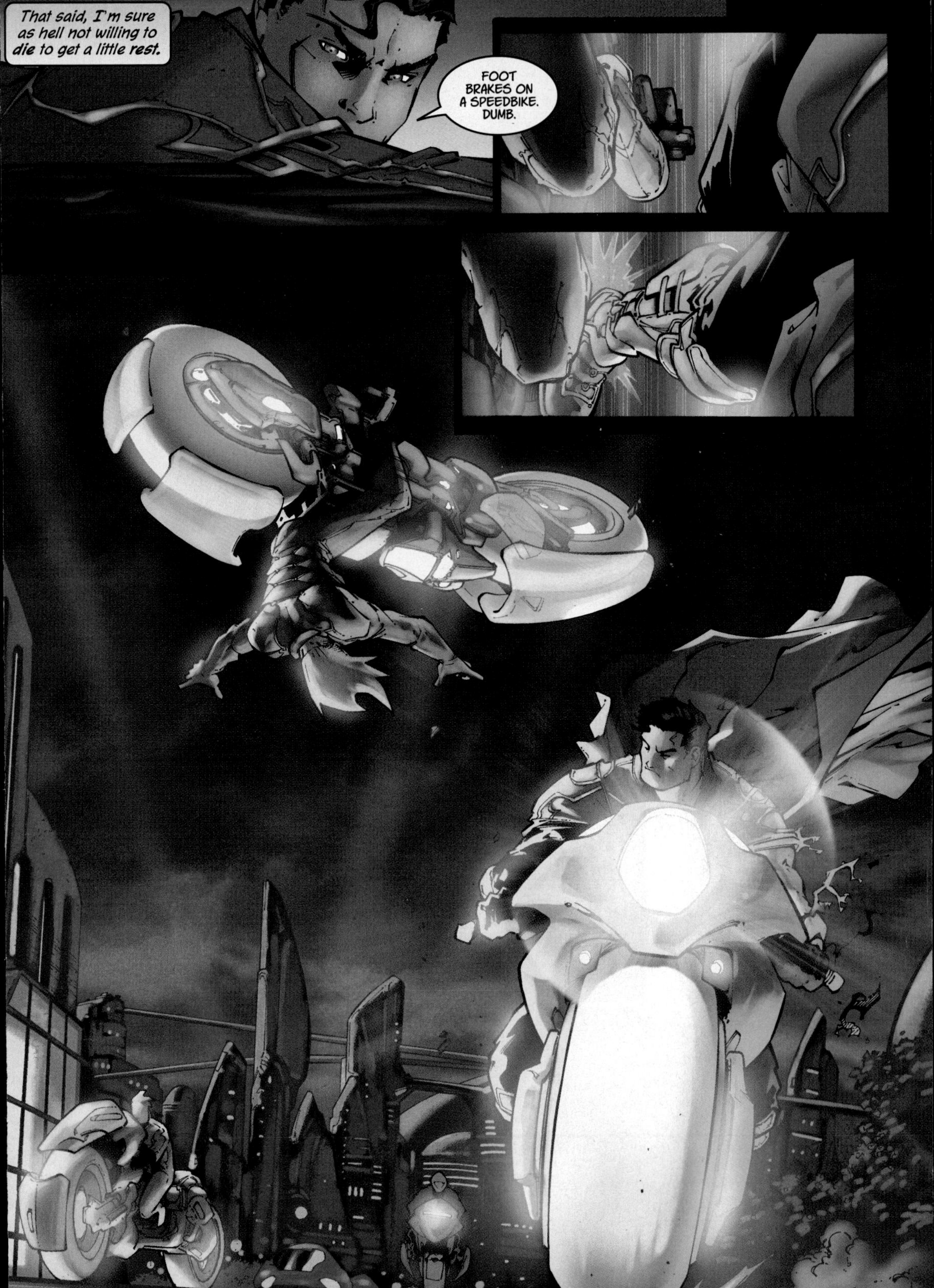
That said, I'm sure as hell not willing to die to get a little rest.
FOOT BRAKES ON A SPEEDBIKE. DUMB.

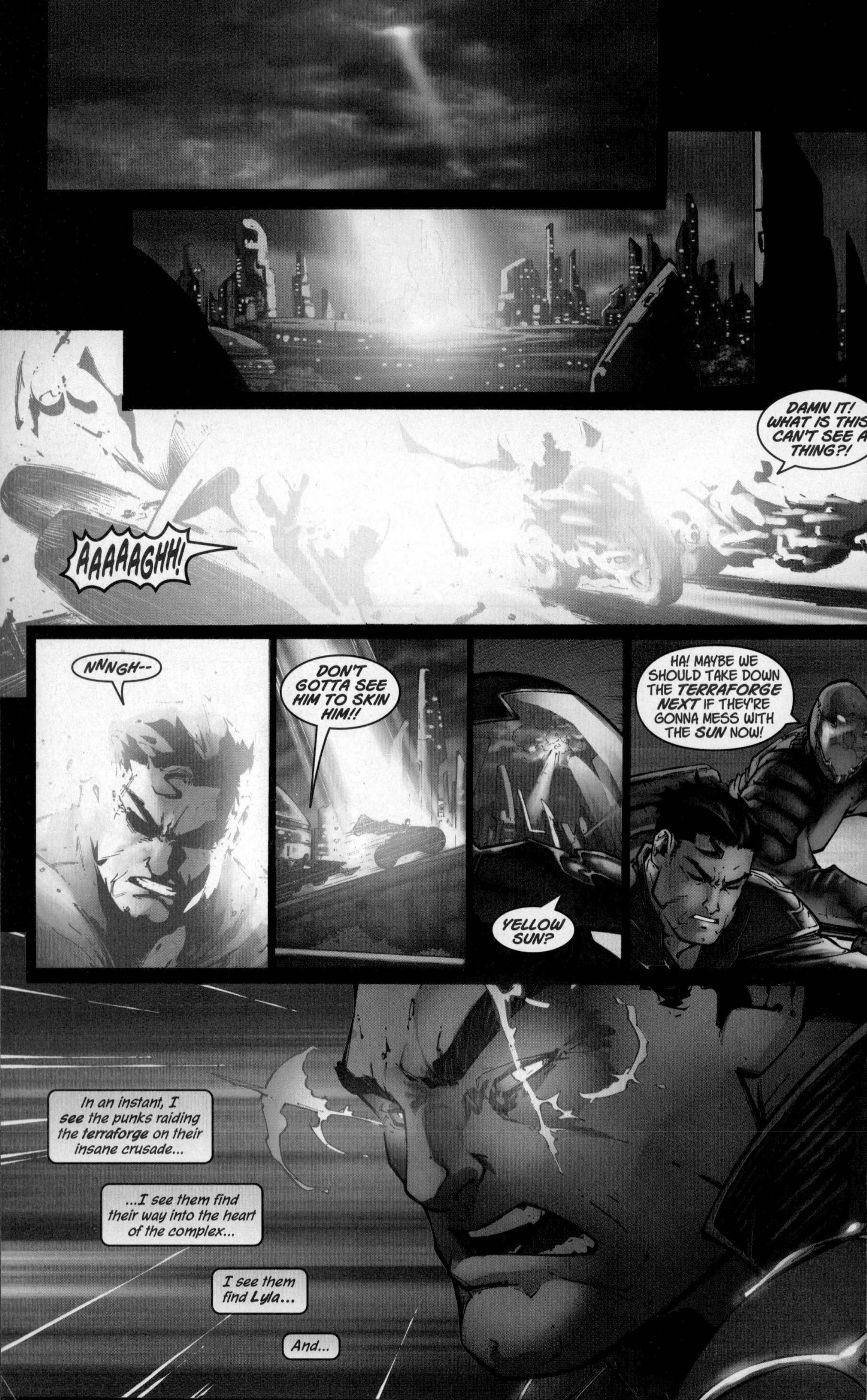
DAMN IT! WHAT IS THIS? CAN'T SEE A THING?!
AAAAAGHH!
NNNGH--
DON'T GOTTA SEE HIM TO SKIN HIM!!
YELLOW SUN?
HA! MAYBE WE SHOULD TAKE DOWN THE TERRAFORGE NEXT IF THEY'RE GONNA MESS WITH THE SUN NOW!
In an instant, I see the punks raiding the terraforge on their insane crusade...
...I see them find their way into the heart of the complex...
I see them find Lyla...
And...

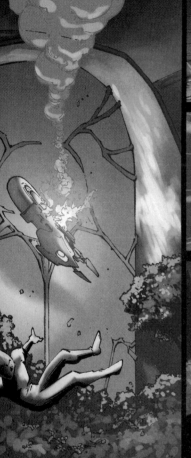

GREAT RAO...

NO ONE SAID HE'D BE ARMED?

DAMMIT! OUR INTEL BITES!

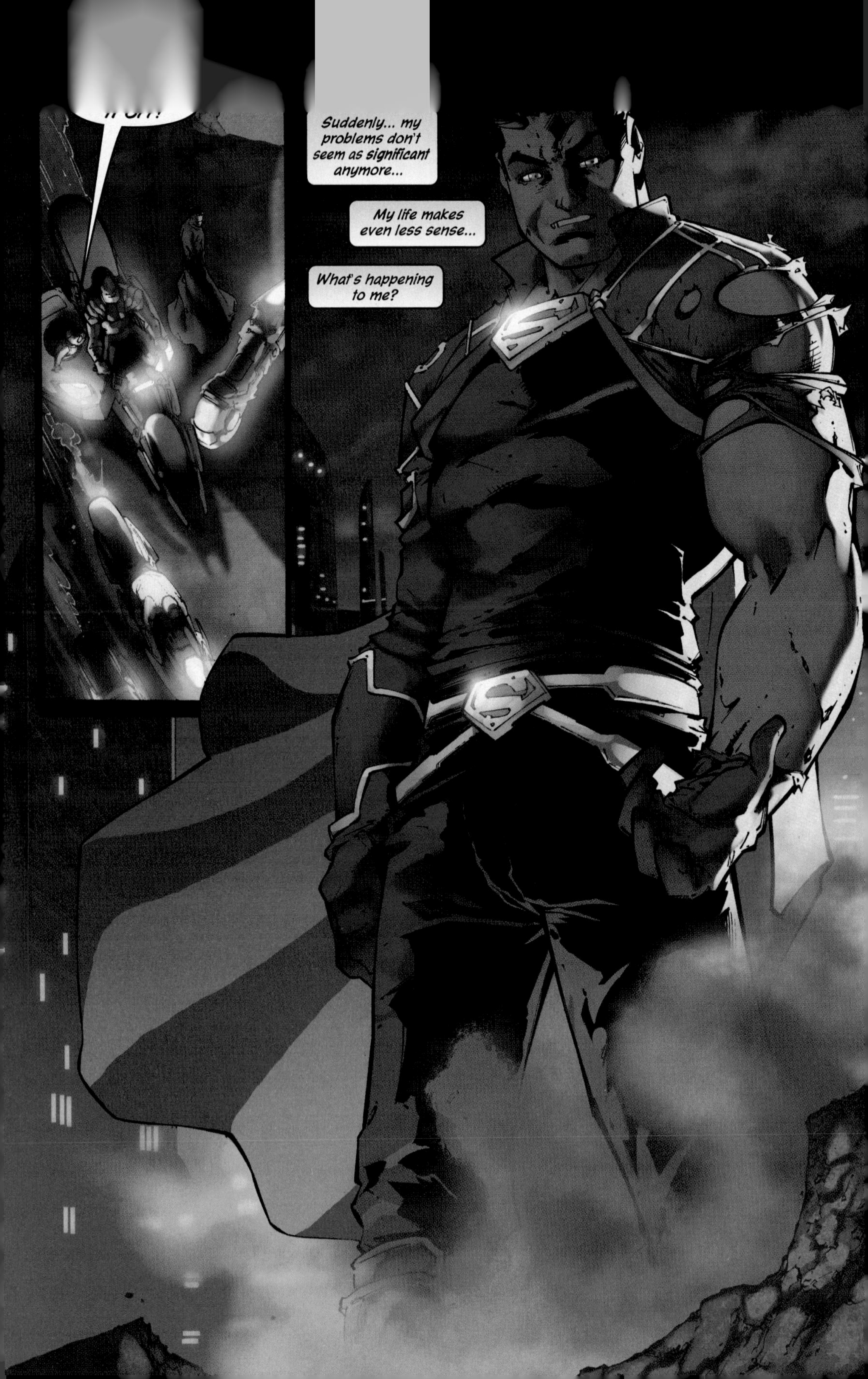
Suddenly... my problems don't seem as significant anymore...
My life makes even less sense...
What's happening to me?

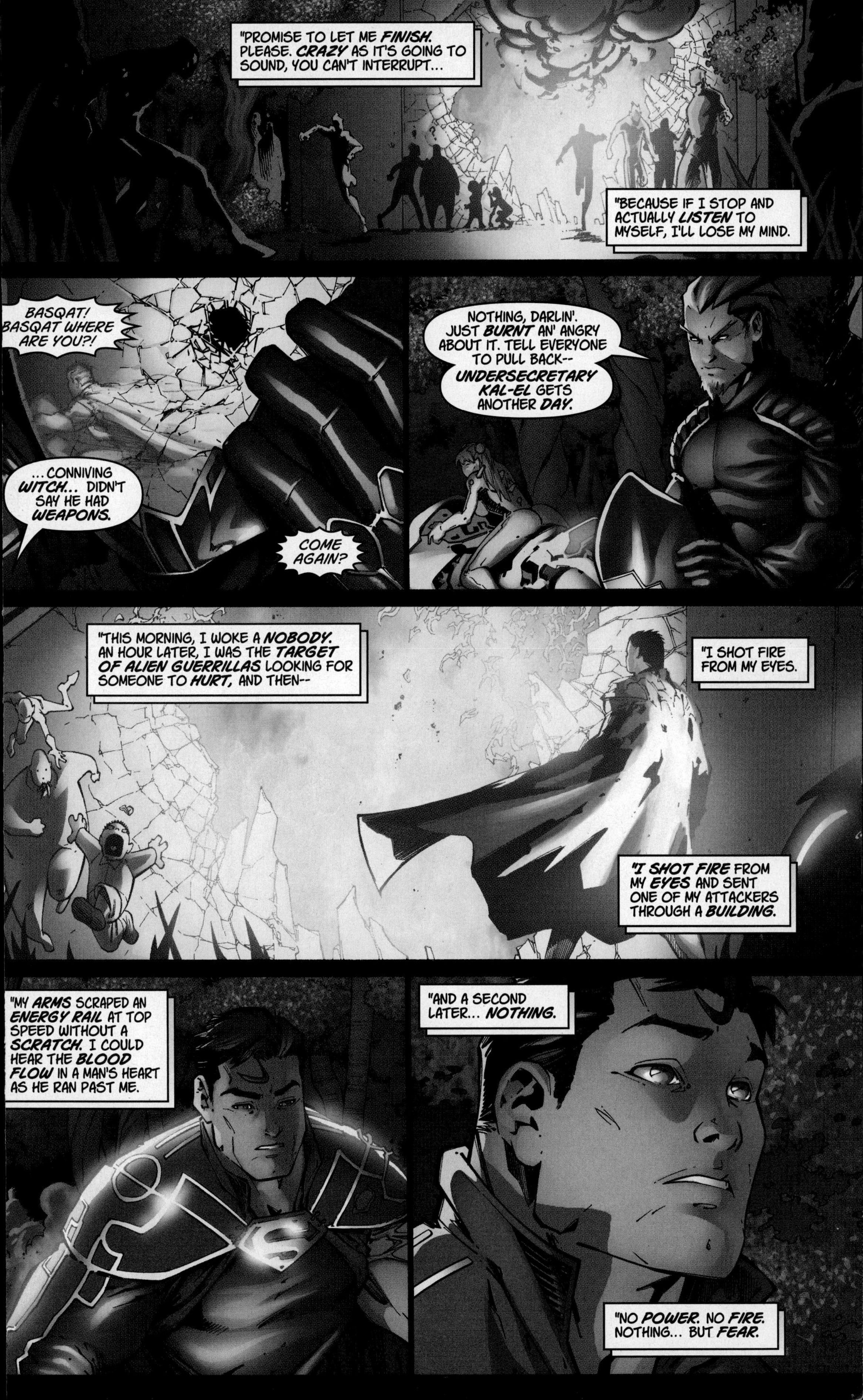
"PROMISE TO LET ME FINISH. PLEASE. CRAZY AS IT'S GOING TO SOUND, YOU CAN'T INTERRUPT...
"BECAUSE IF I STOP AND ACTUALLY LISTEN TO MYSELF, I'LL LOSE MY MIND.
BASQAT! BASQAT WHERE ARE YOU?!
...CONNIVING WITCH... DIDN'T SAY HE HAD WEAPONS.
COME AGAIN?
NOTHING, DARLIN'. JUST BURNT AN' ANGRY ABOUT IT. TELL EVERYONE TO PULL BACK--
UNDERSECRETARY KAL-EL GETS ANOTHER DAY.
"THIS MORNING, I WOKE A NOBODY. AN HOUR LATER, I WAS THE TARGET OF ALIEN GUERRILLAS LOOKING FOR SOMEONE TO HURT, AND THEN--
"I SHOT FIRE FROM MY EYES.
"I SHOT FIRE FROM MY EYES AND SENT ONE OF MY ATTACKERS THROUGH A BUILDING.
"MY ARMS SCRAPED AN ENERGY RAIL AT TOP SPEED WITHOUT A SCRATCH. I COULD HEAR THE BLOOD FLOW IN A MAN'S HEART AS HE RAN PAST ME.
"AND A SECOND LATER... NOTHING.
"NO POWER. NO FIRE. NOTHING... BUT FEAR.

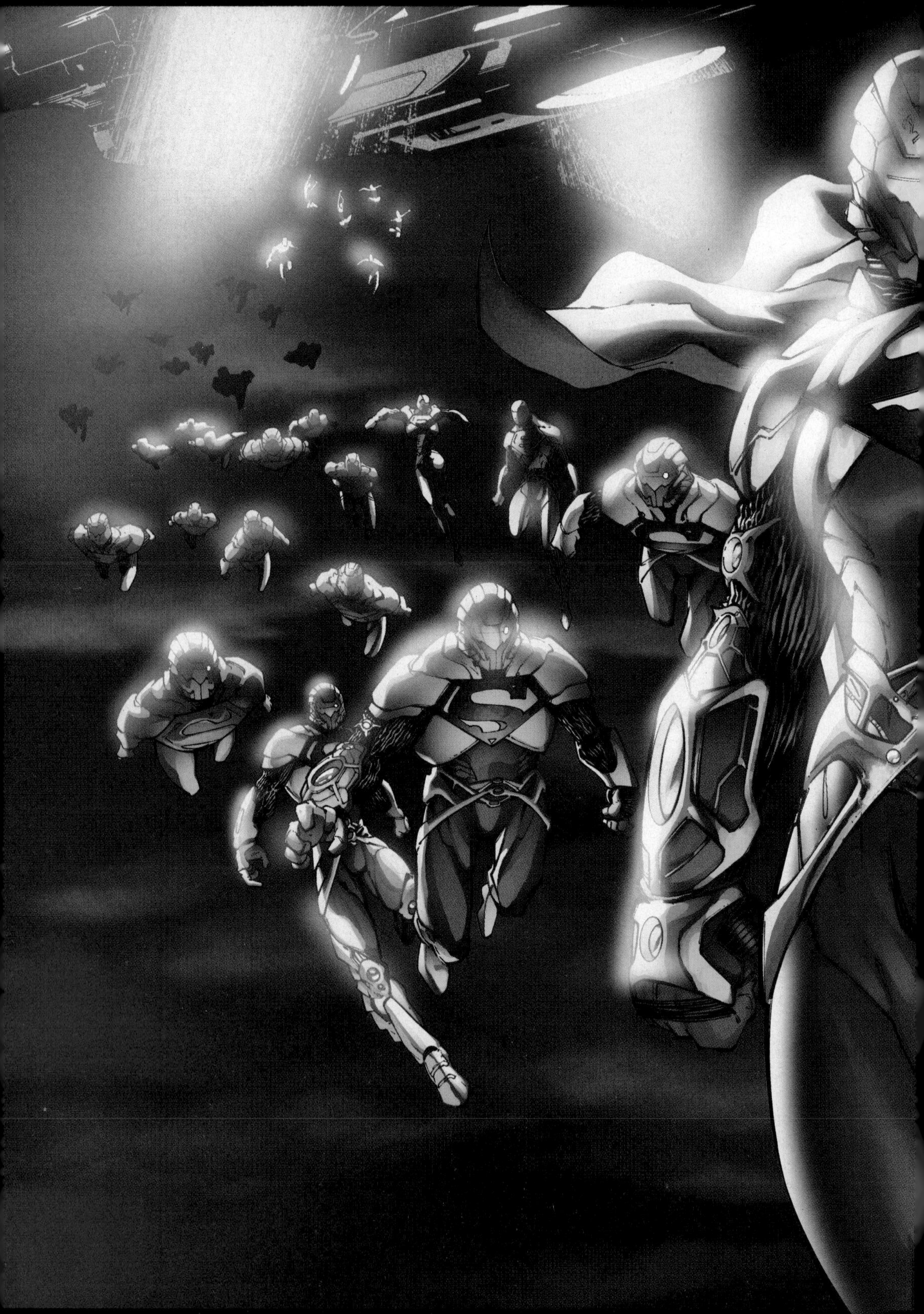

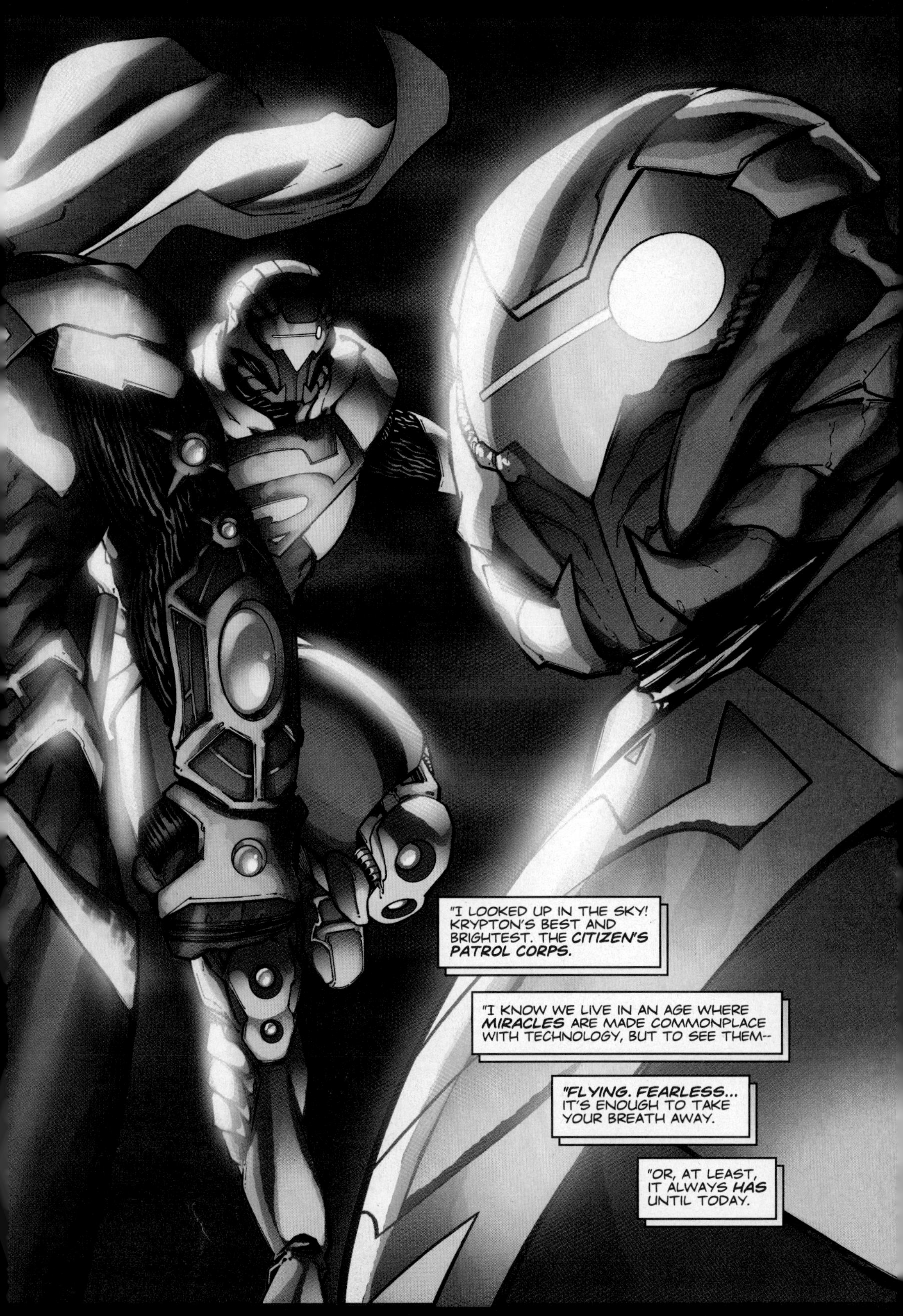
"I LOOKED UP IN THE SKY! KRYPTON'S BEST AND BRIGHTEST. THE CITIZEN'S PATROL CORPS.
"I KNOW WE LIVE IN AN AGE WHERE MIRACLES ARE MADE COMMONPLACE WITH TECHNOLOGY, BUT TO SEE THEM--
"FLYING. FEARLESS... IT'S ENOUGH TO TAKE YOUR BREATH AWAY.
"OR, AT LEAST, IT ALWAYS HAS UNTIL TODAY.

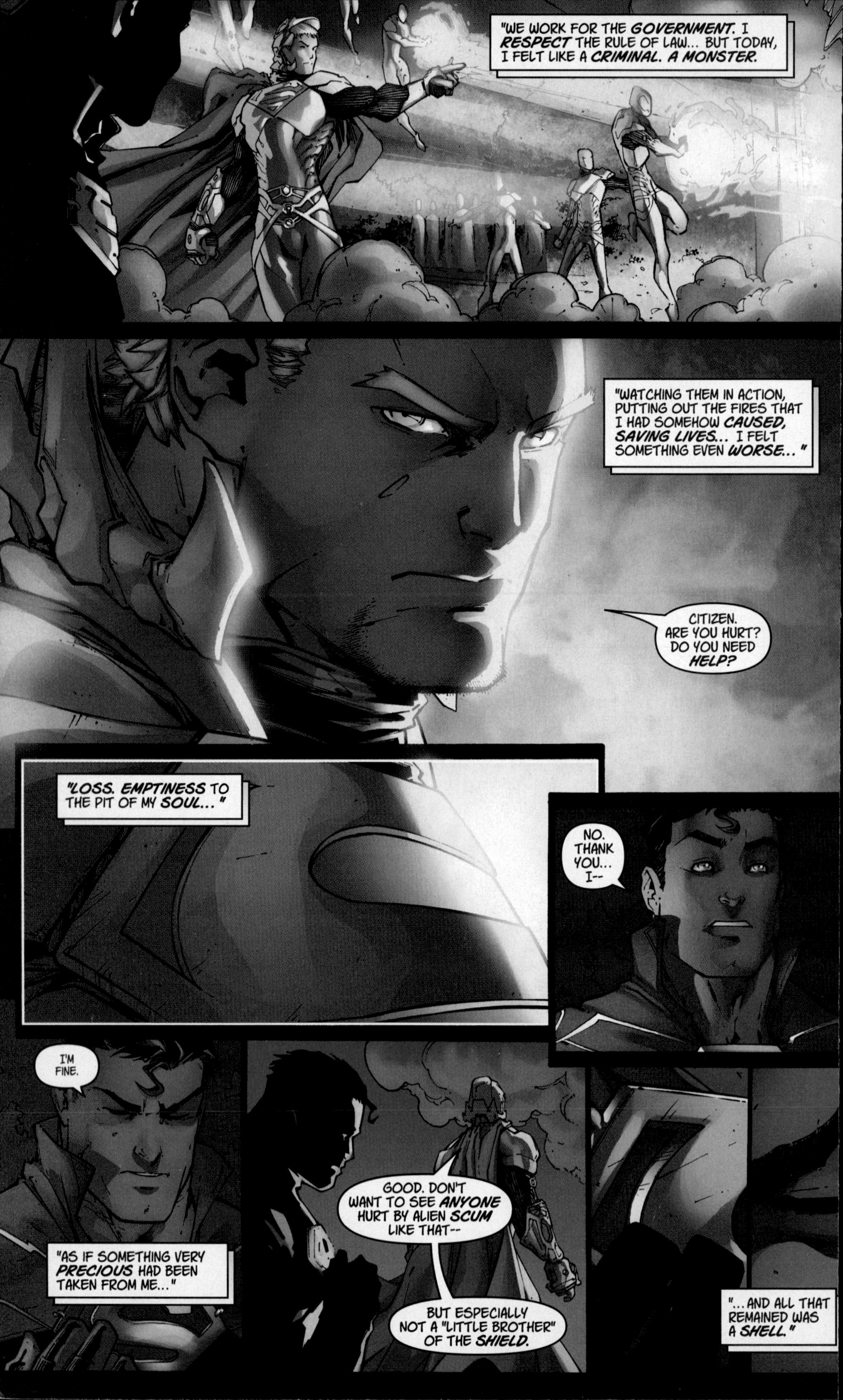
"WE WORK FOR THE GOVERNMENT. I RESPECT THE RULE OF LAW... BUT TODAY, I FELT LIKE A CRIMINAL. A MONSTER.
"WATCHING THEM IN ACTION, PUTTING OUT THE FIRES THAT I HAD SOMEHOW CAUSED, SAVING LIVES... I FELT SOMETHING EVEN WORSE..."
CITIZEN. ARE YOU HURT? DO YOU NEED HELP?
"LOSS. EMPTINESS TO THE PIT OF MY SOUL..."
NO. THANK YOU... I--
I'M FINE.
"AS IF SOMETHING VERY PRECIOUS HAD BEEN TAKEN FROM ME..."
GOOD. DON'T WANT TO SEE ANYONE HURT BY ALIEN SCUM LIKE THAT--
BUT ESPECIALLY NOT A "LITTLE BROTHER" OF THE SHIELD.
"...AND ALL THAT REMAINED WAS A SHELL."

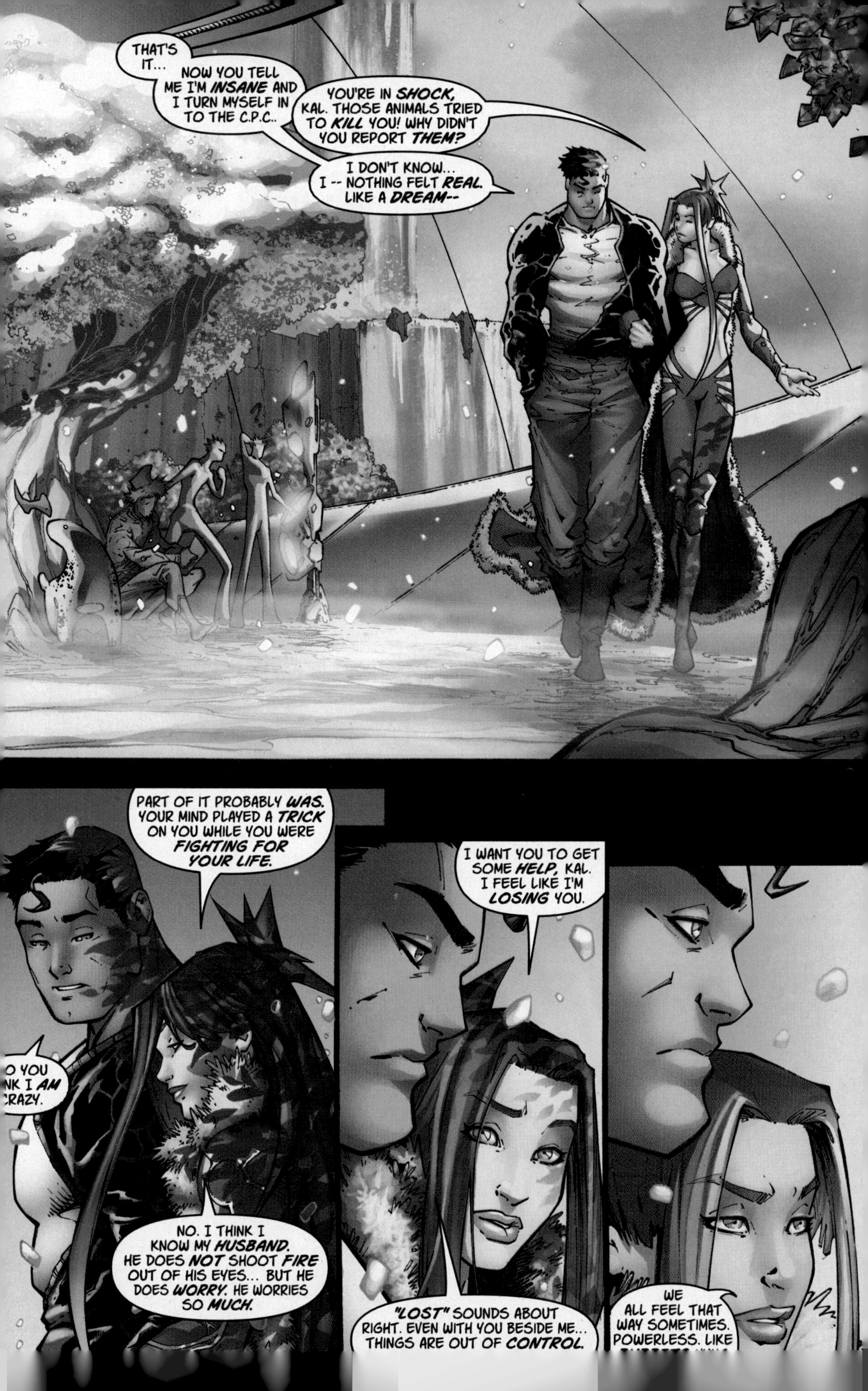
THAT'S IT... NOW YOU TELL ME I'M INSANE AND I TURN MYSELF IN TO THE C.P.C..
YOU'RE IN SHOCK, KAL. THOSE ANIMALS TRIED TO KILL YOU! WHY DIDN'T YOU REPORT THEM?
I DON'T KNOW... I -- NOTHING FELT REAL. LIKE A DREAM--
PART OF IT PROBABLY WAS. YOUR MIND PLAYED A TRICK ON YOU WHILE YOU WERE FIGHTING FOR YOUR LIFE.
O YOU NK I AM CRAZY.
NO. I THINK I KNOW MY HUSBAND. HE DOES NOT SHOOT FIRE OUT OF HIS EYES... BUT HE DOES WORRY. HE WORRIES SO MUCH.
I WANT YOU TO GET SOME HELP, KAL. I FEEL LIKE I'M LOSING YOU.
"LOST" SOUNDS ABOUT RIGHT. EVEN WITH YOU BESIDE ME... THINGS ARE OUT OF CONTROL.
WE ALL FEEL THAT WAY SOMETIMES. POWERLESS. LIKE

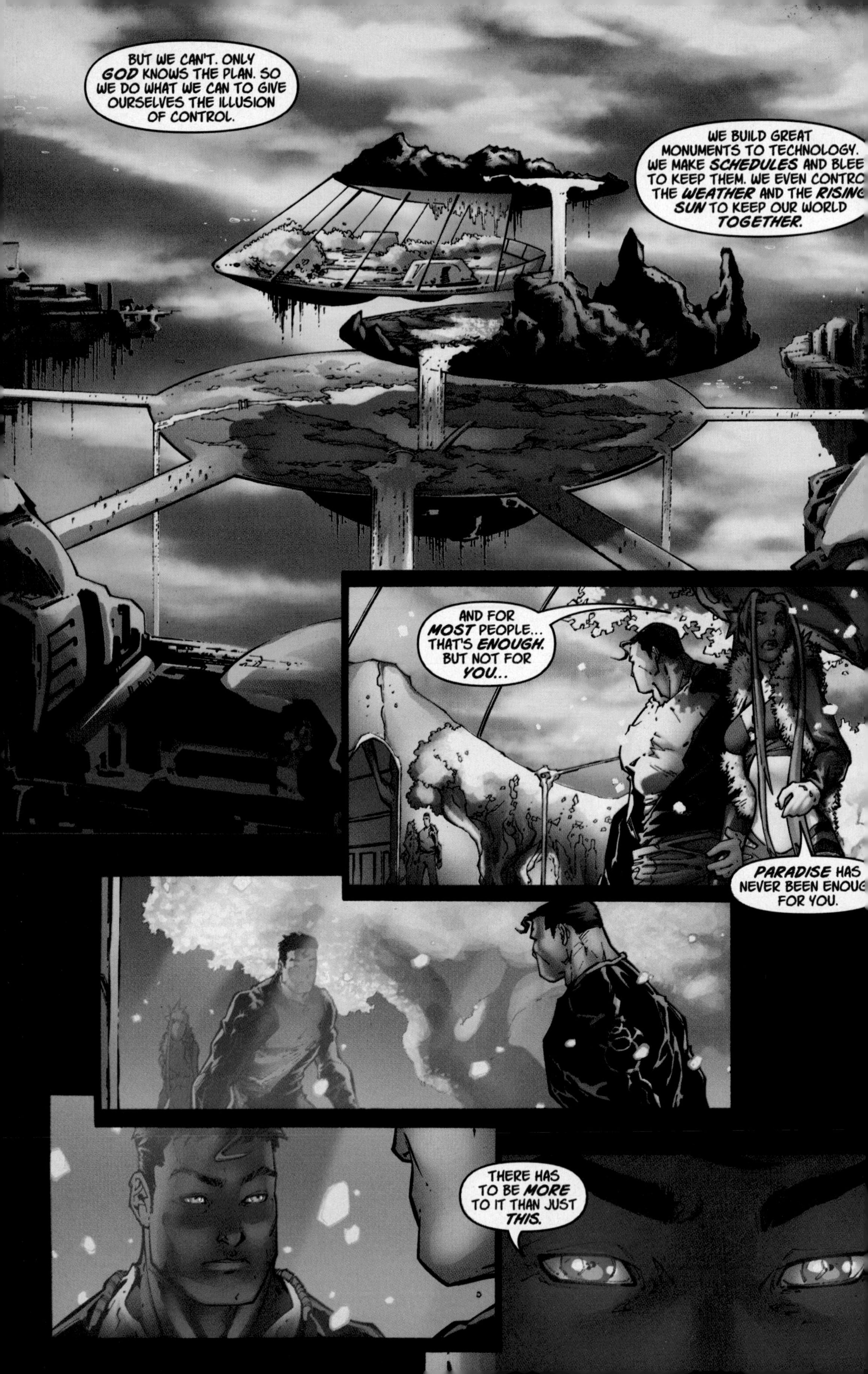
BUT WE CAN'T. ONLY GOD KNOWS THE PLAN. SO WE DO WHAT WE CAN TO GIVE OURSELVES THE ILLUSION OF CONTROL.
WE BUILD GREAT MONUMENTS TO TECHNOLOGY. WE MAKE SCHEDULES AND BLEE TO KEEP THEM. WE EVEN CONTRO THE WEATHER AND THE RISING SUN TO KEEP OUR WORLD TOGETHER.
AND FOR MOST PEOPLE... THAT'S ENOUGH. BUT NOT FOR YOU...
PARADISE HAS NEVER BEEN ENOUG FOR YOU.
THERE HAS TO BE MORE TO IT THAN JUST THIS.

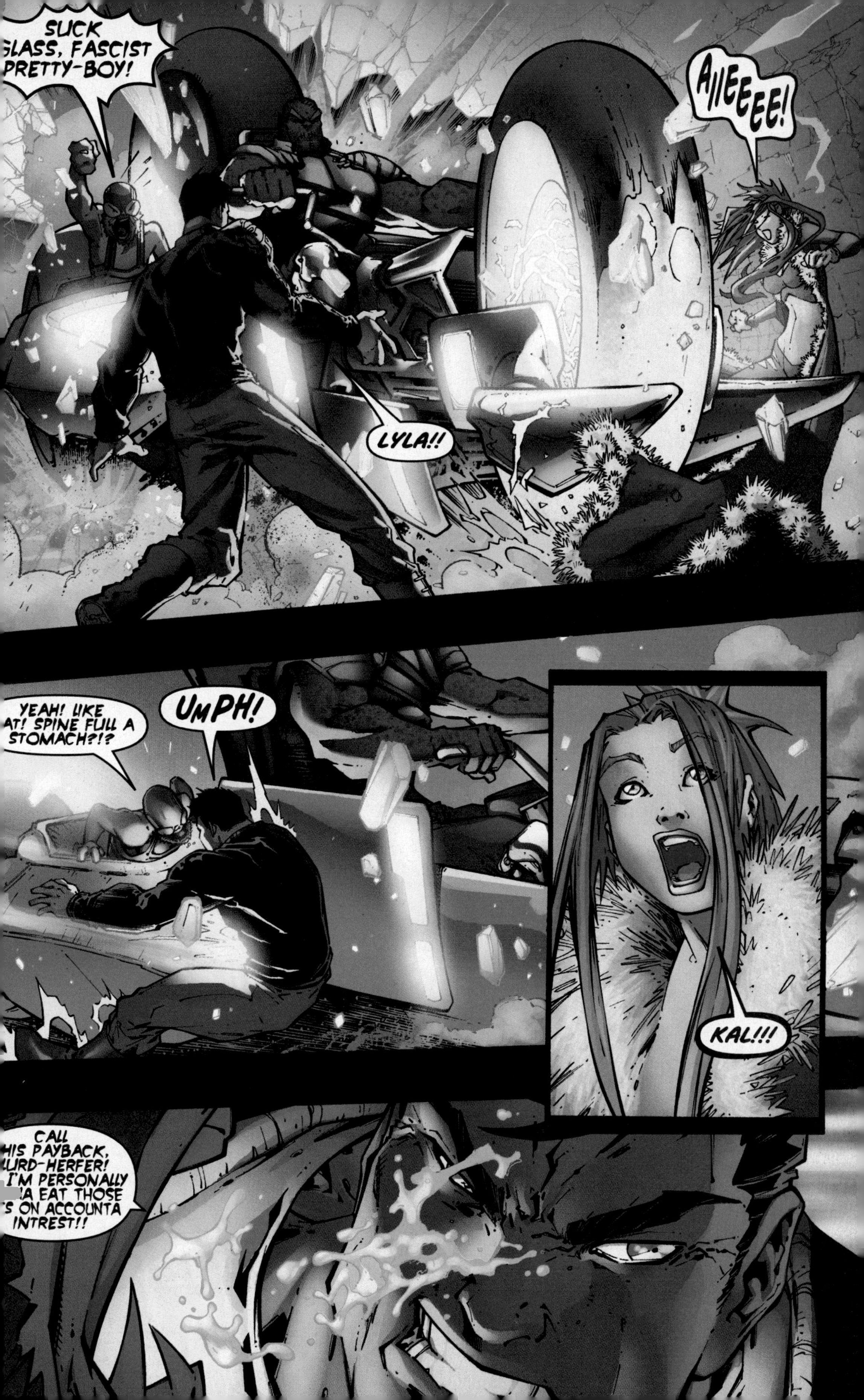
SUCK GLASS, FASCIST PRETTY-BOY!
AIIEEEEE!
LYLA!!
YEAH! LIKE AT! SPINE FULL A STOMACH?!?
UMPH!
KAL!!!
CALL HIS PAYBACK, URD-HERFER! I'M PERSONALLY A EAT THOSE S ON ACCOUNTA INTREST!!

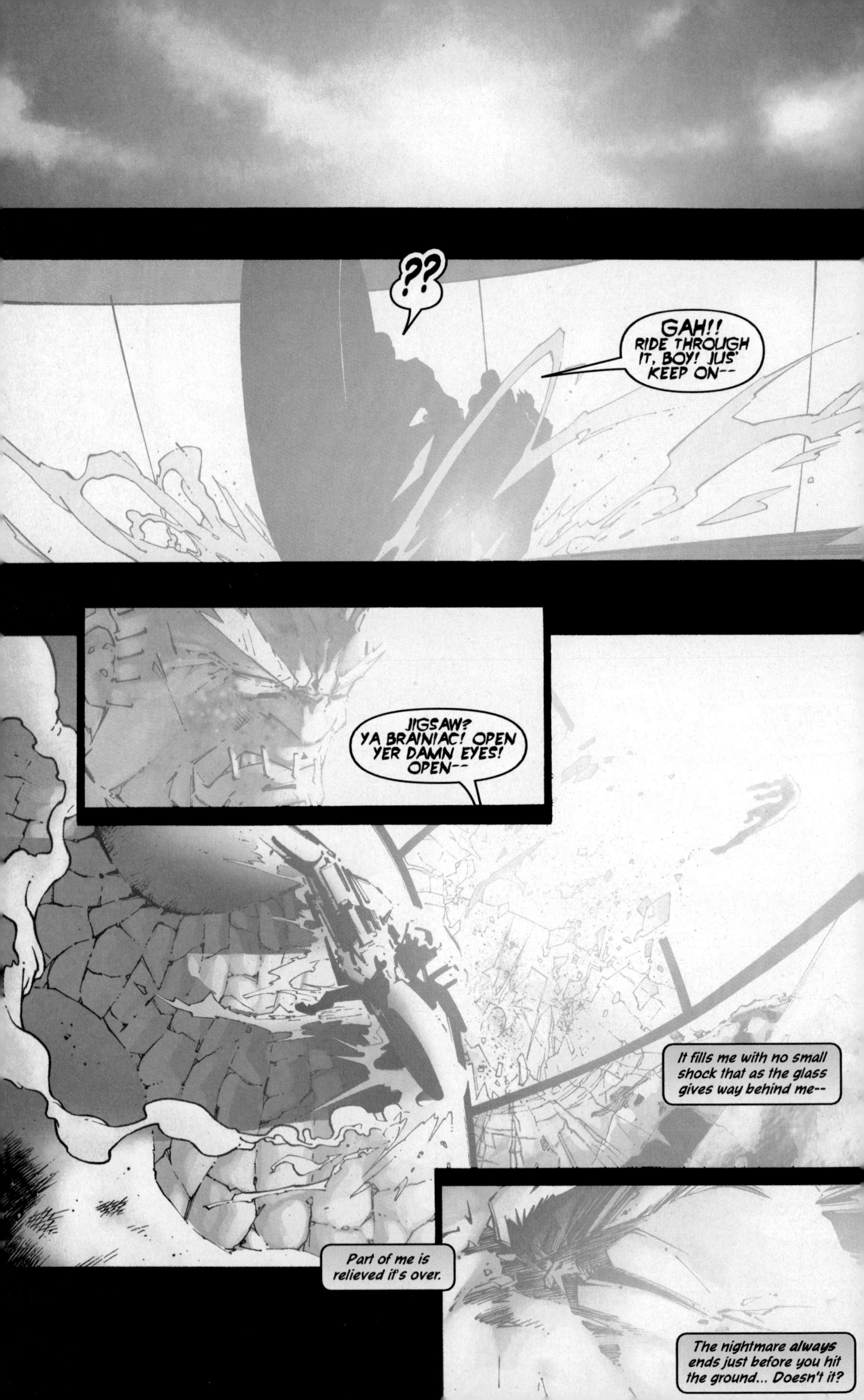
??
GAH!! RIDE THROUGH IT, BOY! JUS' KEEP ON--
JIGSAW? YA BRAINIAC! OPEN YER DAMN EYES! OPEN--
It fills me with no small shock that as the glass gives way behind me--
Part of me is relieved it's over.
The nightmare always ends just before you hit the ground... Doesn't it?

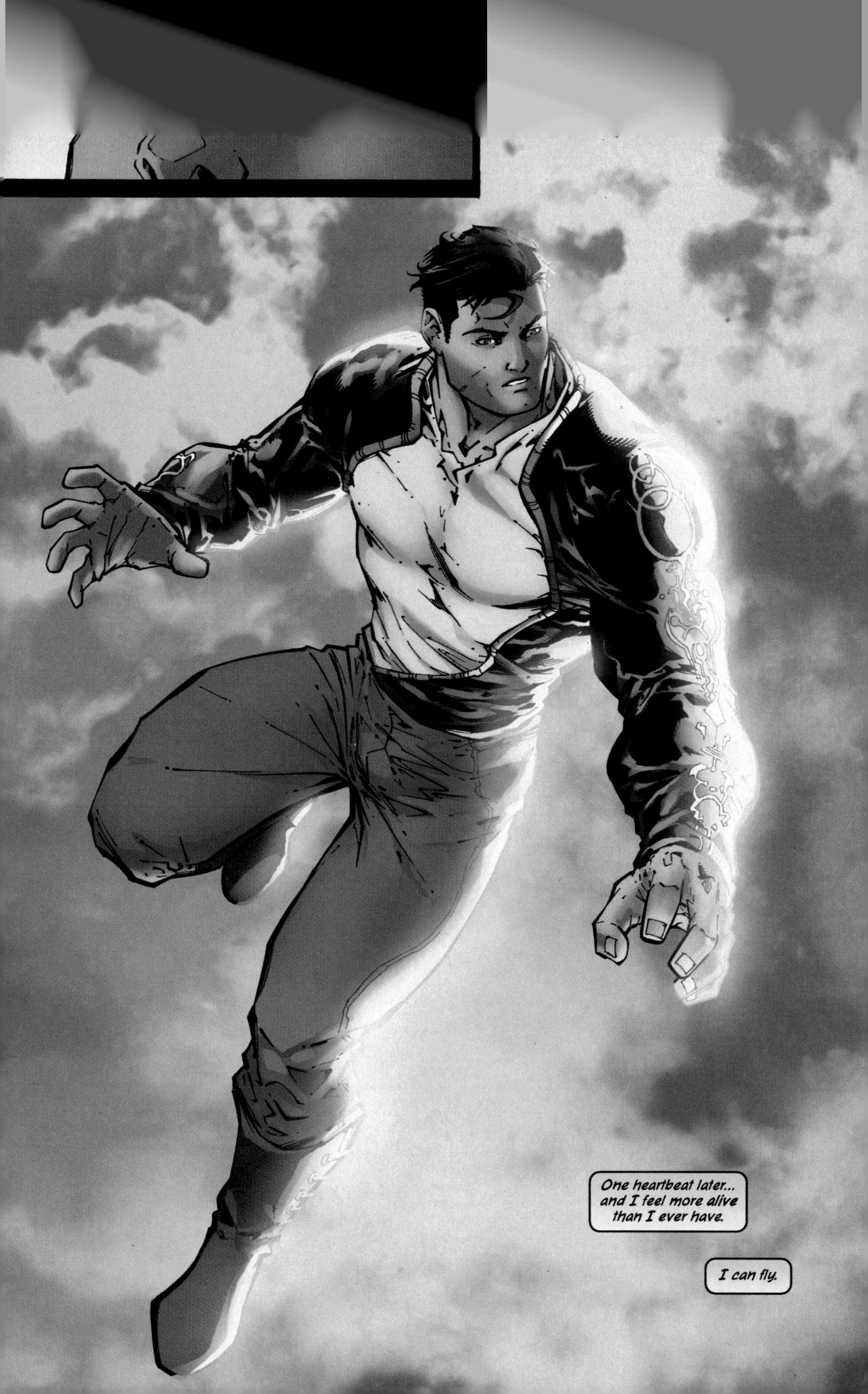
One heartbeat later... and I feel more alive than I ever have.
I can fly.

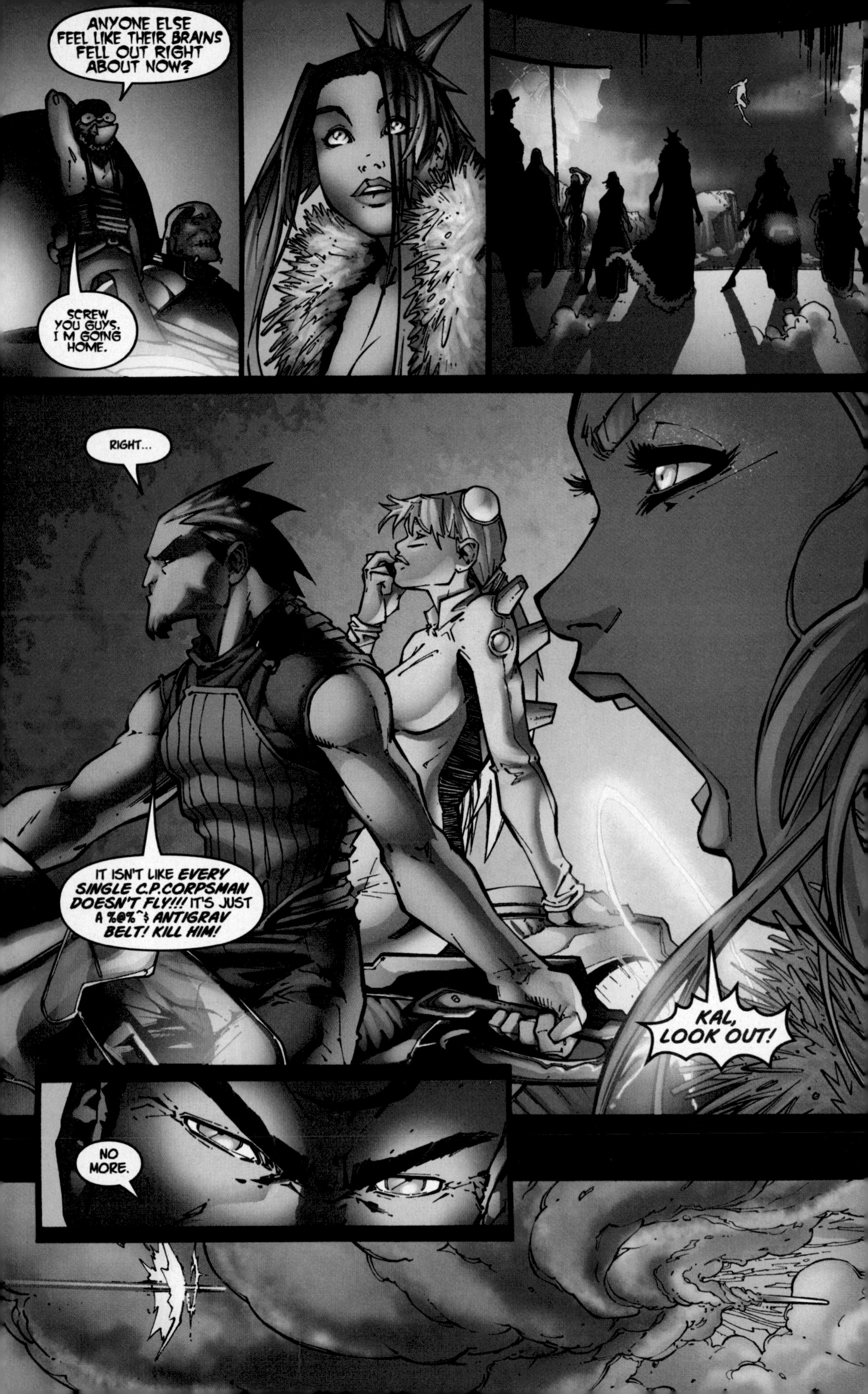

ANYONE ELSE FEEL LIKE THEIR BRAINS FELL OUT RIGHT ABOUT NOW?
SCREW YOU GUYS. I M GOING HOME.
RIGHT...
IT ISN'T LIKE EVERY SINGLE C.P.CORPSMAN DOESN'T FLY!!! IT'S JUST A %@%^$ ANTIGRAV BELT! KILL HIM!
KAL, LOOK OUT!
NO MORE.

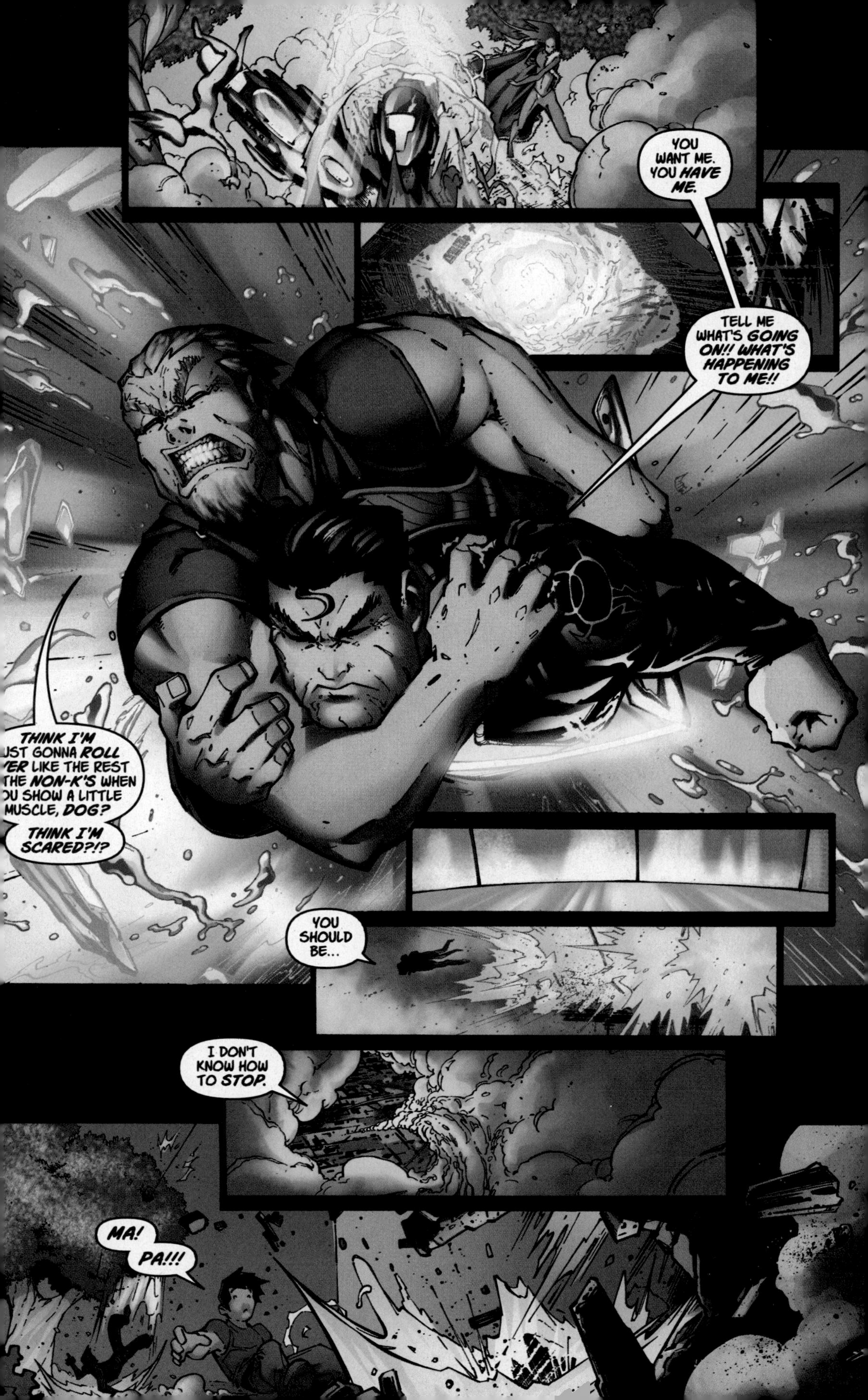

YOU WANT ME. YOU *HAVE* ME.
TELL ME WHAT'S *GOING ON!! WHAT'S HAPPENING TO ME!!*
THINK I'M UST GONNA *ROLL* *VER* LIKE THE REST THE *NON-K'S* WHEN OU SHOW A LITTLE MUSCLE, *DOG?*
THINK I'M SCARED?!?
YOU SHOULD BE...
I DON'T KNOW HOW TO *STOP.*
MA!
PA!!!

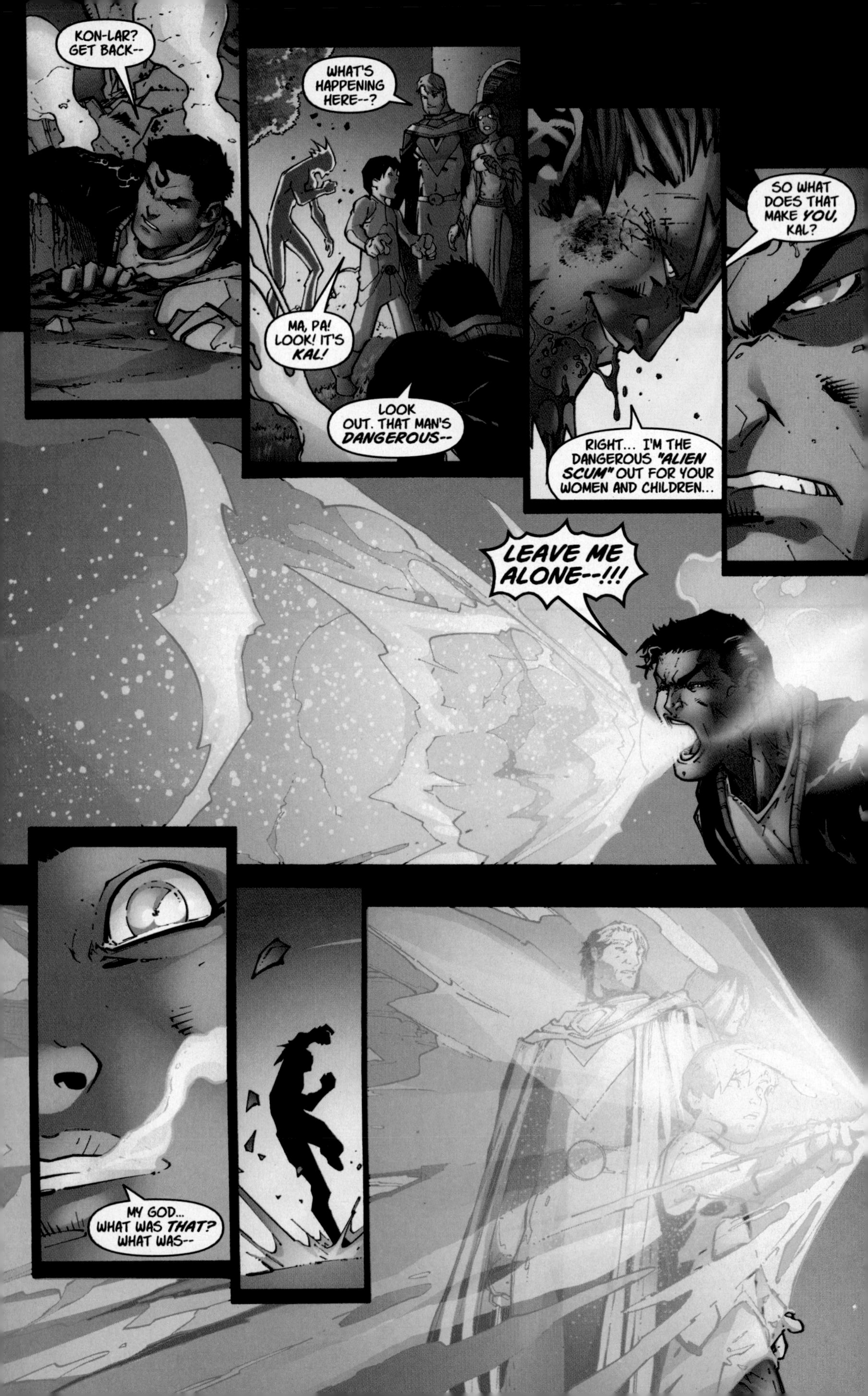
KON-LAR? GET BACK--
WHAT'S HAPPENING HERE--?
MA, PA! LOOK! IT'S KAL!
LOOK OUT. THAT MAN'S DANGEROUS--
RIGHT... I'M THE DANGEROUS "ALIEN SCUM" OUT FOR YOUR WOMEN AND CHILDREN...
SO WHAT DOES THAT MAKE YOU, KAL?
LEAVE ME ALONE--!!!
MY GOD... WHAT WAS THAT? WHAT WAS--

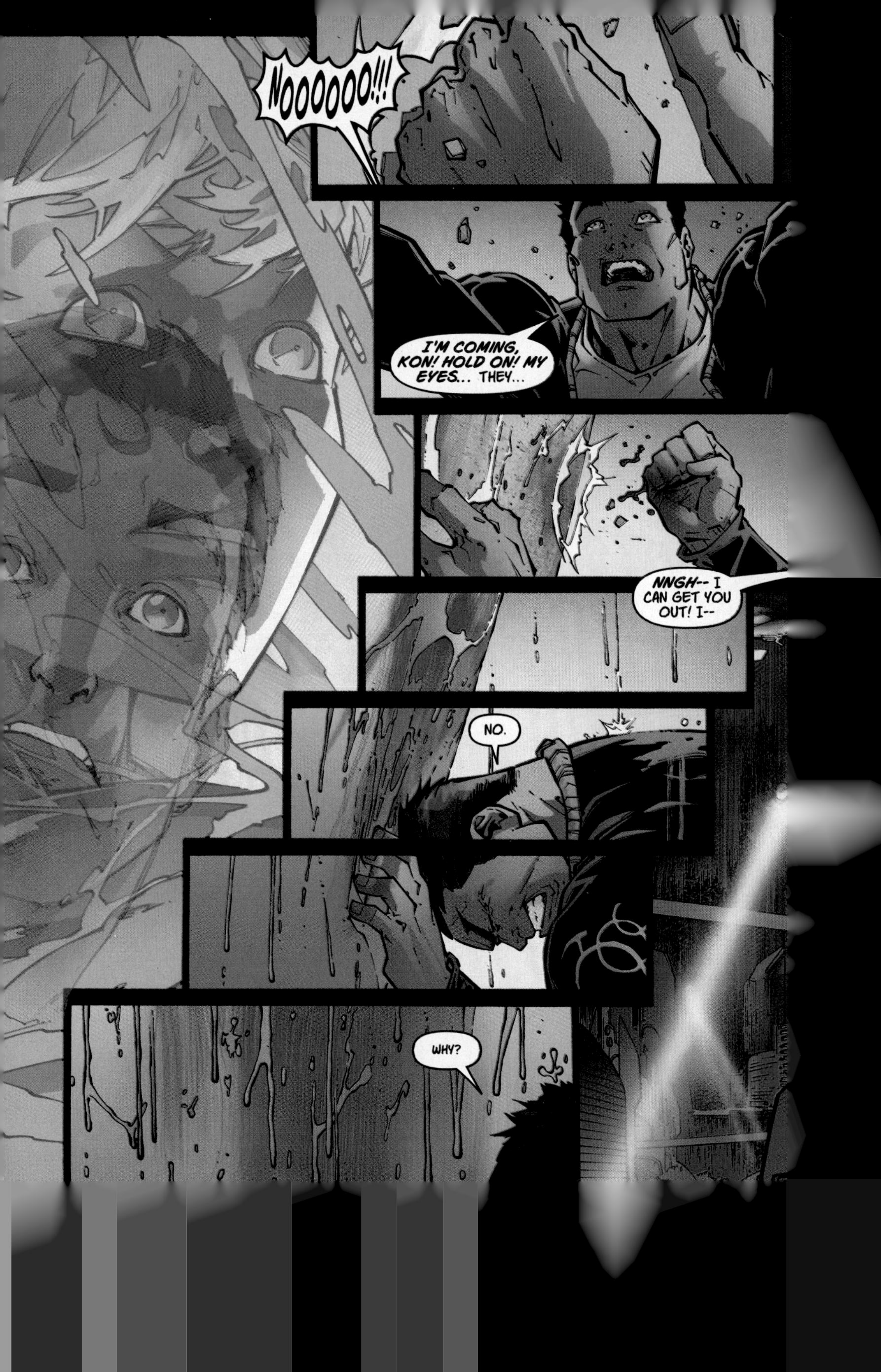
NOOOOOO!!!
I'M COMING, KON! HOLD ON! MY EYES... THEY...
NNGH-- I CAN GET YOU OUT! I--
NO.
WHY?

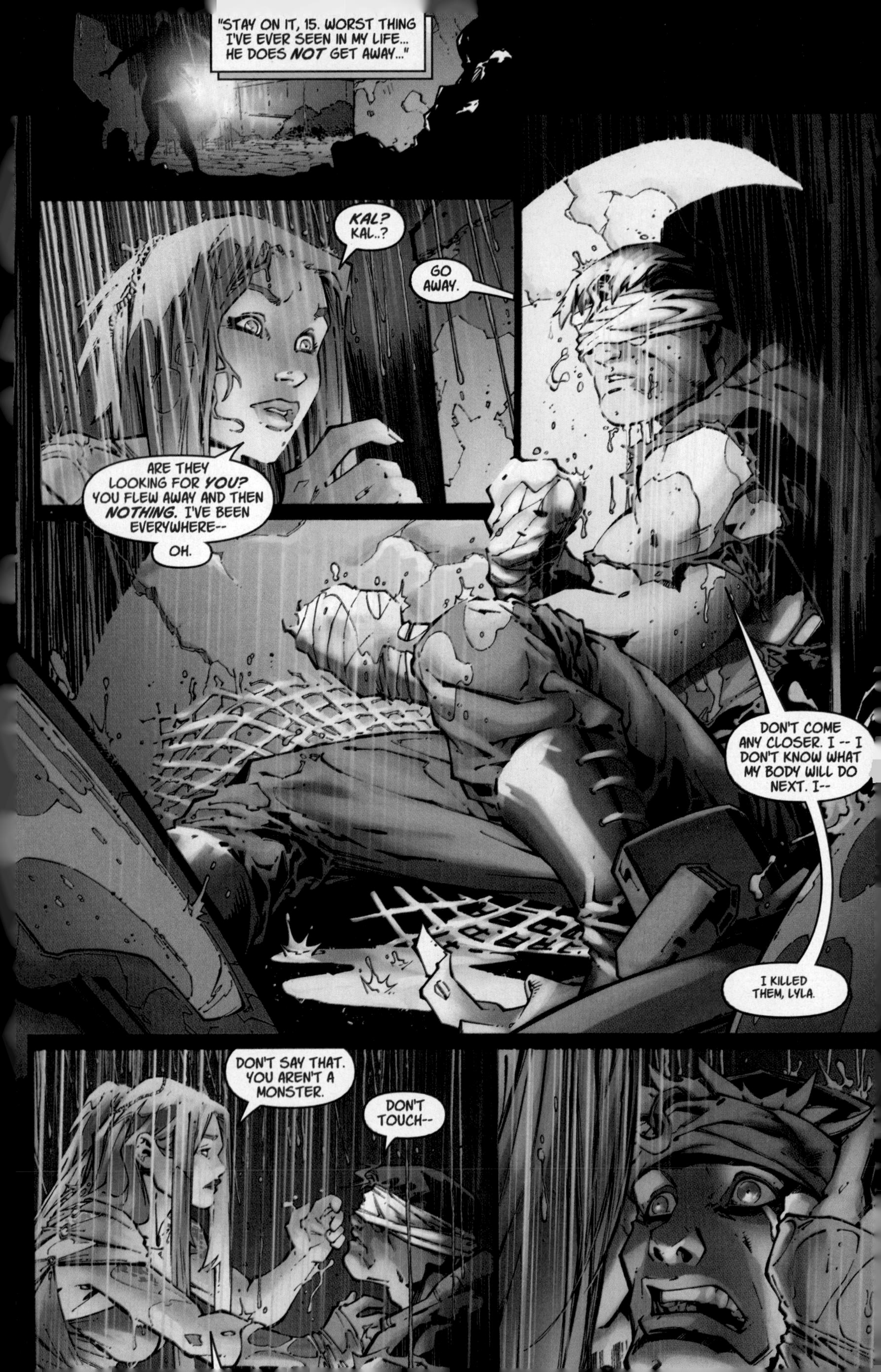
"STAY ON IT, 15. WORST THING I'VE EVER SEEN IN MY LIFE... HE DOES NOT GET AWAY..."
KAL? KAL..?
GO AWAY.
ARE THEY LOOKING FOR YOU? YOU FLEW AWAY AND THEN NOTHING. I'VE BEEN EVERYWHERE--
OH.
DON'T COME ANY CLOSER. I -- I DON'T KNOW WHAT MY BODY WILL DO NEXT. I--
I KILLED THEM, LYLA.
DON'T SAY THAT. YOU AREN'T A MONSTER.
DON'T TOUCH--

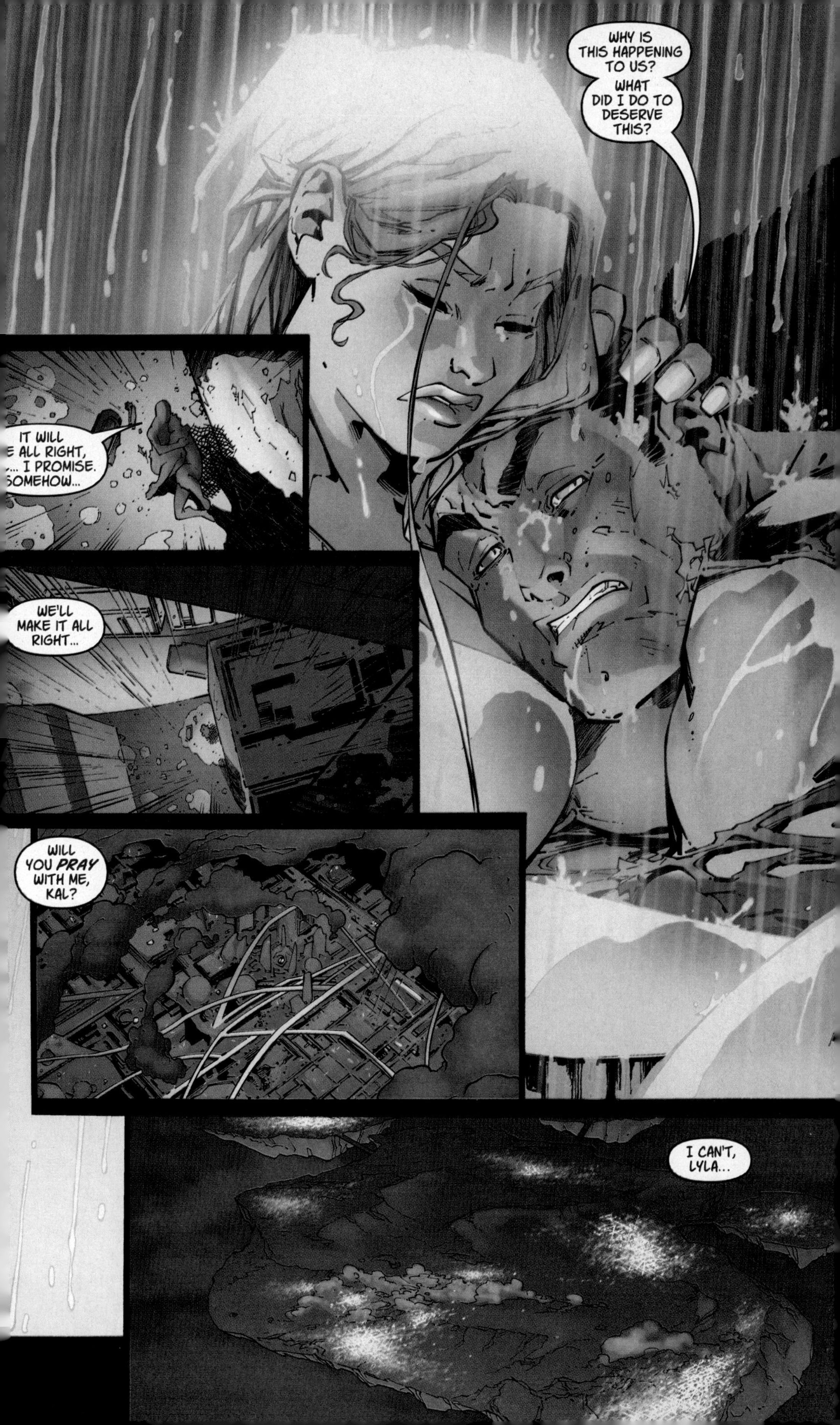
WHY IS THIS HAPPENING TO US? WHAT DID I DO TO DESERVE THIS?
IT WILL E ALL RIGHT, ... I PROMISE. SOMEHOW...
WE'LL MAKE IT ALL RIGHT...
WILL YOU *PRAY* WITH ME, KAL?
I CAN'T, LYLA...

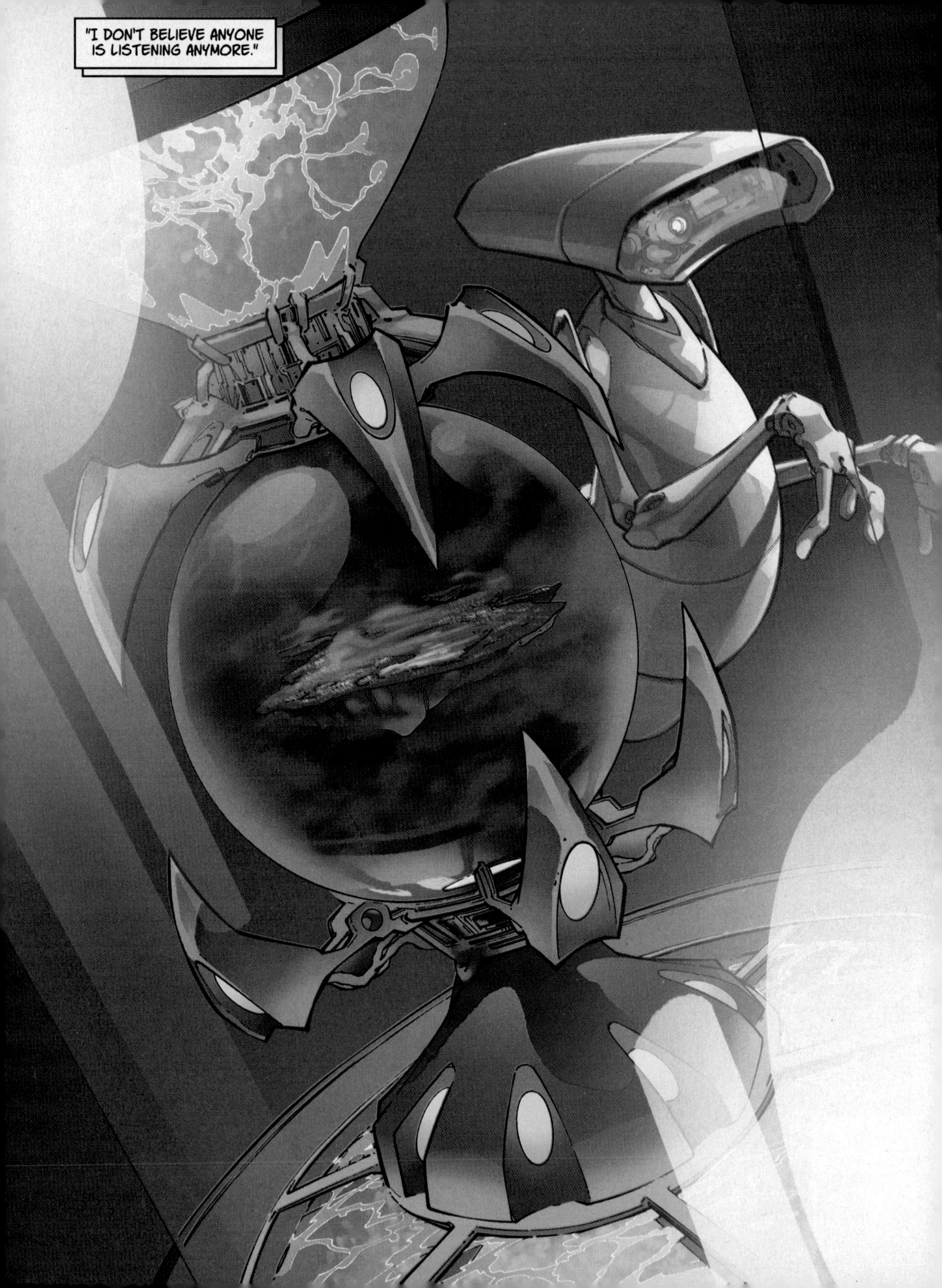
"I DON'T BELIEVE ANYONE IS LISTENING ANYMORE."

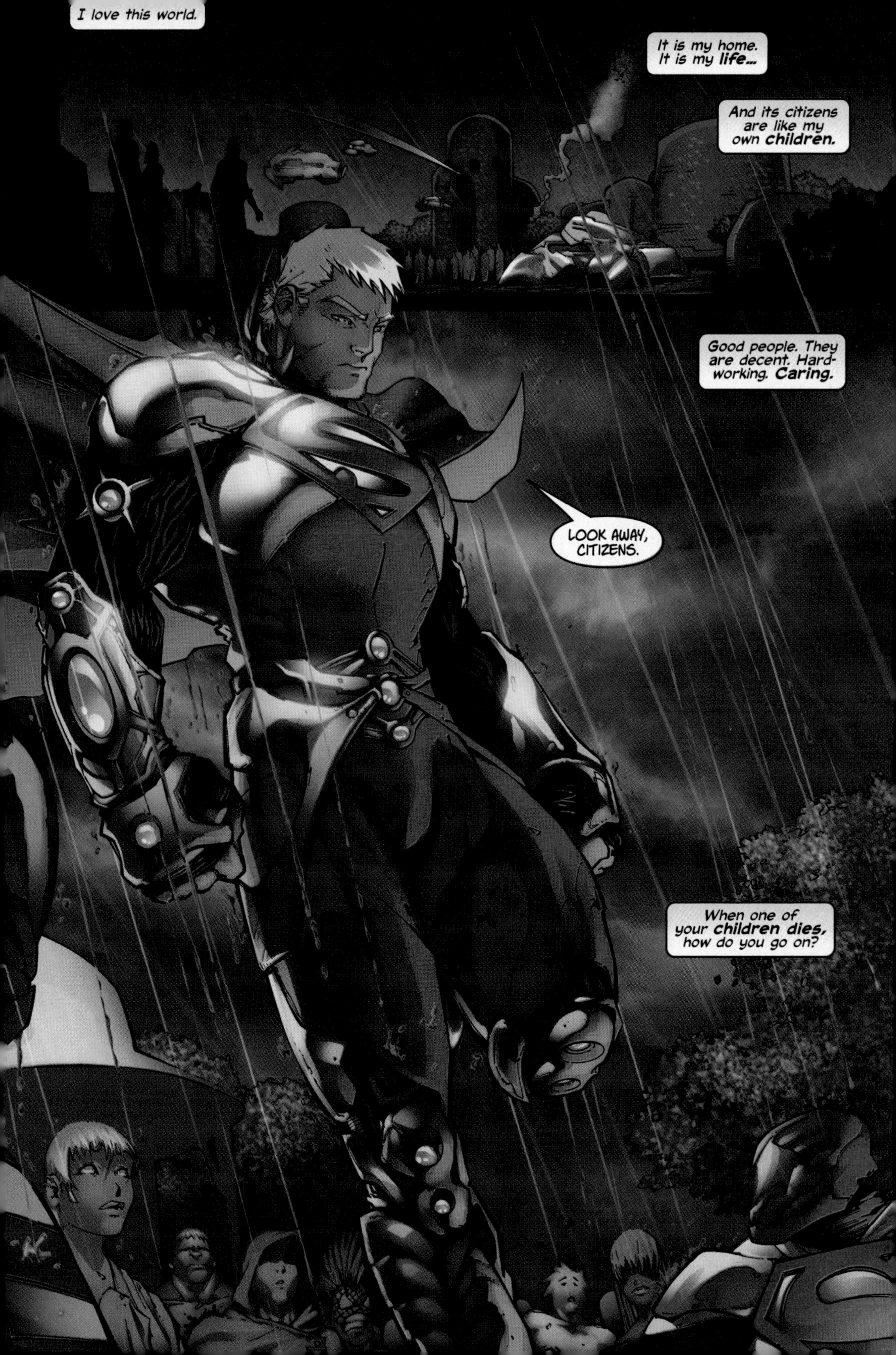
I love this world.
It is my home. It is my life...
And its citizens are like my own children.
Good people. They are decent. Hard-working. Caring.
LOOK AWAY, CITIZENS.
When one of your children dies, how do you go on?

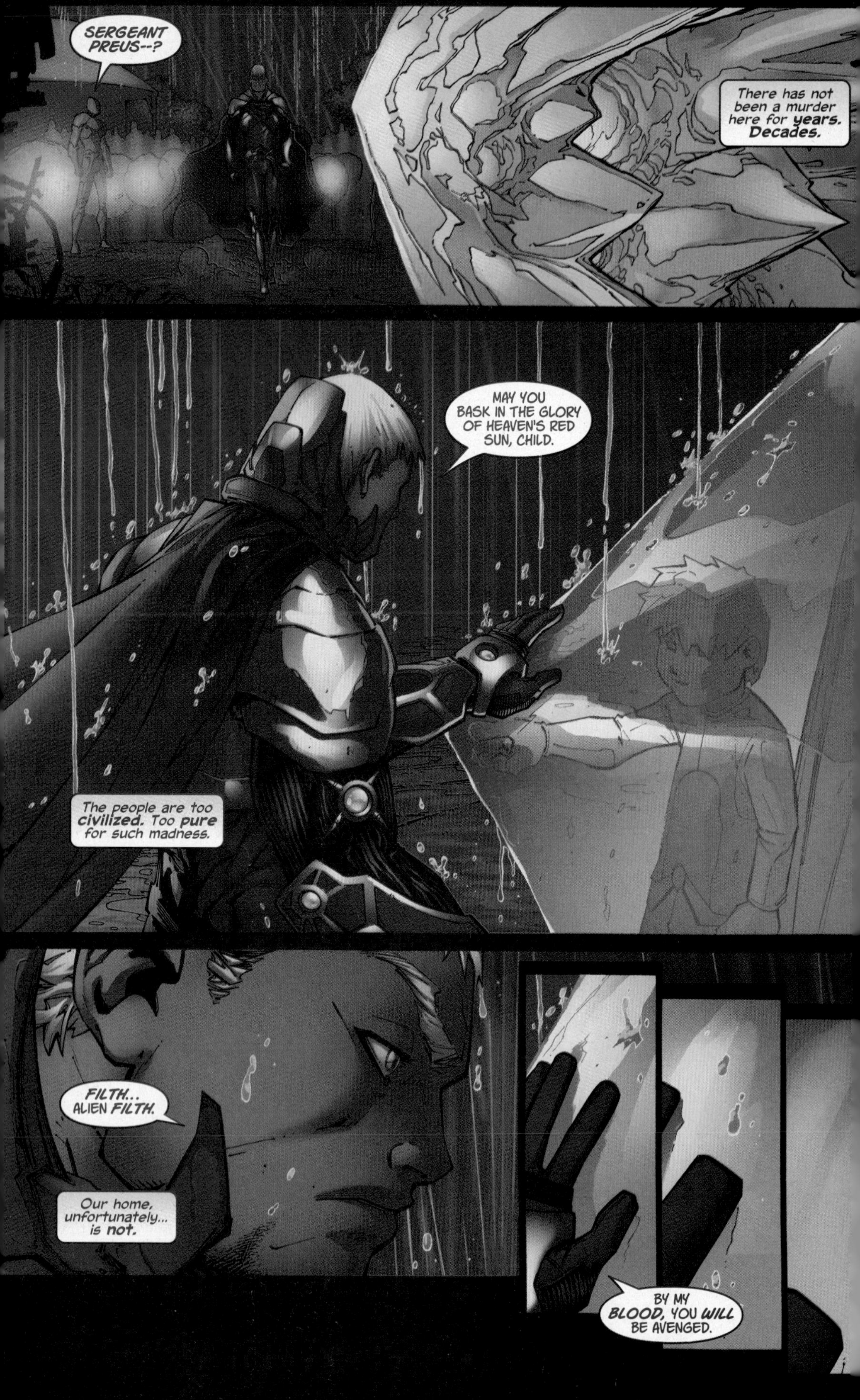
SERGEANT PREUS--?
There has not been a murder here for **years. Decades.**
MAY YOU BASK IN THE GLORY OF HEAVEN'S RED SUN, CHILD.
The people are too **civilized.** Too **pure** for such madness.
FILTH... ALIEN FILTH.
Our home, unfortunately... is **not.**
BY MY BLOOD, YOU WILL BE AVENGED.

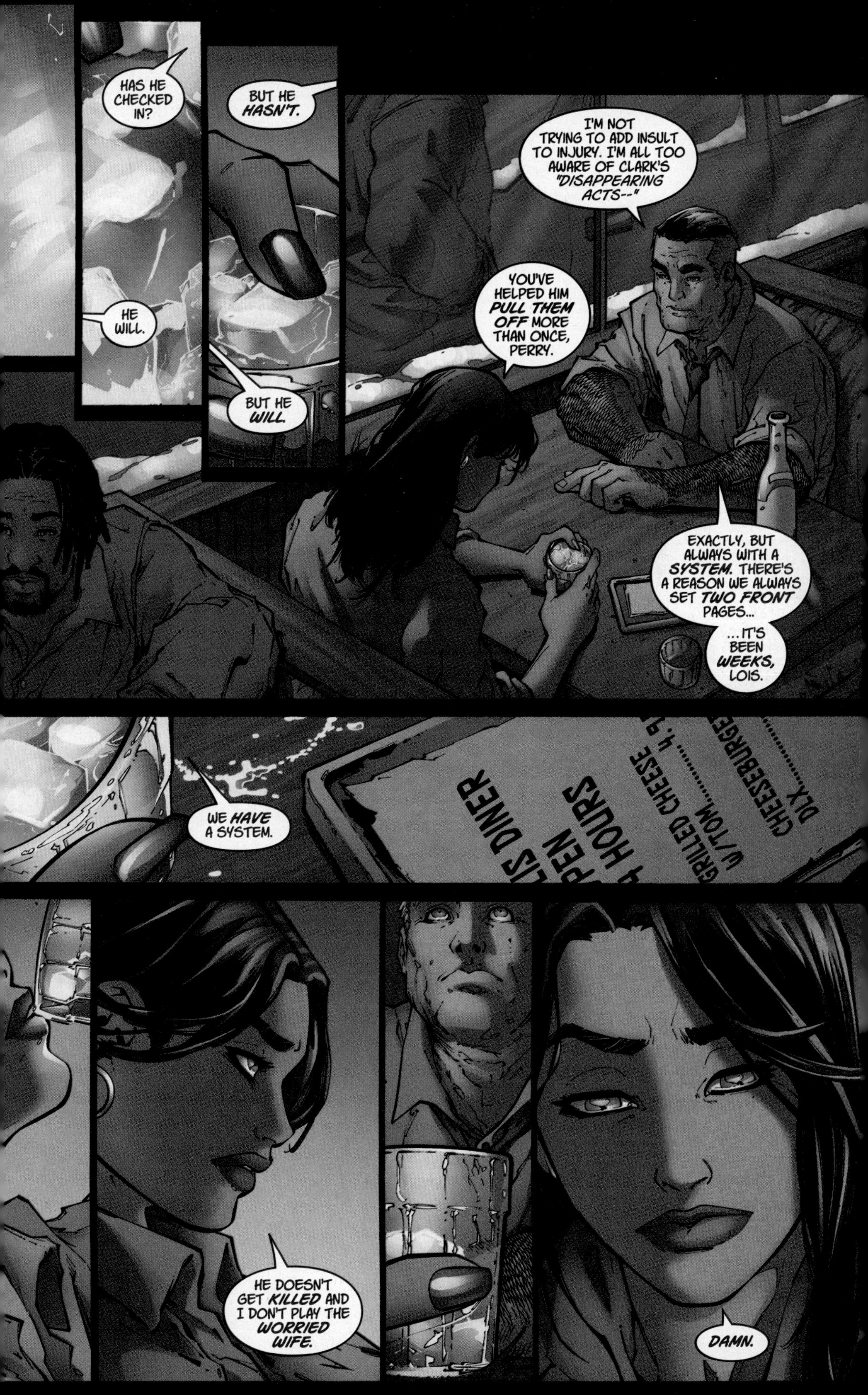
HAS HE CHECKED IN?
HE WILL.
BUT HE HASN'T.
BUT HE WILL.
I'M NOT TRYING TO ADD INSULT TO INJURY. I'M ALL TOO AWARE OF CLARK'S "DISAPPEARING ACTS--"
YOU'VE HELPED HIM PULL THEM OFF MORE THAN ONCE, PERRY.
EXACTLY, BUT ALWAYS WITH A SYSTEM. THERE'S A REASON WE ALWAYS SET TWO FRONT PAGES...
...IT'S BEEN WEEKS, LOIS.
WE HAVE A SYSTEM.
DINER
HOURS
GRILLED CHEESE
W/TOM
CHEESEBURGER
DLX
HE DOESN'T GET KILLED AND I DON'T PLAY THE WORRIED WIFE.
DAMN.

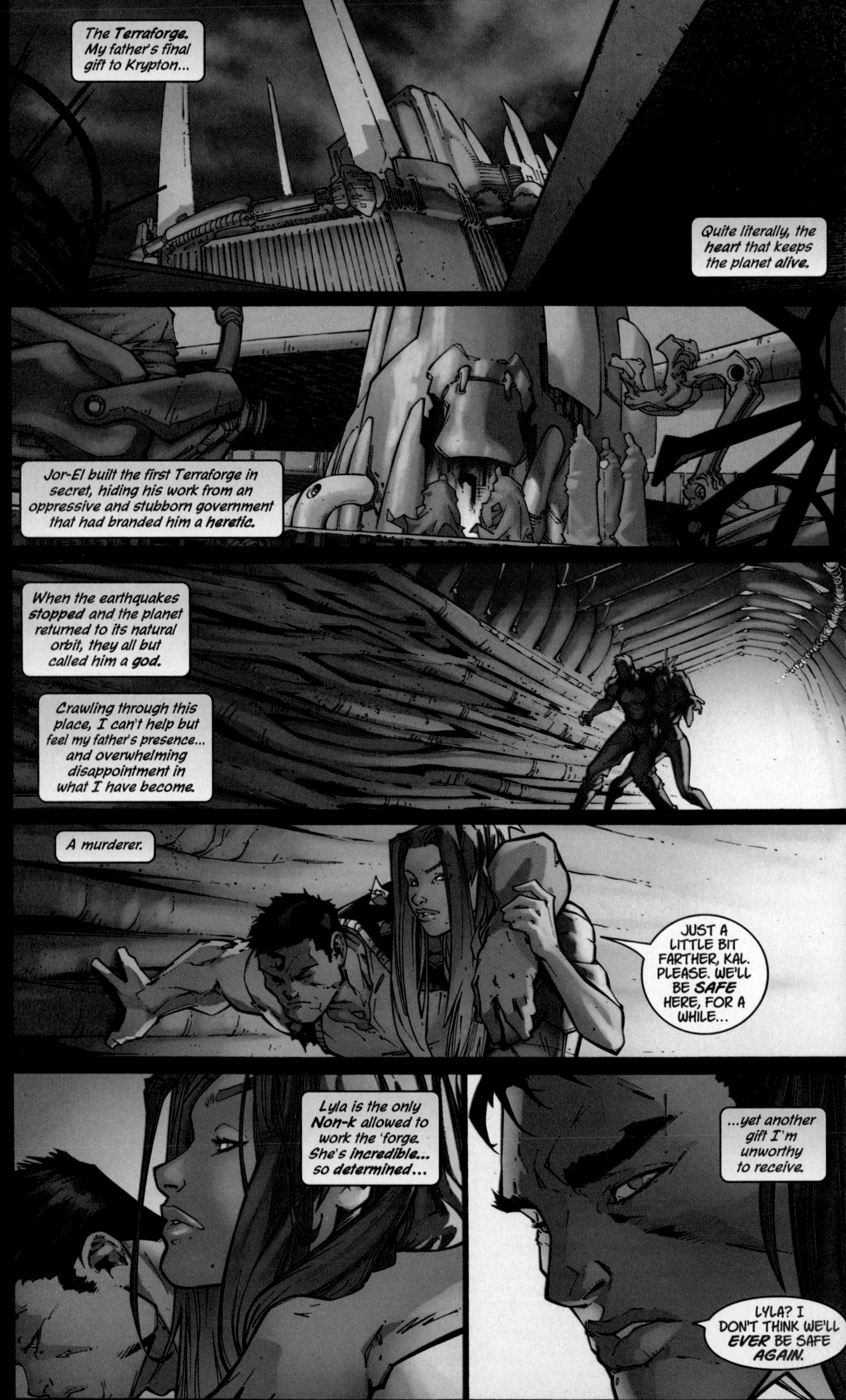
The Terraforge. My father's final gift to Krypton...
Quite literally, the heart that keeps the planet alive.
Jor-El built the first Terraforge in secret, hiding his work from an oppressive and stubborn government that had branded him a heretic.
When the earthquakes stopped and the planet returned to its natural orbit, they all but called him a god.
Crawling through this place, I can't help but feel my father's presence... and overwhelming disappointment in what I have become.
A murderer.
JUST A LITTLE BIT FARTHER, KAL. PLEASE. WE'LL BE SAFE HERE, FOR A WHILE...
Lyla is the only Non-k allowed to work the 'forge. She's incredible... so determined...
...yet another gift I'm unworthy to receive.
LYLA? I DON'T THINK WE'LL EVER BE SAFE AGAIN.

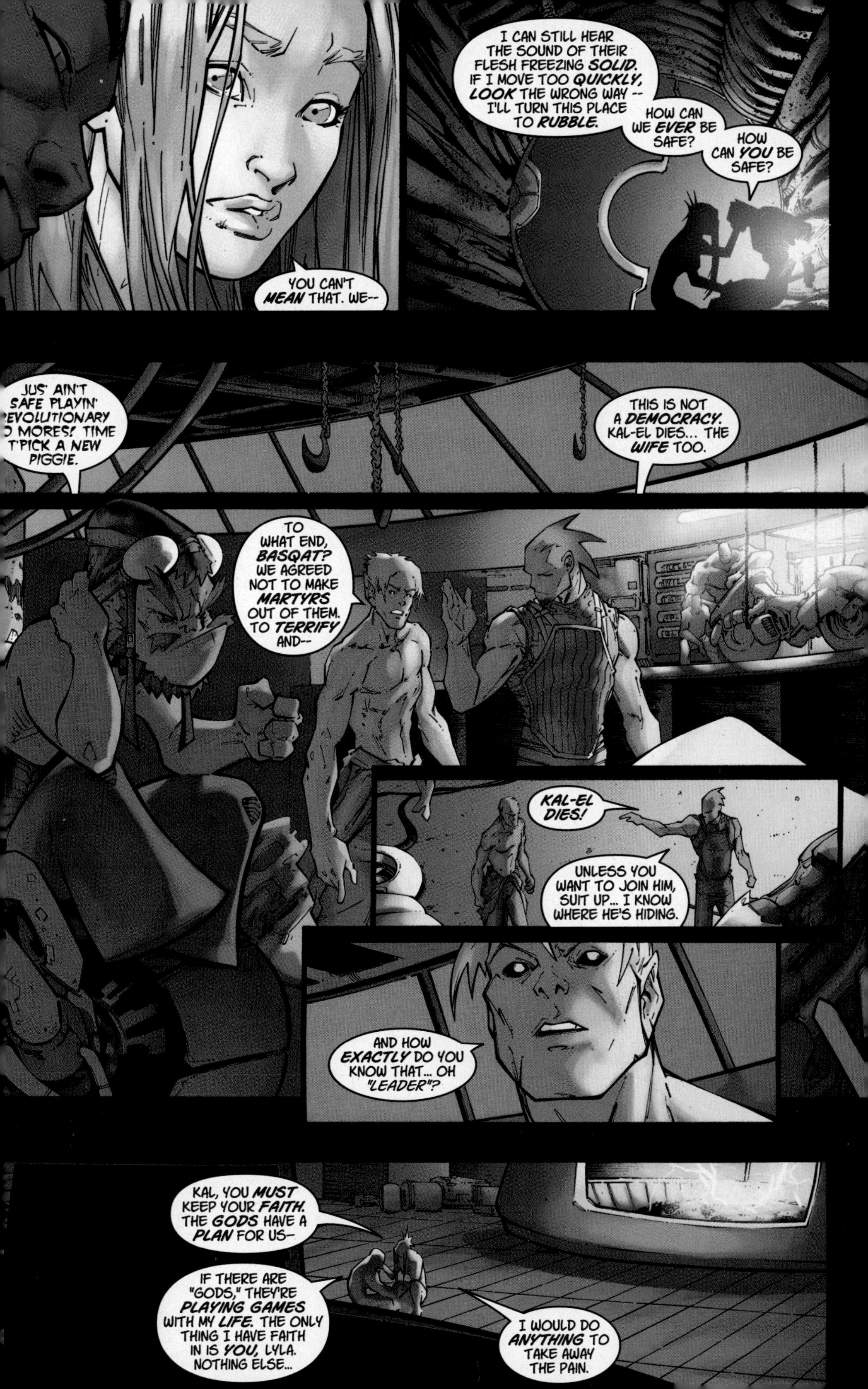
YOU CAN'T MEAN THAT. WE--
I CAN STILL HEAR THE SOUND OF THEIR FLESH FREEZING SOLID. IF I MOVE TOO QUICKLY, LOOK THE WRONG WAY -- I'LL TURN THIS PLACE TO RUBBLE.
HOW CAN WE EVER BE SAFE?
HOW CAN YOU BE SAFE?
JUS' AIN'T SAFE PLAYIN' REVOLUTIONARY NO MORES! TIME T'PICK A NEW PIGGIE.
THIS IS NOT A DEMOCRACY. KAL-EL DIES... THE WIFE TOO.
TO WHAT END, BASQAT? WE AGREED NOT TO MAKE MARTYRS OUT OF THEM. TO TERRIFY AND--
KAL-EL DIES!
UNLESS YOU WANT TO JOIN HIM, SUIT UP... I KNOW WHERE HE'S HIDING.
AND HOW EXACTLY DO YOU KNOW THAT... OH "LEADER"?
KAL, YOU MUST KEEP YOUR FAITH. THE GODS HAVE A PLAN FOR US-
IF THERE ARE "GODS," THEY'RE PLAYING GAMES WITH MY LIFE. THE ONLY THING I HAVE FAITH IN IS YOU, LYLA. NOTHING ELSE...
I WOULD DO ANYTHING TO TAKE AWAY THE PAIN.

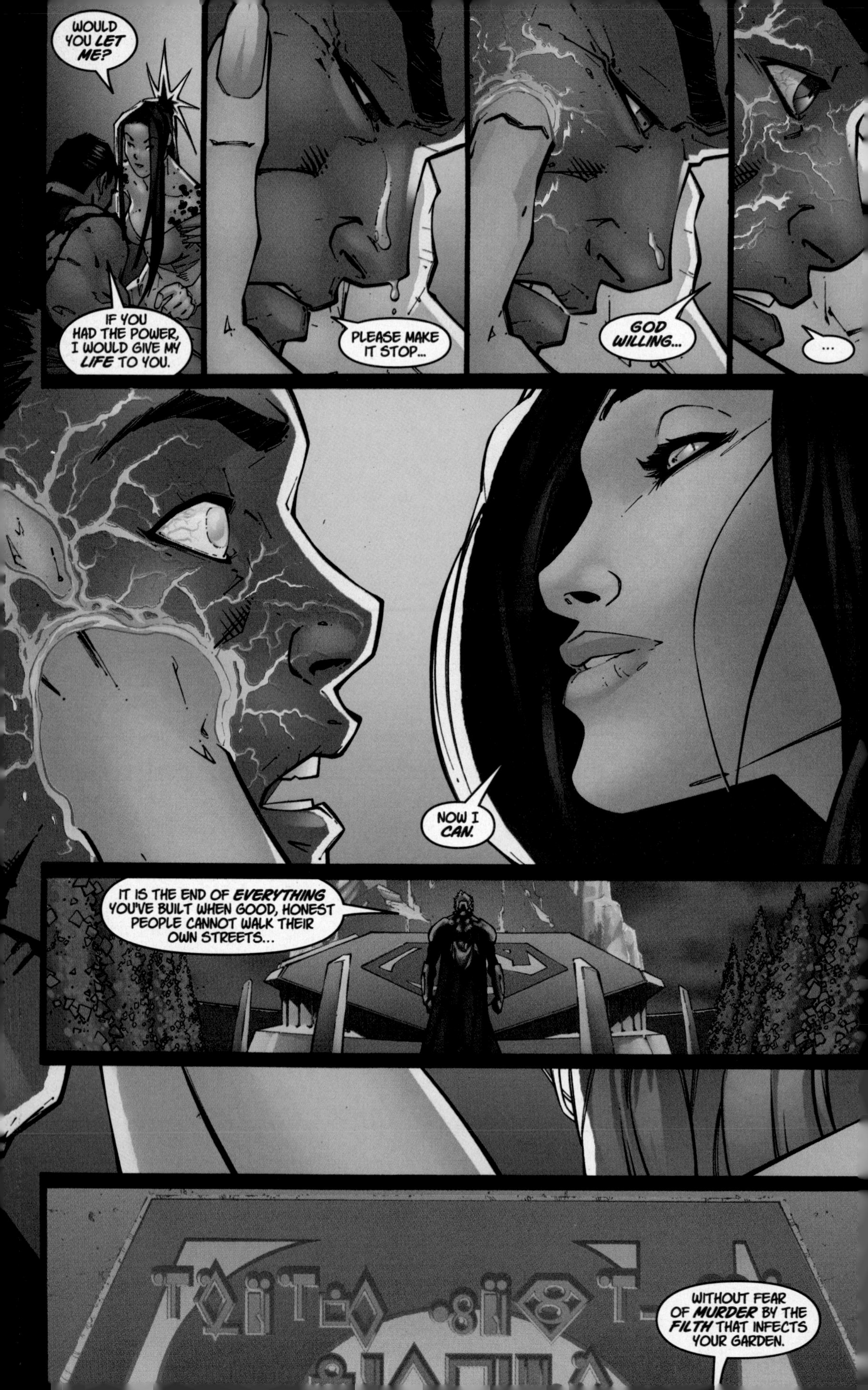
WOULD YOU LET ME?
IF YOU HAD THE POWER, I WOULD GIVE MY LIFE TO YOU.
PLEASE MAKE IT STOP...
GOD WILLING...
...
NOW I CAN.
IT IS THE END OF EVERYTHING YOU'VE BUILT WHEN GOOD, HONEST PEOPLE CANNOT WALK THEIR OWN STREETS...
WITHOUT FEAR OF MURDER BY THE FILTH THAT INFECTS YOUR GARDEN.

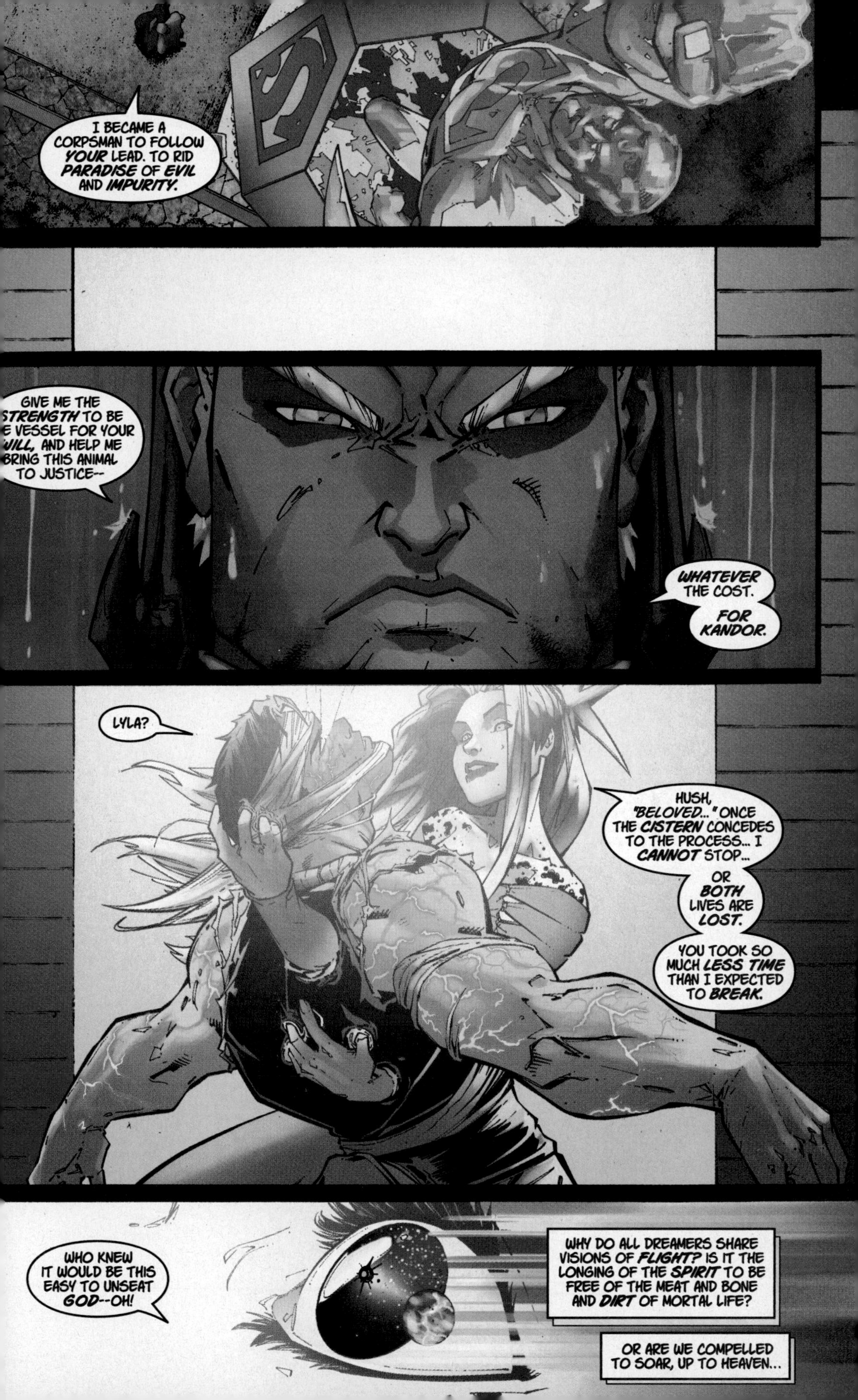
I BECAME A CORPSMAN TO FOLLOW YOUR LEAD. TO RID PARADISE OF EVIL AND IMPURITY.
GIVE ME THE STRENGTH TO BE E VESSEL FOR YOUR WILL, AND HELP ME BRING THIS ANIMAL TO JUSTICE--
WHATEVER THE COST.
FOR KANDOR.
LYLA?
HUSH, "BELOVED..." ONCE THE CISTERN CONCEDES TO THE PROCESS... I CANNOT STOP...
OR BOTH LIVES ARE LOST.
YOU TOOK SO MUCH LESS TIME THAN I EXPECTED TO BREAK.
WHO KNEW IT WOULD BE THIS EASY TO UNSEAT GOD--OH!
WHY DO ALL DREAMERS SHARE VISIONS OF FLIGHT? IS IT THE LONGING OF THE SPIRIT TO BE FREE OF THE MEAT AND BONE AND DIRT OF MORTAL LIFE?
OR ARE WE COMPELLED TO SOAR, UP TO HEAVEN...

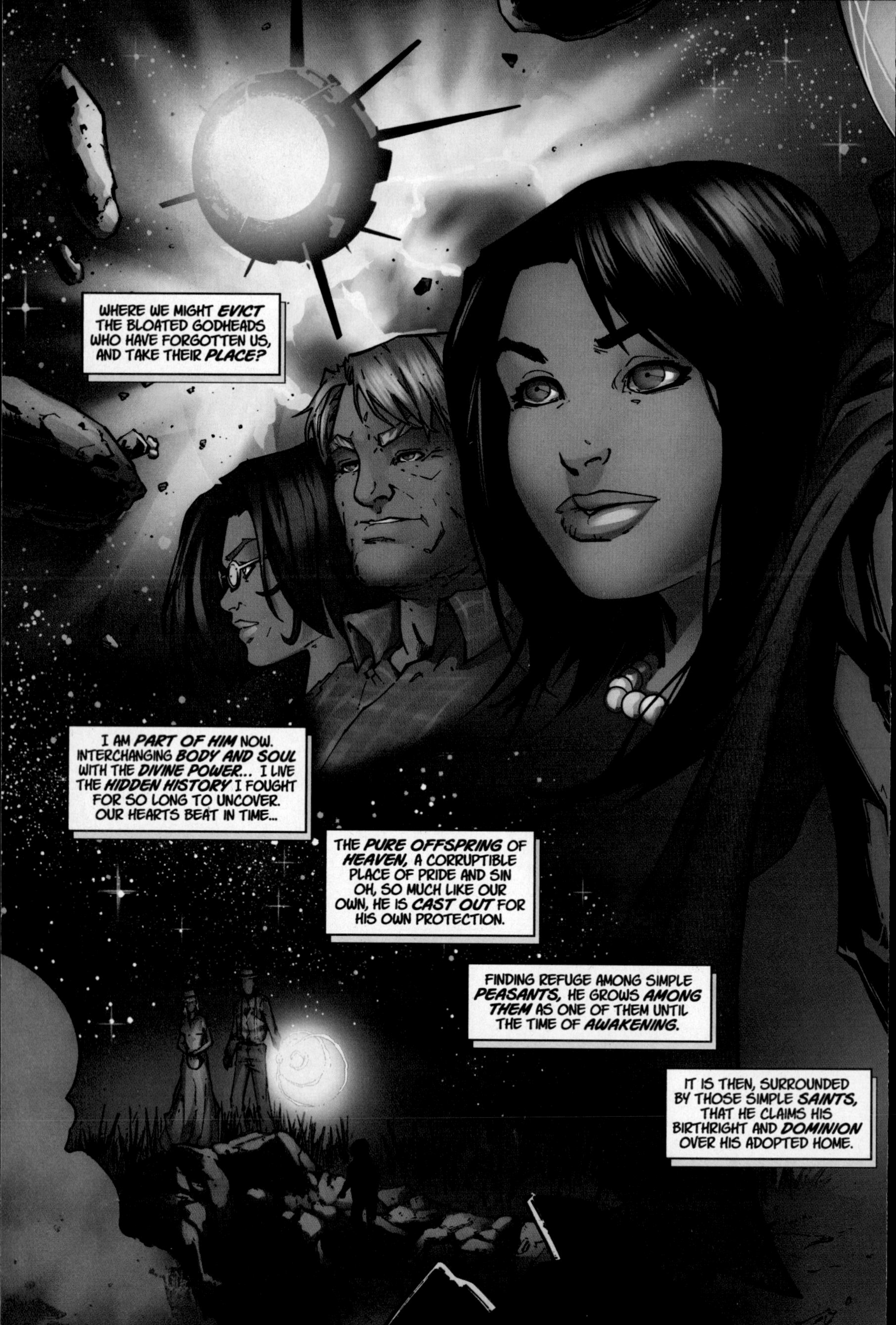
WHERE WE MIGHT *EVICT* THE BLOATED GODHEADS WHO HAVE FORGOTTEN US, AND TAKE THEIR *PLACE?*
I AM *PART OF HIM* NOW. INTERCHANGING *BODY AND SOUL* WITH THE *DIVINE POWER*... I LIVE THE *HIDDEN HISTORY* I FOUGHT FOR SO LONG TO UNCOVER. OUR HEARTS BEAT IN TIME...
THE *PURE OFFSPRING* OF *HEAVEN,* A CORRUPTIBLE PLACE OF PRIDE AND SIN OH, SO MUCH LIKE OUR OWN, HE IS *CAST OUT* FOR HIS OWN PROTECTION.
FINDING REFUGE AMONG SIMPLE *PEASANTS,* HE GROWS *AMONG THEM* AS ONE OF THEM UNTIL THE TIME OF *AWAKENING.*
IT IS THEN, SURROUNDED BY THOSE SIMPLE *SAINTS,* THAT HE CLAIMS HIS BIRTHRIGHT AND *DOMINION* OVER HIS ADOPTED HOME.

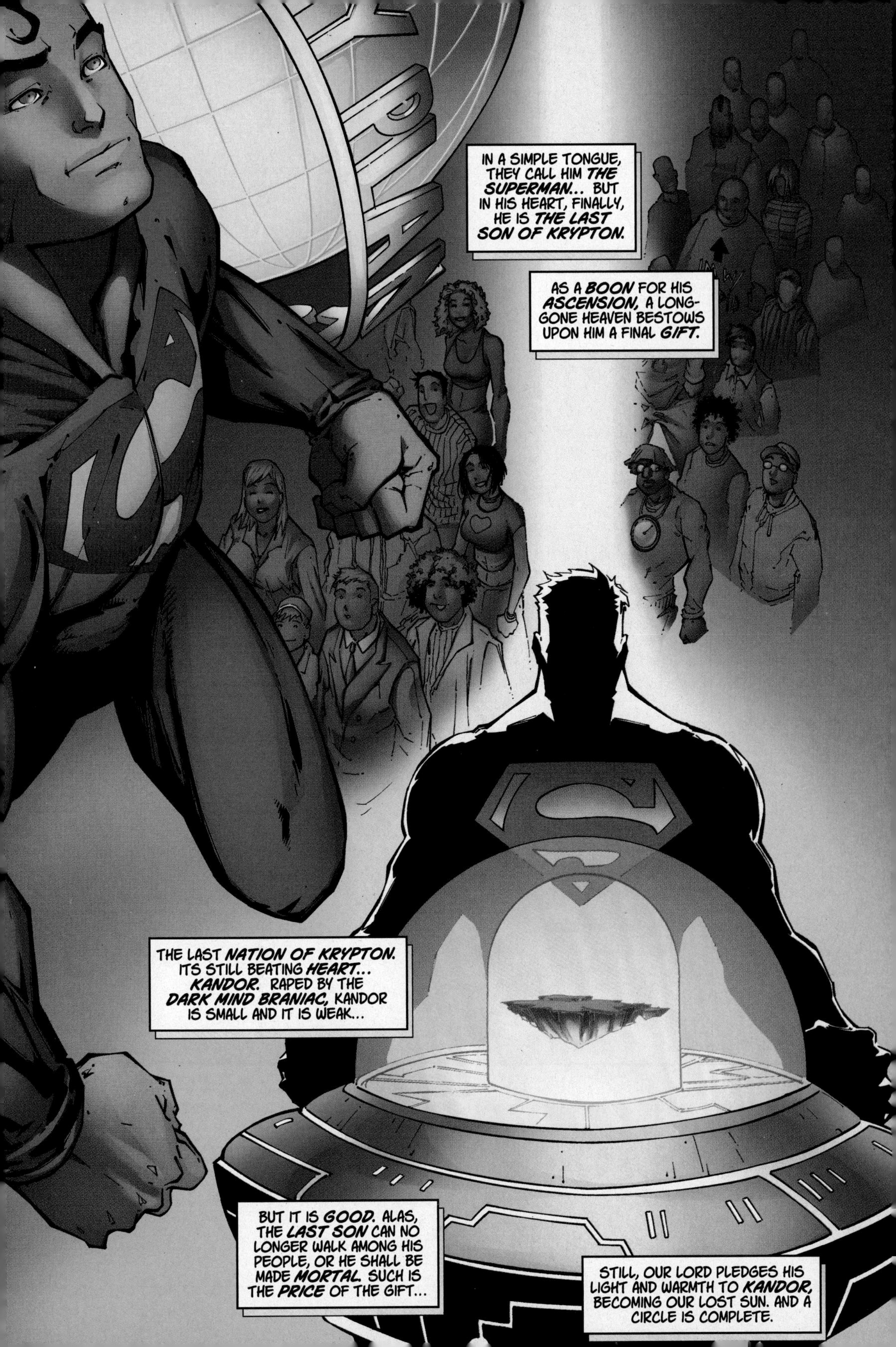

IN A SIMPLE TONGUE, THEY CALL HIM THE SUPERMAN... BUT IN HIS HEART, FINALLY, HE IS THE LAST SON OF KRYPTON.
AS A BOON FOR HIS ASCENSION, A LONG-GONE HEAVEN BESTOWS UPON HIM A FINAL GIFT.
THE LAST NATION OF KRYPTON. ITS STILL BEATING HEART... KANDOR. RAPED BY THE DARK MIND BRANIAC, KANDOR IS SMALL AND IT IS WEAK...
BUT IT IS GOOD. ALAS, THE LAST SON CAN NO LONGER WALK AMONG HIS PEOPLE, OR HE SHALL BE MADE MORTAL. SUCH IS THE PRICE OF THE GIFT...
STILL, OUR LORD PLEDGES HIS LIGHT AND WARMTH TO KANDOR, BECOMING OUR LOST SUN. AND A CIRCLE IS COMPLETE.

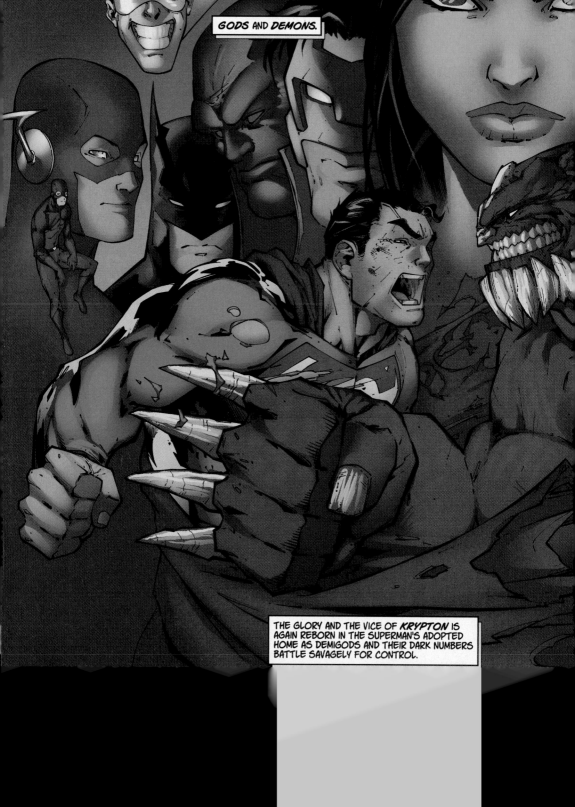

THE SUN GIVES LIFE. SUCH IS ITS NATURE. WHAT LIFE IS BORN OF A DIVINE SUN?

GODS AND DEMONS.

THE GLORY AND THE VICE OF KRYPTON IS AGAIN REBORN IN THE SUPERMAN'S ADOPTED HOME AS DEMIGODS AND THEIR DARK NUMBERS BATTLE SAVAGELY FOR CONTROL.

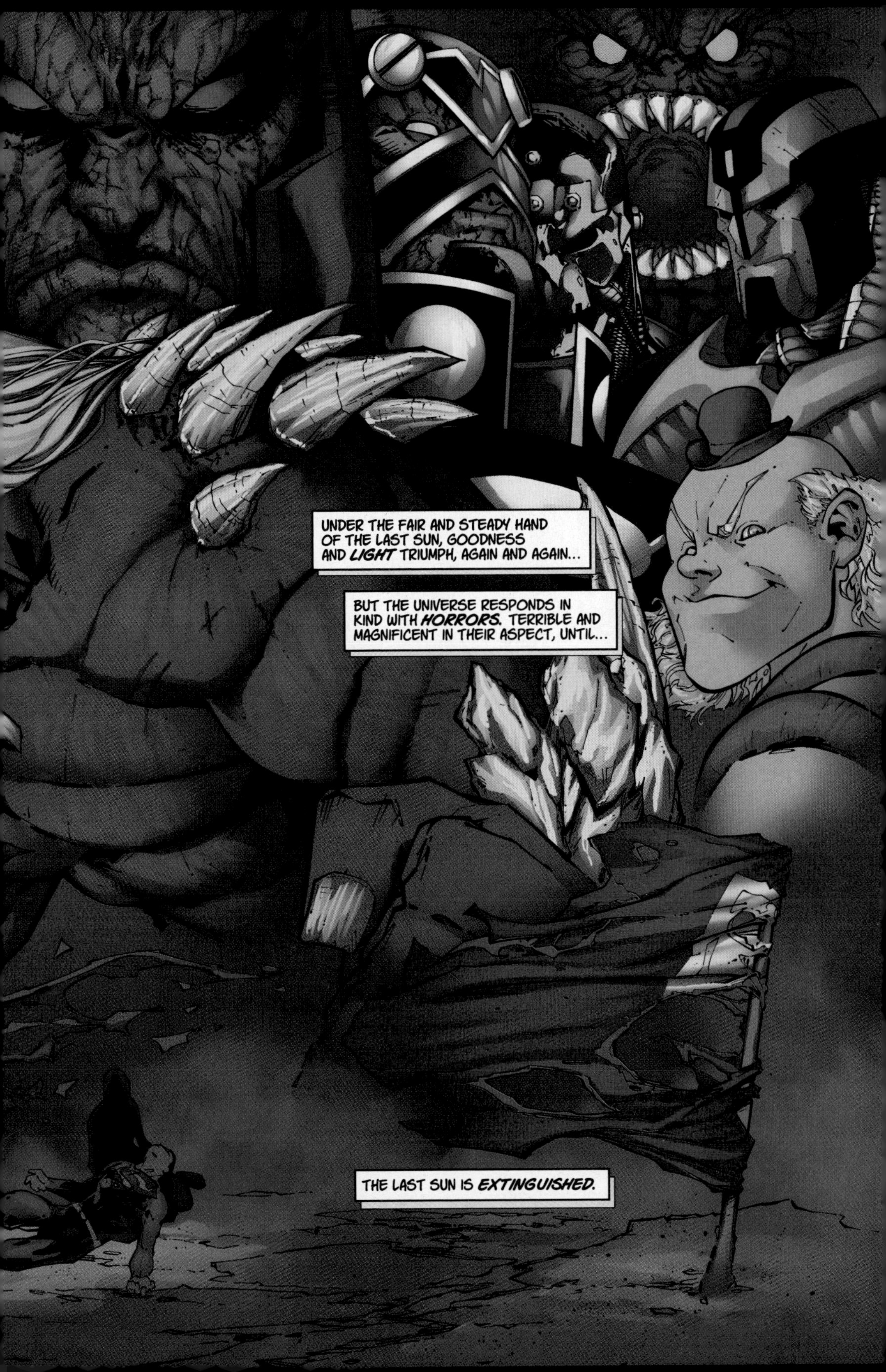
UNDER THE FAIR AND STEADY HAND OF THE LAST SUN, GOODNESS AND LIGHT TRIUMPH, AGAIN AND AGAIN...
BUT THE UNIVERSE RESPONDS IN KIND WITH HORRORS. TERRIBLE AND MAGNIFICENT IN THEIR ASPECT, UNTIL...
THE LAST SUN IS EXTINGUISHED.

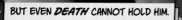

BUT EVEN *DEATH* CANNOT HOLD HIM.

THE LAST SUN IS *RESURRECTED,* AND LIGHT RETURNS TO THE WORLD HE CALLS HOME...

UNITING ALL PEOPLE. TURNING OUT *DARKNESS* WHERE IT FESTERS...

A *PARADISE* IS BORN. HE TAKES HIS *BRIDE,* A NATIVE DEMIGODDESS. THEY ARE AT *BLISS*...

WHILE *KANDOR...* BEAUTIFUL *KANDOR* ENJOYS NAUGHT BUT *NEGLIGENCE* FOR OVER A CENTURY.

A *CENTURY* DURING WHICH YOU BECAME NO MORE THAN A *MYTH.*

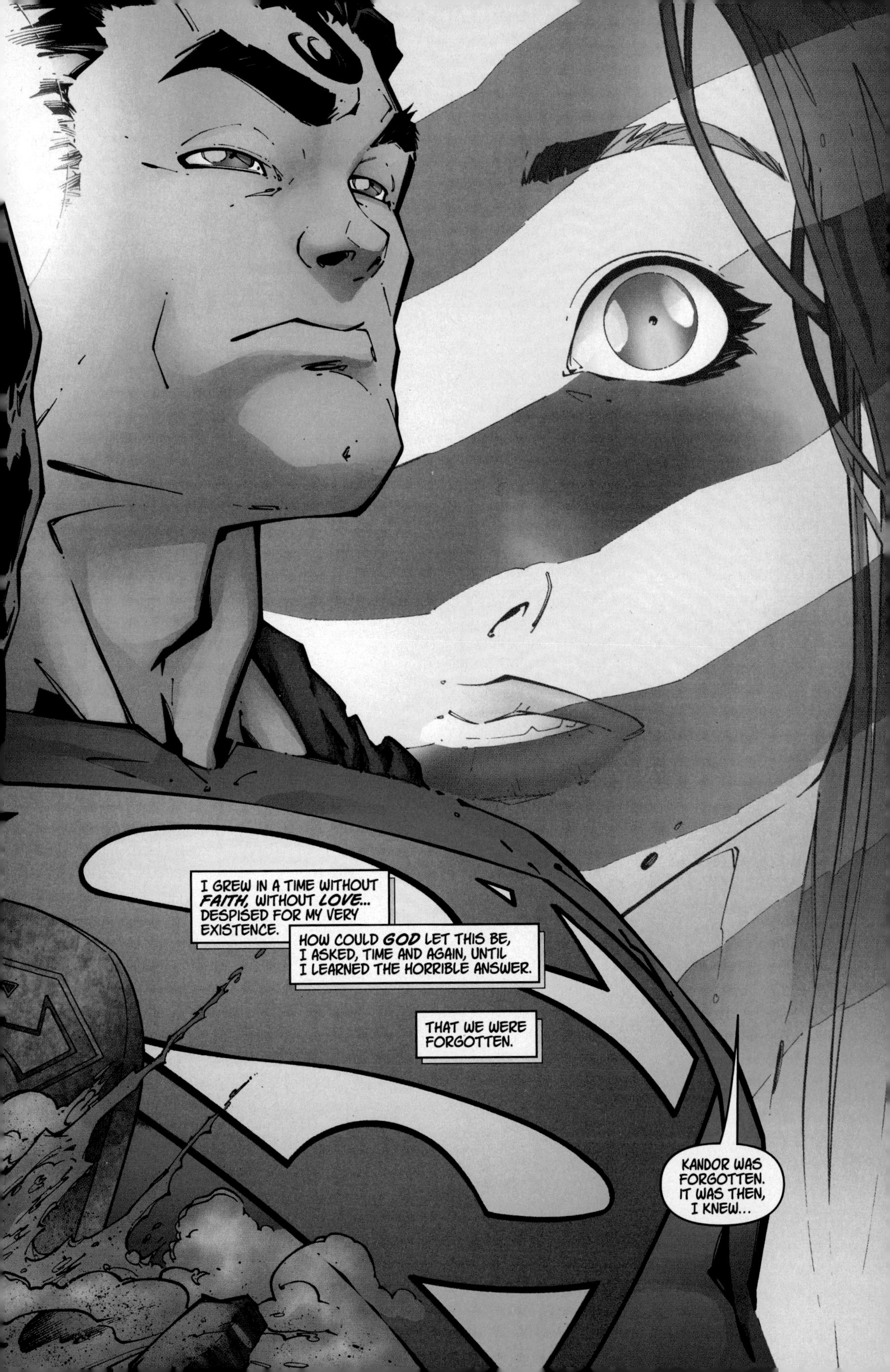
I GREW IN A TIME WITHOUT FAITH, WITHOUT LOVE... DESPISED FOR MY VERY EXISTENCE.
HOW COULD GOD LET THIS BE, I ASKED, TIME AND AGAIN, UNTIL I LEARNED THE HORRIBLE ANSWER.
THAT WE WERE FORGOTTEN.
KANDOR WAS FORGOTTEN. IT WAS THEN, I KNEW...

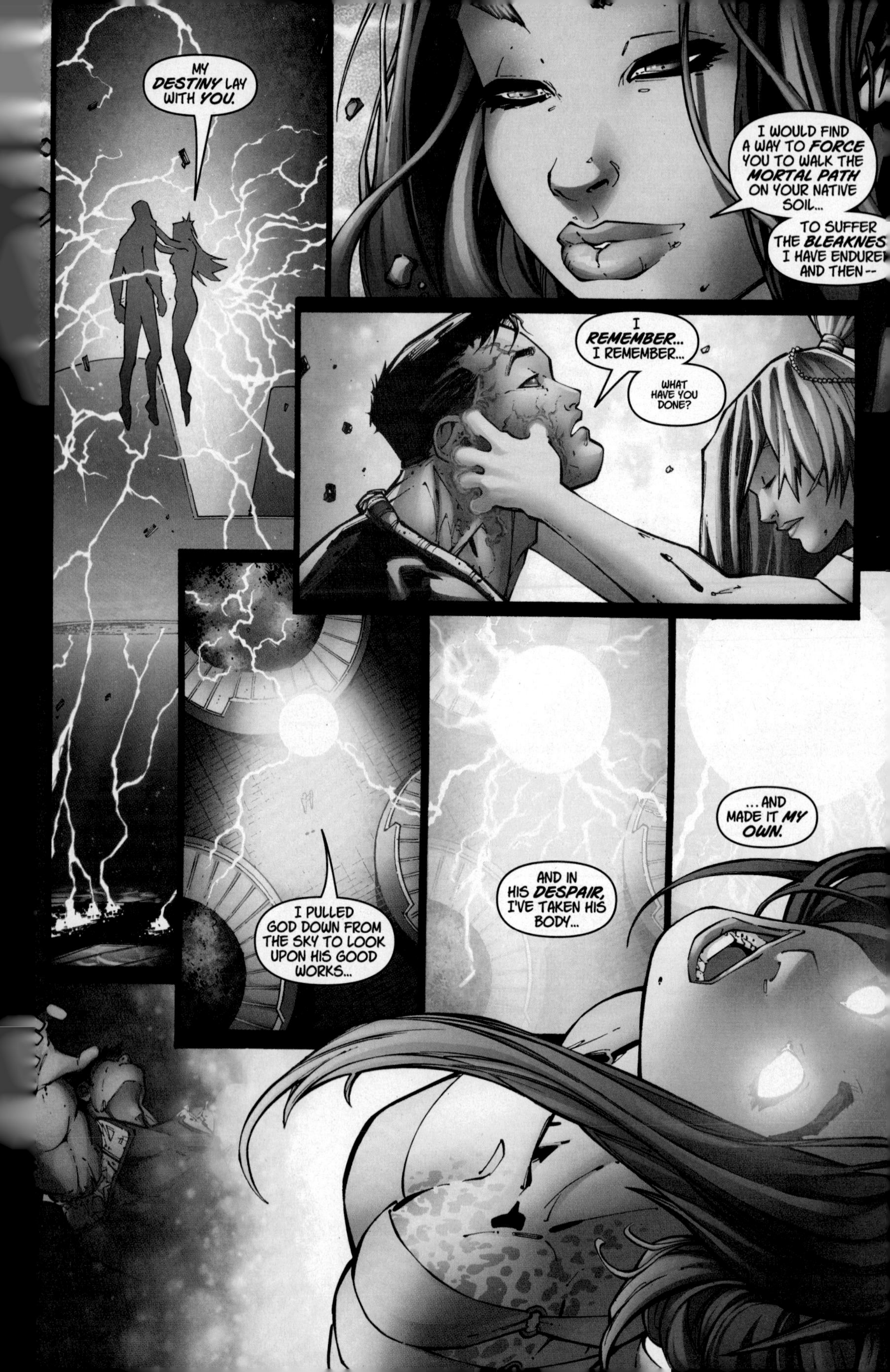
MY DESTINY LAY WITH YOU.
I WOULD FIND A WAY TO FORCE YOU TO WALK THE MORTAL PATH ON YOUR NATIVE SOIL...
TO SUFFER THE BLEAKNES I HAVE ENDURE AND THEN--
I REMEMBER... I REMEMBER...
WHAT HAVE YOU DONE?
I PULLED GOD DOWN FROM THE SKY TO LOOK UPON HIS GOOD WORKS...
AND IN HIS DESPAIR, I'VE TAKEN HIS BODY...
...AND MADE IT MY OWN.

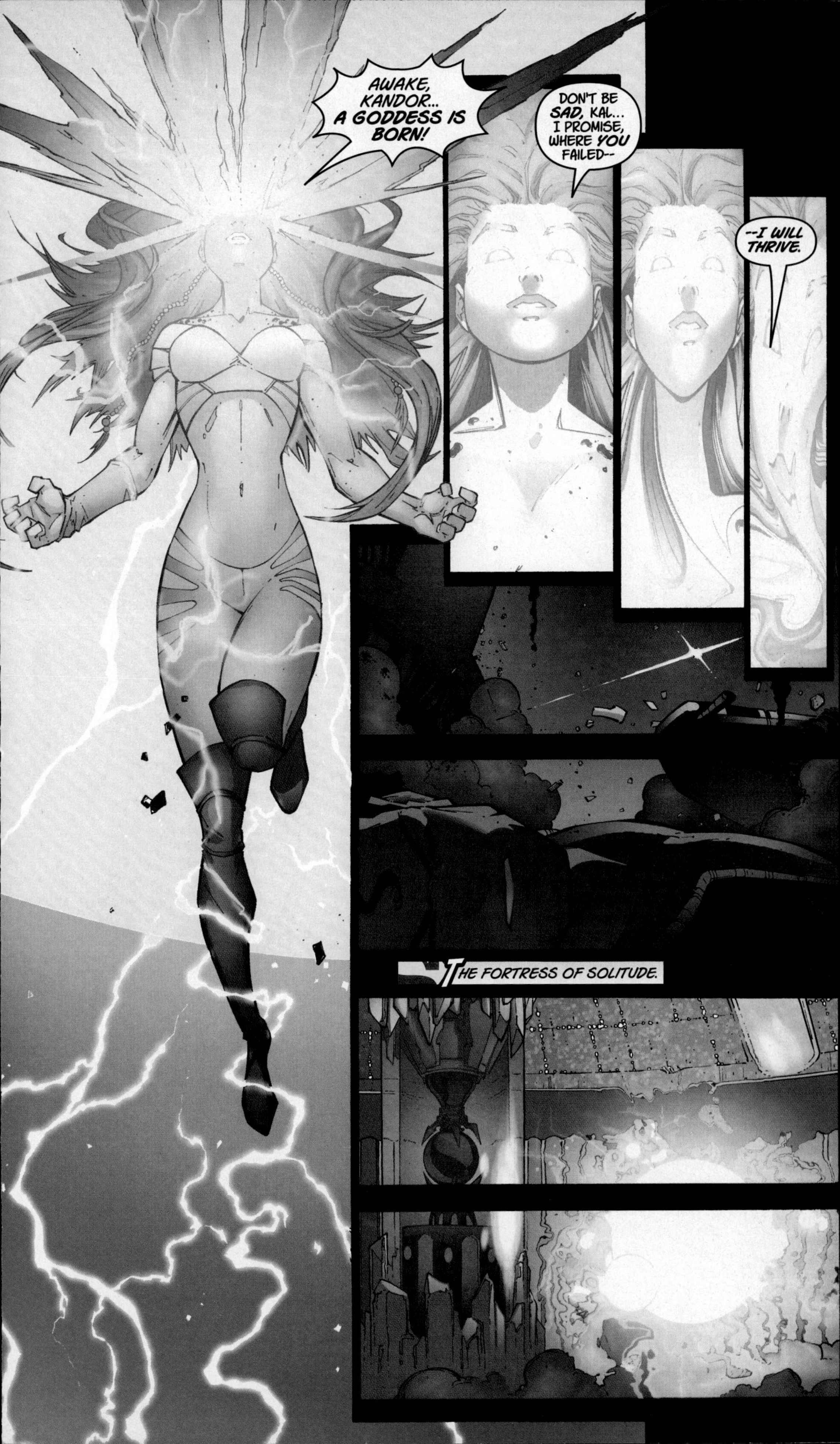
AWAKE, KANDOR... A GODDESS IS BORN!
DON'T BE SAD, KAL... I PROMISE, WHERE YOU FAILED--
--I WILL THRIVE.
THE FORTRESS OF SOLITUDE.

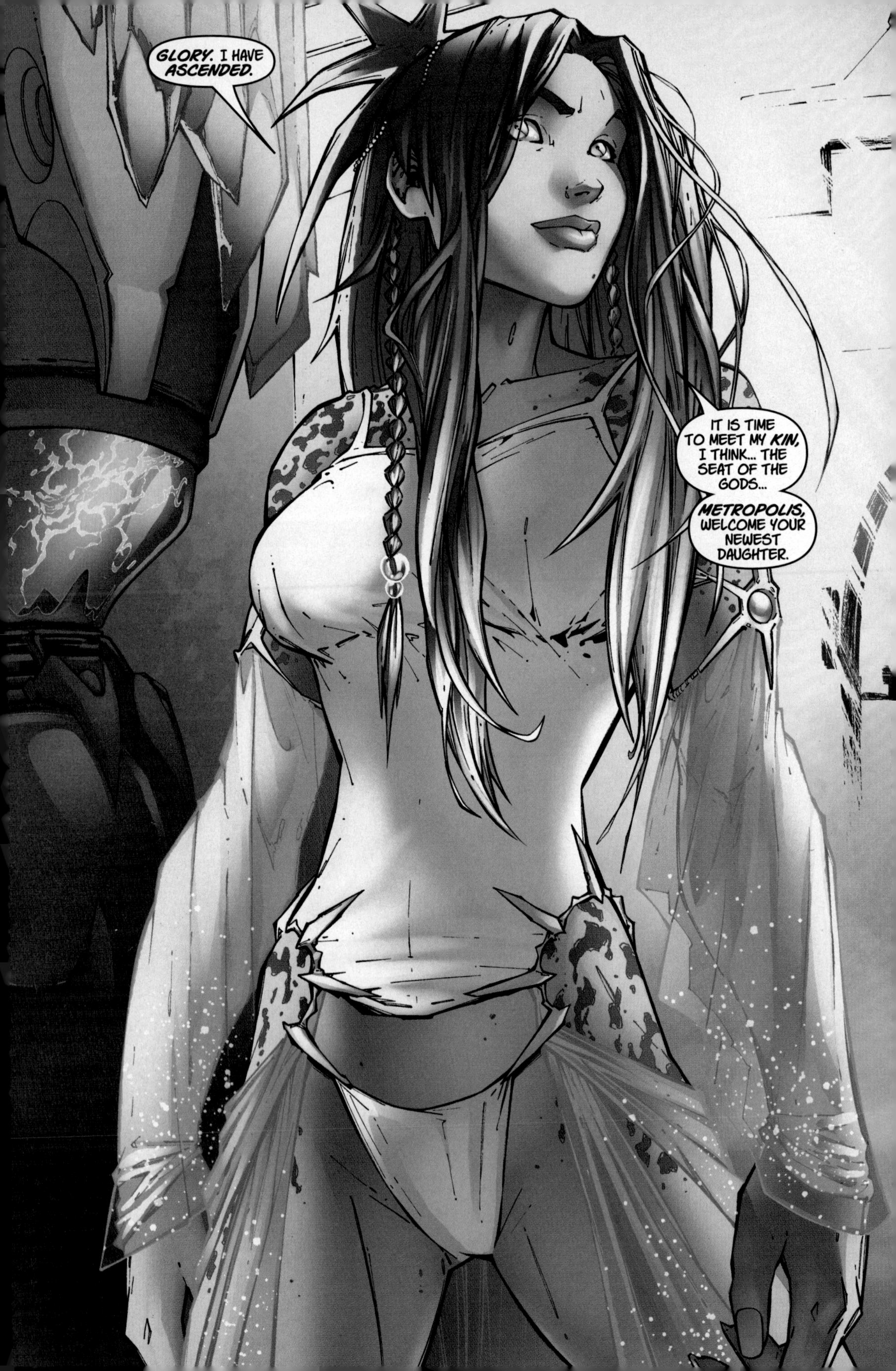
GLORY. I HAVE ASCENDED.
IT IS TIME TO MEET MY KIN, I THINK... THE SEAT OF THE GODS...
METROPOLIS, WELCOME YOUR NEWEST DAUGHTER.

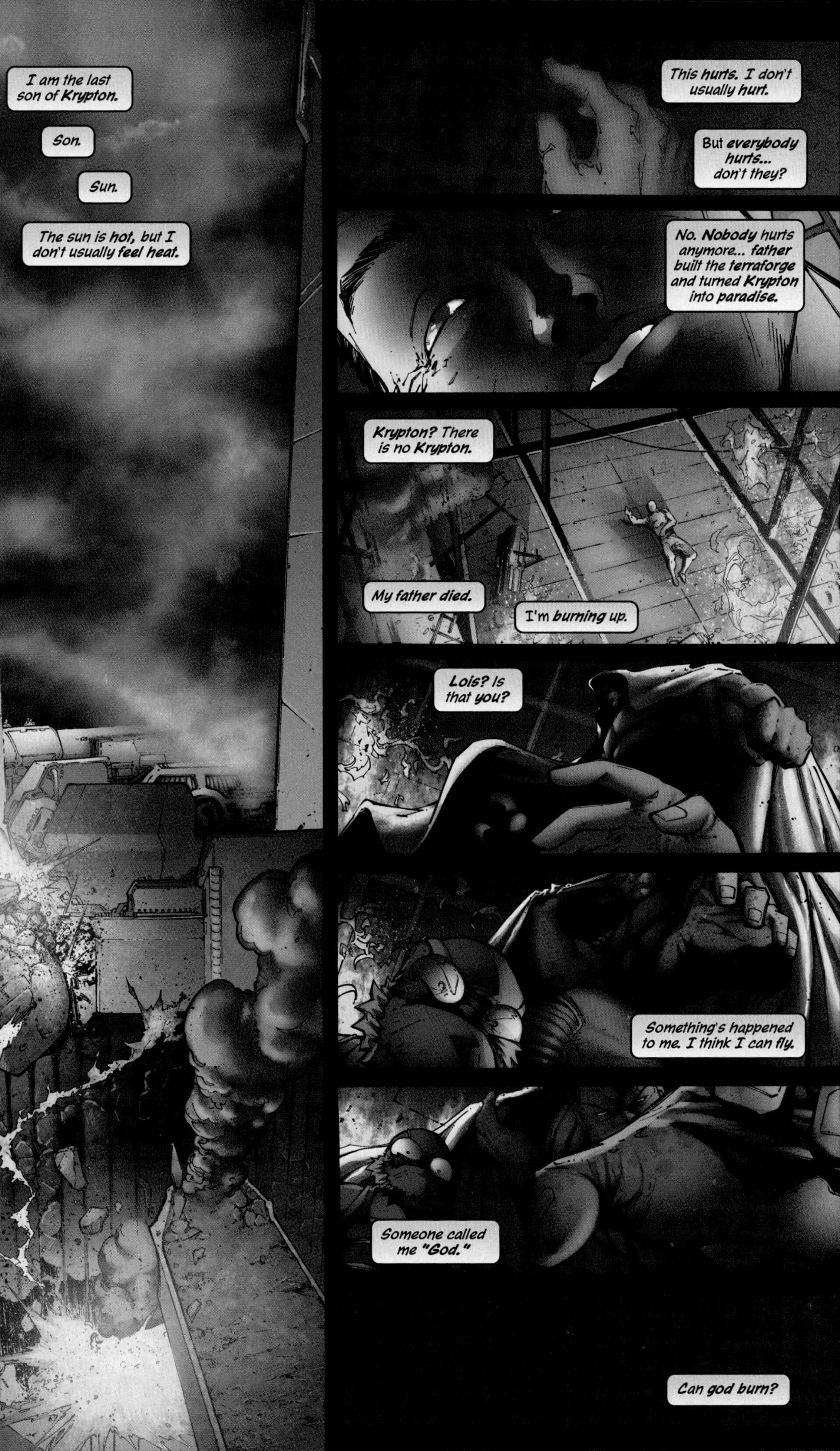
I am the last son of Krypton.
Son.
Sun.
The sun is hot, but I don't usually feel heat.
This hurts. I don't usually hurt.
But everybody hurts... don't they?
No. Nobody hurts anymore... father built the terraforge and turned Krypton into paradise.
Krypton? There is no Krypton.
My father died.
I'm burning up.
Lois? Is that you?
Something's happened to me. I think I can fly.
Someone called me "God."
Can god burn?

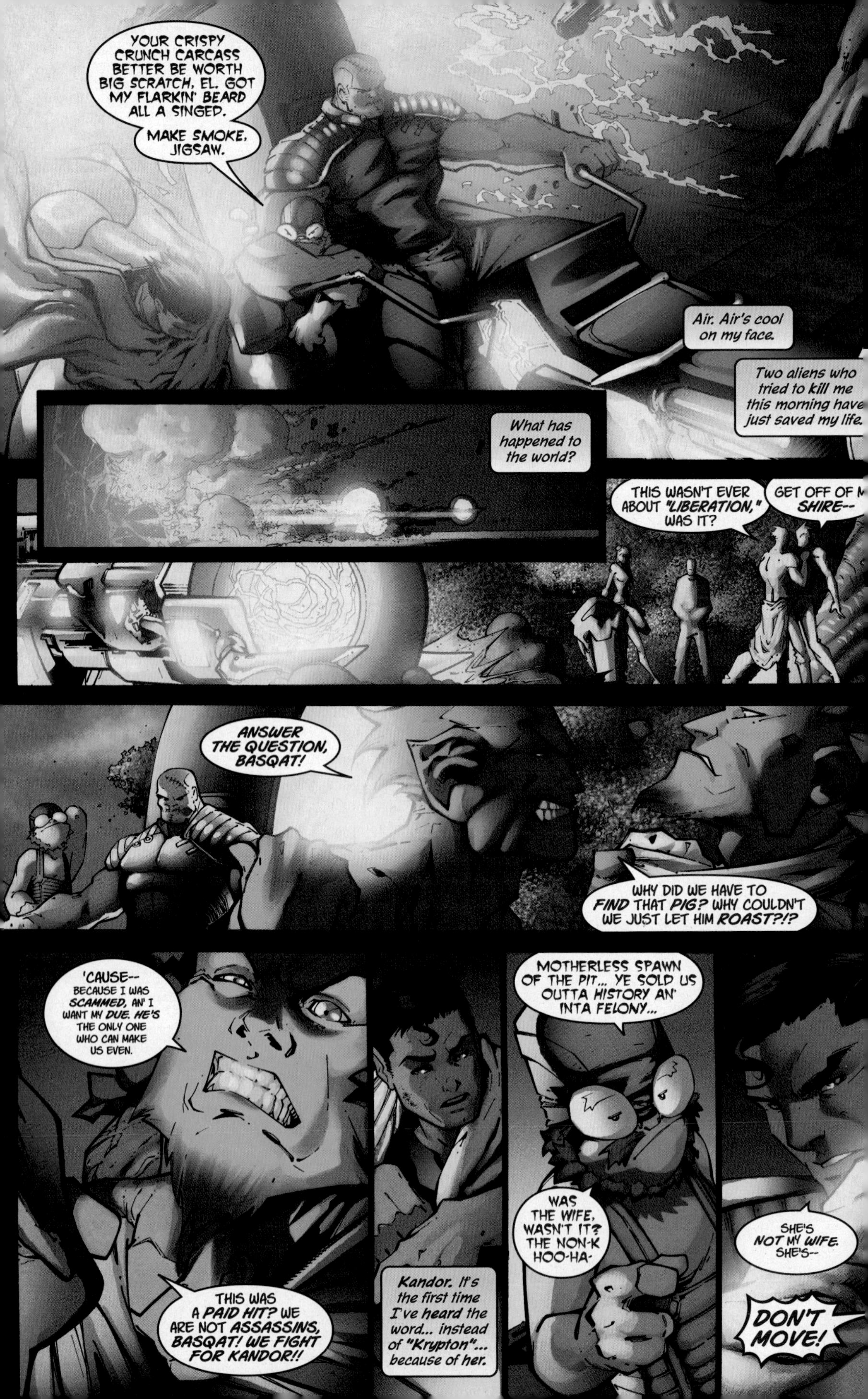

YOUR CRISPY CRUNCH CARCASS BETTER BE WORTH BIG SCRATCH, EL. GOT MY FLARKIN' BEARD ALL A SINGED.
MAKE SMOKE, JIGSAW.
Air. Air's cool on my face.
Two aliens who tried to kill me this morning have just saved my life.
What has happened to the world?
THIS WASN'T EVER ABOUT "LIBERATION," WAS IT?
GET OFF OF M SHIRE--
ANSWER THE QUESTION, BASQAT!
WHY DID WE HAVE TO FIND THAT PIG? WHY COULDN'T WE JUST LET HIM ROAST?!?
'CAUSE-- BECAUSE I WAS SCAMMED, AN' I WANT MY DUE. HE'S THE ONLY ONE WHO CAN MAKE US EVEN.
THIS WAS A PAID HIT? WE ARE NOT ASSASSINS, BASQAT! WE FIGHT FOR KANDOR!!
Kandor. It's the first time I've heard the word... instead of "Krypton"... because of her.
MOTHERLESS SPAWN OF THE PIT... YE SOLD US OUTTA HISTORY AN' INTA FELONY...
WAS THE WIFE, WASN'T IT? THE NON-K HOO-HA-
SHE'S NOT MY WIFE. SHE'S--
DON'T MOVE!

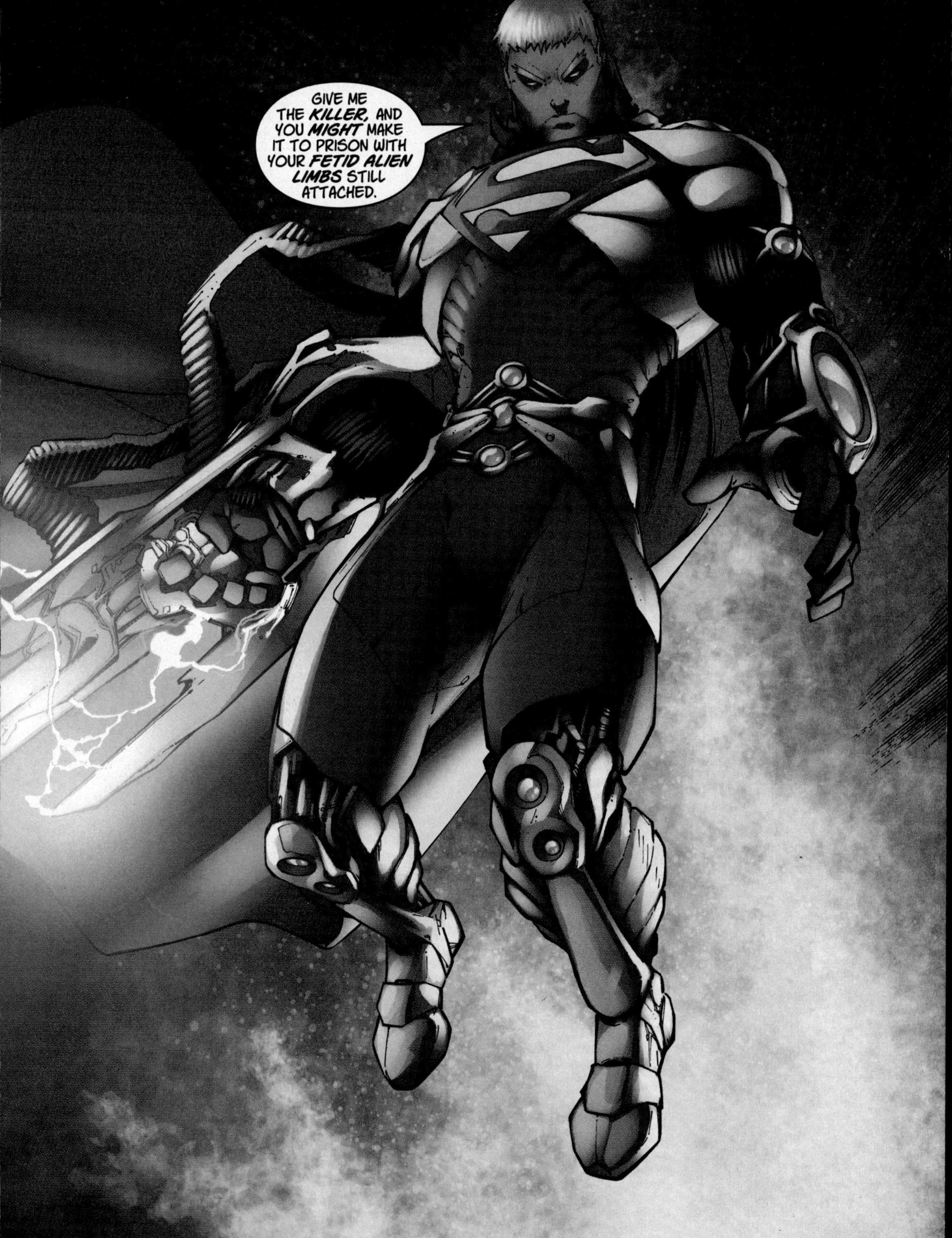
GIVE ME THE KILLER, AND YOU MIGHT MAKE IT TO PRISON WITH YOUR FETID ALIEN LIMBS STILL ATTACHED.

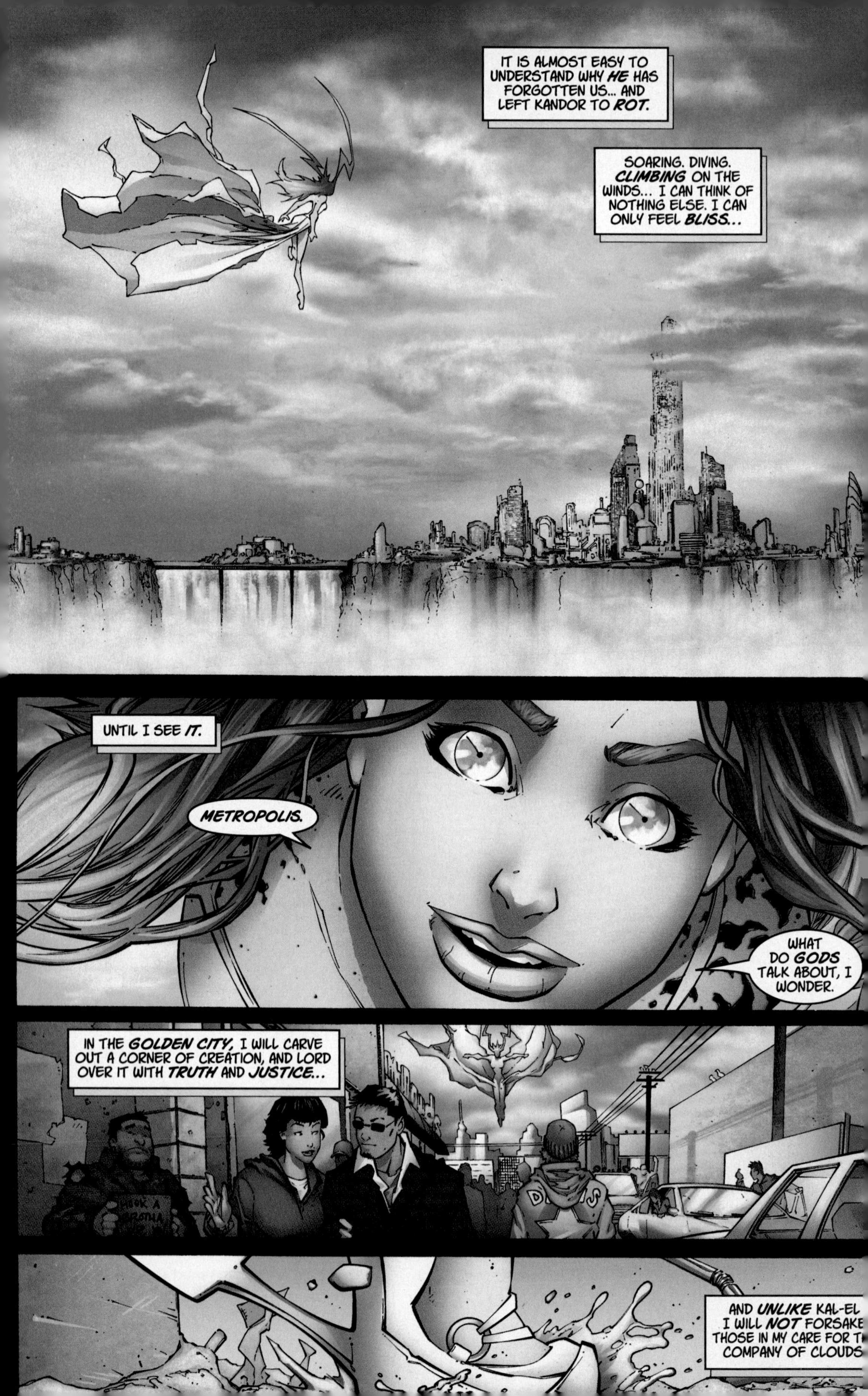
IT IS ALMOST EASY TO UNDERSTAND WHY *HE* HAS FORGOTTEN US... AND LEFT KANDOR TO *ROT*.
SOARING. DIVING. *CLIMBING* ON THE WINDS... I CAN THINK OF NOTHING ELSE. I CAN ONLY FEEL *BLISS*...
UNTIL I SEE *IT*.
METROPOLIS.
WHAT DO *GODS* TALK ABOUT, I WONDER.
IN THE *GOLDEN CITY*, I WILL CARVE OUT A CORNER OF CREATION, AND LORD OVER IT WITH *TRUTH* AND *JUSTICE*...
AND *UNLIKE* KAL-EL I WILL *NOT* FORSAKE THOSE IN MY CARE FOR THE COMPANY OF CLOUDS

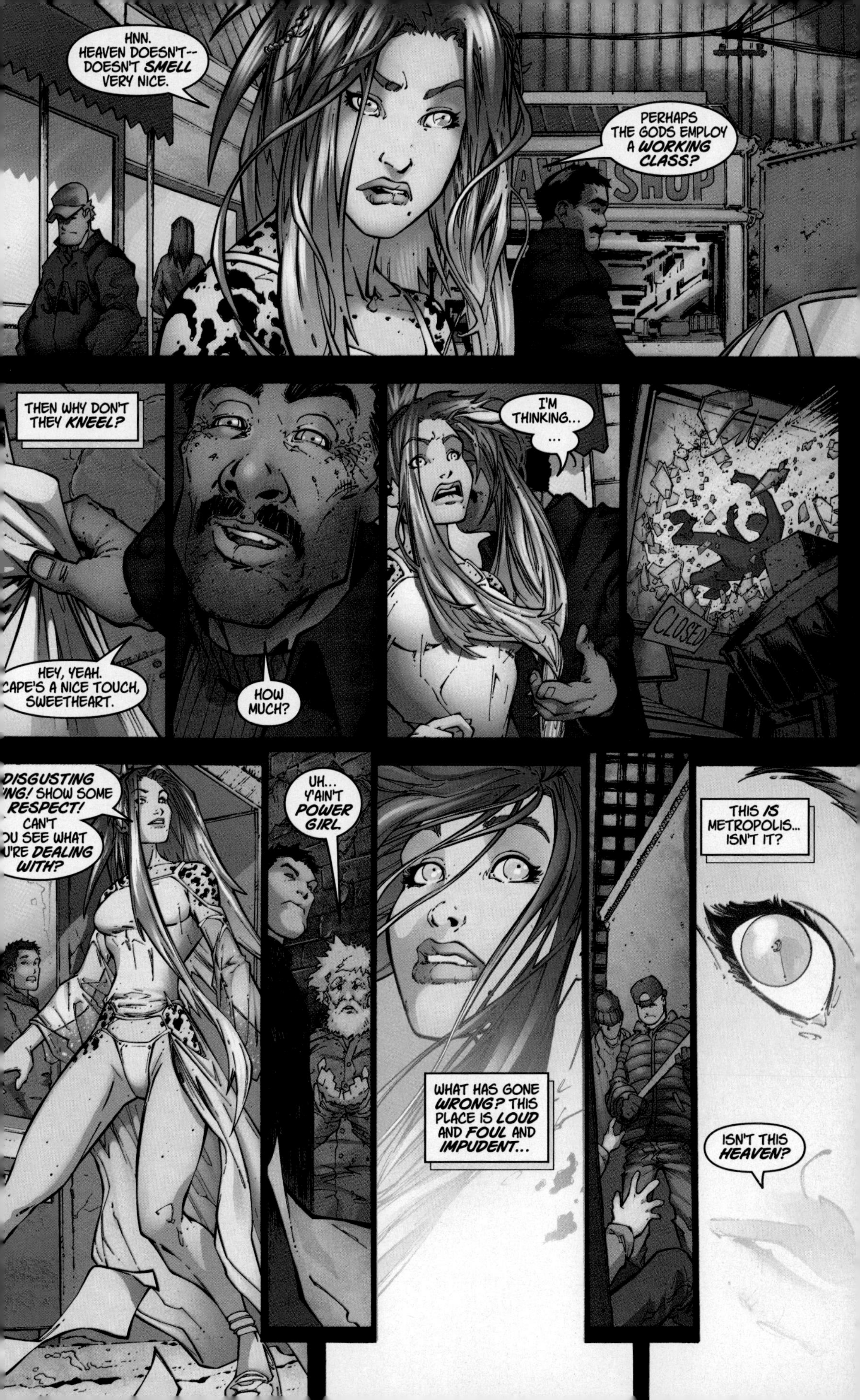
HNN.
HEAVEN DOESN'T--
DOESN'T SMELL
VERY NICE.
PERHAPS
THE GODS EMPLOY
A WORKING
CLASS?
THEN WHY DON'T
THEY KNEEL?
HEY, YEAH.
CAPE'S A NICE TOUCH,
SWEETHEART.
HOW
MUCH?
I'M
THINKING...
...
CLOSED
DISGUSTING
NG! SHOW SOME
RESPECT!
CAN'T
OU SEE WHAT
U'RE DEALING
WITH?
UH...
Y'AIN'T
POWER
GIRL.
WHAT HAS GONE
WRONG? THIS
PLACE IS LOUD
AND FOUL AND
IMPUDENT...
THIS IS
METROPOLIS...
ISN'T IT?
ISN'T THIS
HEAVEN?

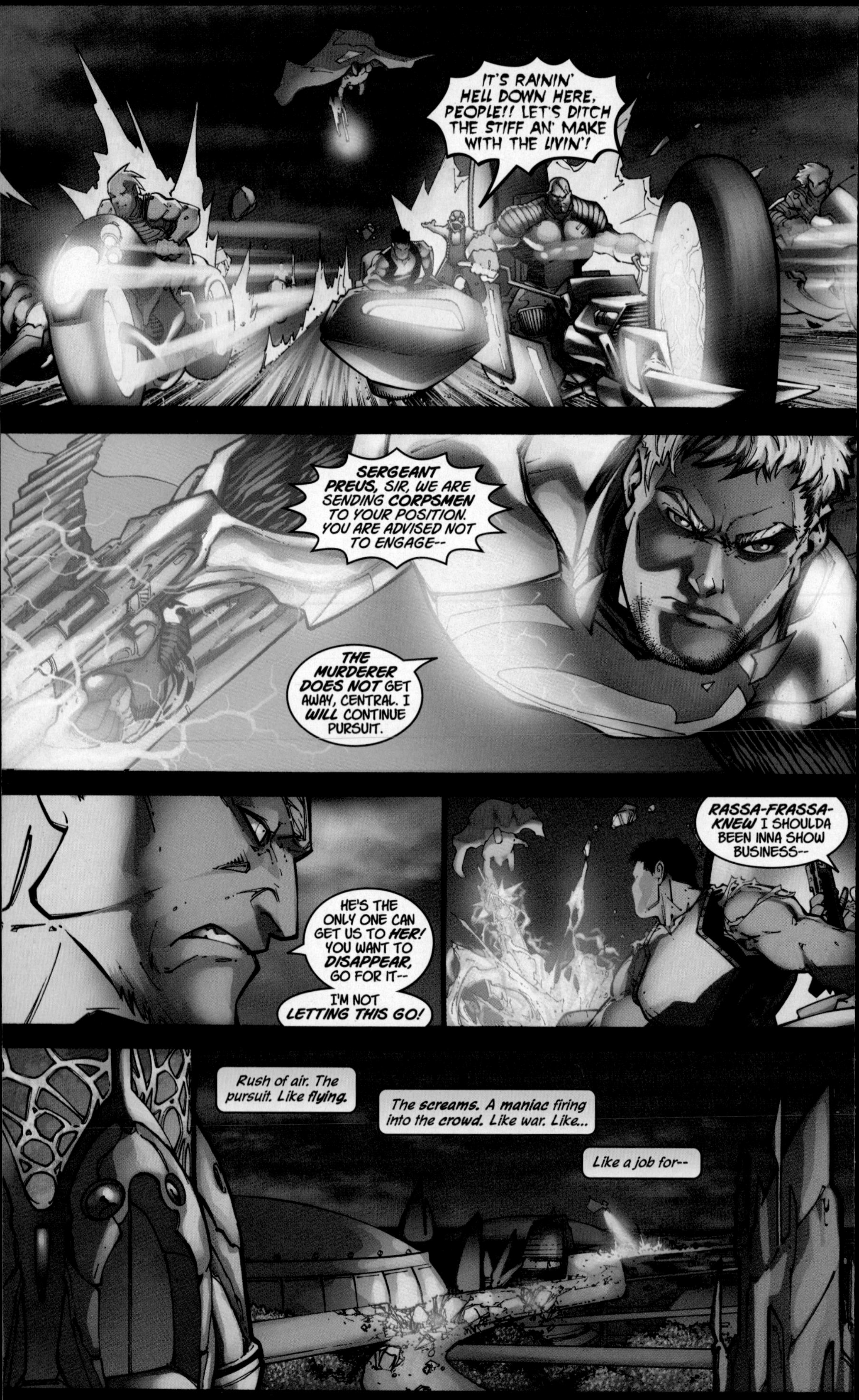
IT'S RAININ' HELL DOWN HERE, PEOPLE!! LET'S DITCH THE STIFF AN' MAKE WITH THE LIVIN'!
SERGEANT PREUS, SIR, WE ARE SENDING CORPSMEN TO YOUR POSITION. YOU ARE ADVISED NOT TO ENGAGE--
THE MURDERER DOES NOT GET AWAY, CENTRAL. I WILL CONTINUE PURSUIT.
HE'S THE ONLY ONE CAN GET US TO HER! YOU WANT TO DISAPPEAR, GO FOR IT--
I'M NOT LETTING THIS GO!
RASSA-FRASSA-KNEW I SHOULDA BEEN INNA SHOW BUSINESS--
Rush of air. The pursuit. Like flying.
The screams. A maniac firing into the crowd. Like war. Like...
Like a job for--

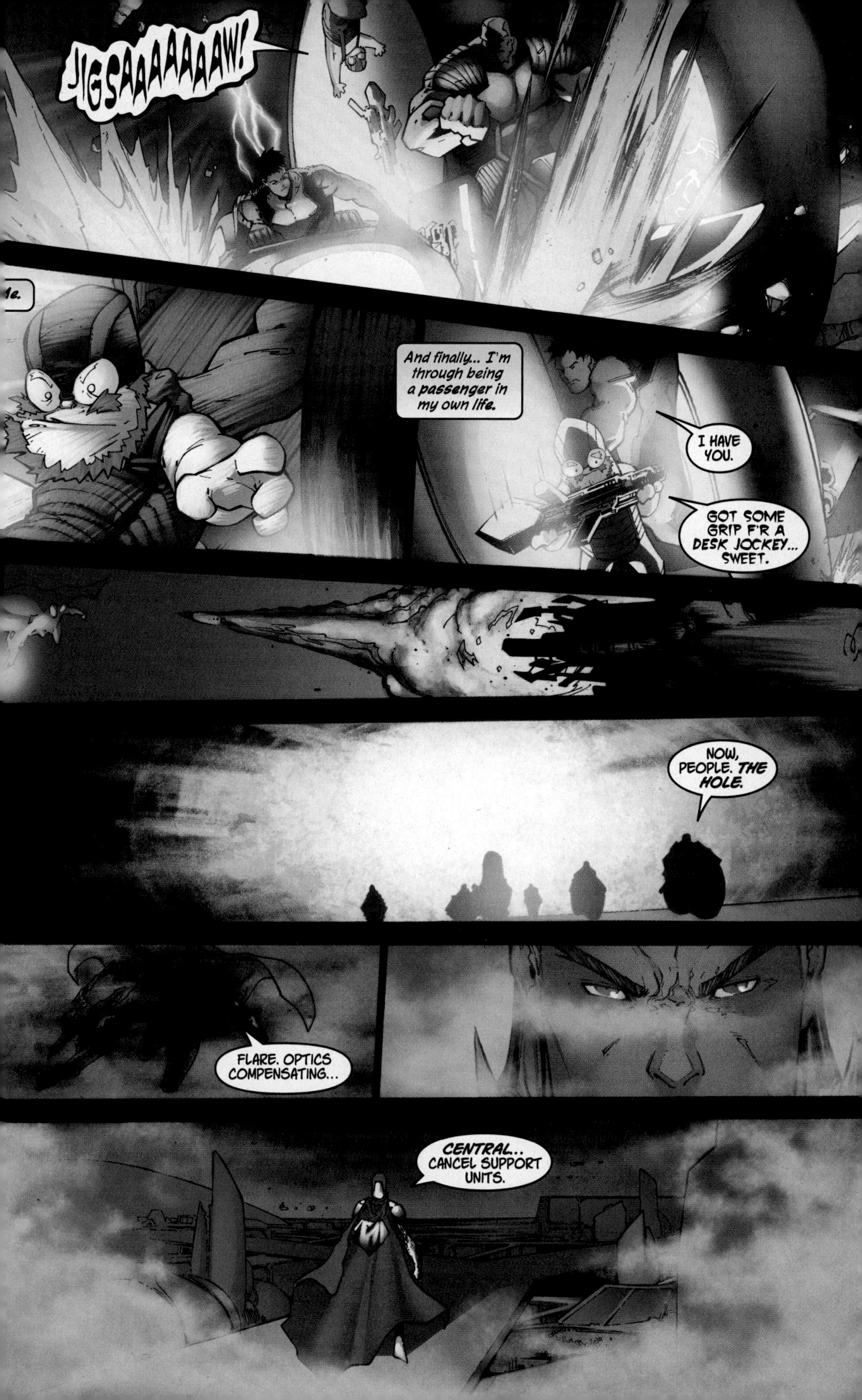
JIGSAAAAAAAW!
And finally... I'm through being a passenger in my own life.
I HAVE YOU.
GOT SOME GRIP F'R A DESK JOCKEY... SWEET.
NOW, PEOPLE. THE HOLE.
FLARE. OPTICS COMPENSATING...
CENTRAL... CANCEL SUPPORT UNITS.

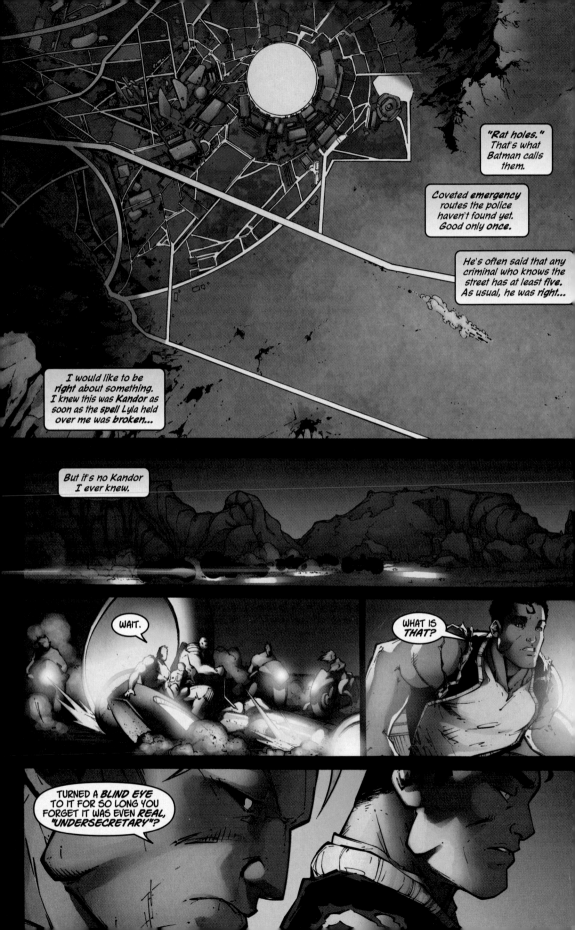

"Rat holes." That's what Batman calls them.

Coveted *emergency* routes the police haven't found yet. Good only *once*.

He's often said that any criminal who knows the street has at least *five*. As usual, he was *right...*

I would like to be *right* about something. I knew this was *Kandor* as soon as the spell *Lyla* held over me was *broken...*

But it's no Kandor I ever knew.

WAIT.

WHAT IS *THAT?*

TURNED A *BLIND EYE* TO IT FOR SO LONG YOU FORGET IT WAS EVEN *REAL,* *"UNDERSECRETARY"?*

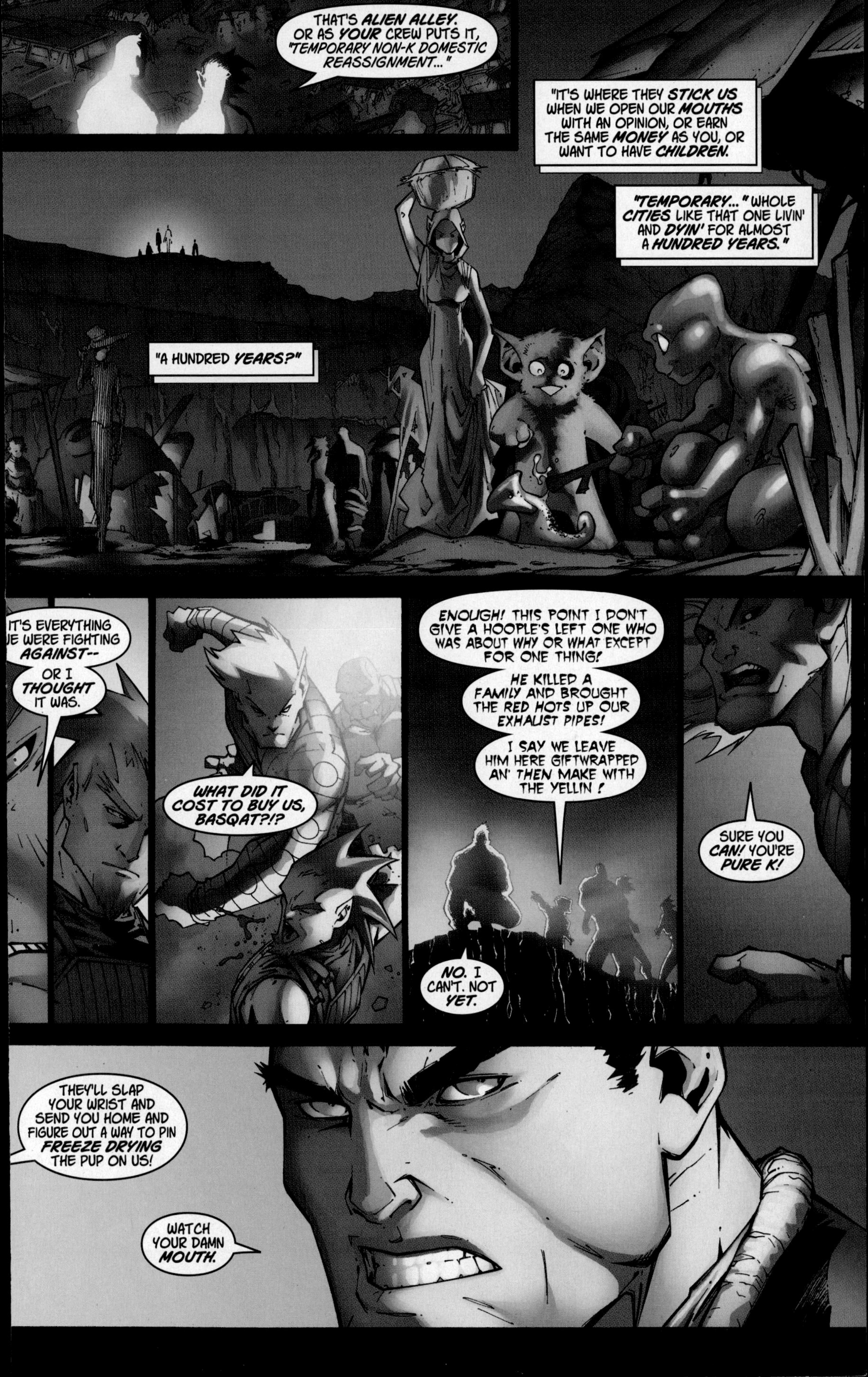
THAT'S ALIEN ALLEY. OR AS YOUR CREW PUTS IT, "TEMPORARY NON-K DOMESTIC REASSIGNMENT..."
"IT'S WHERE THEY STICK US WHEN WE OPEN OUR MOUTHS WITH AN OPINION, OR EARN THE SAME MONEY AS YOU, OR WANT TO HAVE CHILDREN.
"TEMPORARY..." WHOLE CITIES LIKE THAT ONE LIVIN' AND DYIN' FOR ALMOST A HUNDRED YEARS."
"A HUNDRED YEARS?"
IT'S EVERYTHING WE WERE FIGHTING AGAINST--
OR I THOUGHT IT WAS.
WHAT DID IT COST TO BUY US, BASQAT?!?
ENOUGH! THIS POINT I DON'T GIVE A HOOPLE'S LEFT ONE WHO WAS ABOUT WHY OR WHAT EXCEPT FOR ONE THING!
HE KILLED A FAMILY AND BROUGHT THE RED HOTS UP OUR EXHAUST PIPES!
I SAY WE LEAVE HIM HERE GIFTWRAPPED AN' THEN MAKE WITH THE YELLIN'!
NO. I CAN'T. NOT YET.
SURE YOU CAN! YOU'RE PURE K!
THEY'LL SLAP YOUR WRIST AND SEND YOU HOME AND FIGURE OUT A WAY TO PIN FREEZE DRYING THE PUP ON US!
WATCH YOUR DAMN MOUTH.

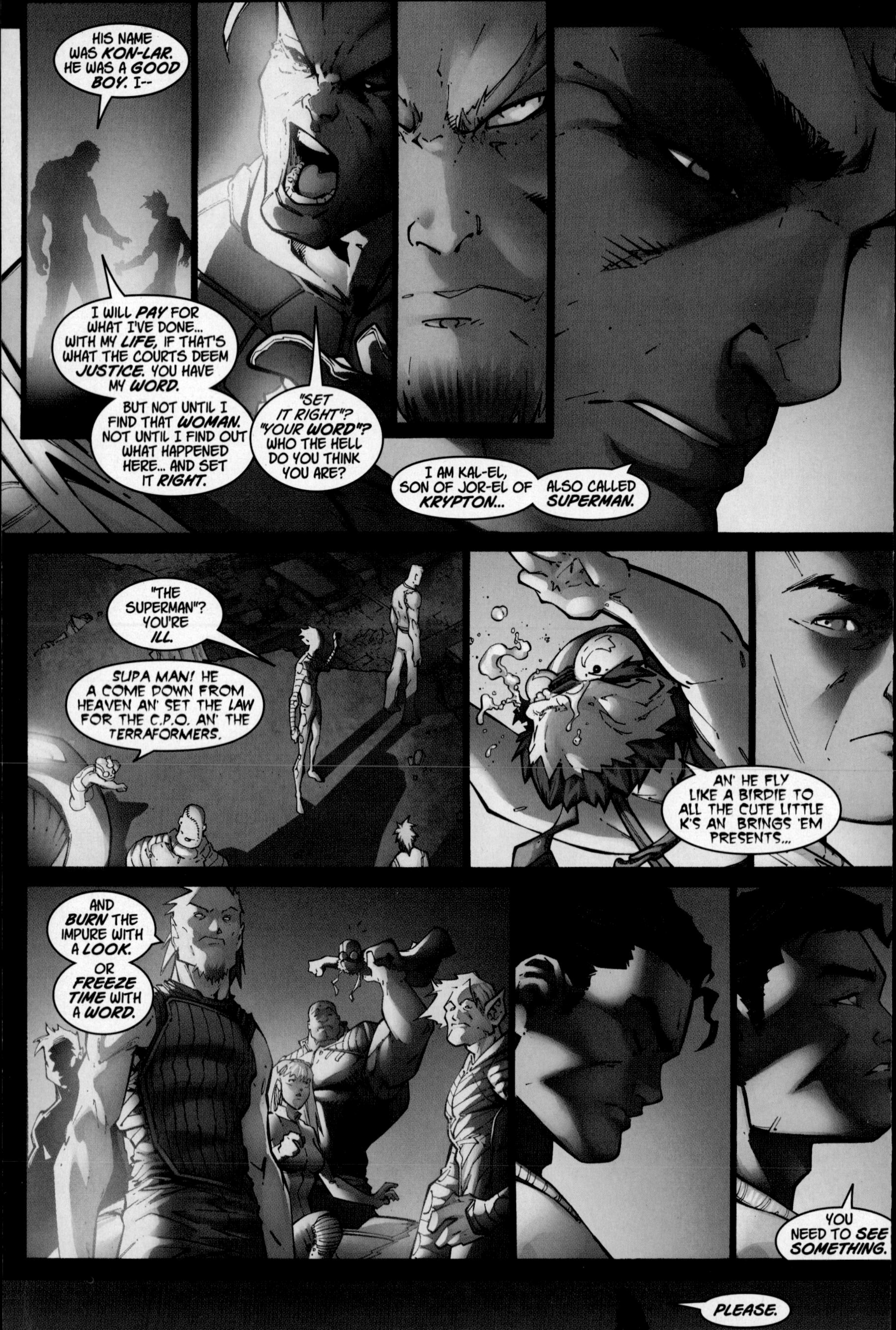
HIS NAME WAS KON-LAR. HE WAS A GOOD BOY. I--
I WILL PAY FOR WHAT I'VE DONE... WITH MY LIFE, IF THAT'S WHAT THE COURTS DEEM JUSTICE. YOU HAVE MY WORD.
BUT NOT UNTIL I FIND THAT WOMAN. NOT UNTIL I FIND OUT WHAT HAPPENED HERE... AND SET IT RIGHT.
"SET IT RIGHT"? "YOUR WORD"? WHO THE HELL DO YOU THINK YOU ARE?
I AM KAL-EL, SON OF JOR-EL OF KRYPTON...
ALSO CALLED SUPERMAN.
"THE SUPERMAN"? YOU'RE ILL.
SUPA MAN! HE A COME DOWN FROM HEAVEN AN' SET THE LAW FOR THE C.P.O. AN' THE TERRAFORMERS.
AN' HE FLY LIKE A BIRDIE TO ALL THE CUTE LITTLE K'S AN BRINGS 'EM PRESENTS...
AND BURN THE IMPURE WITH A LOOK.
OR FREEZE TIME WITH A WORD.
YOU NEED TO SEE SOMETHING.
PLEASE.

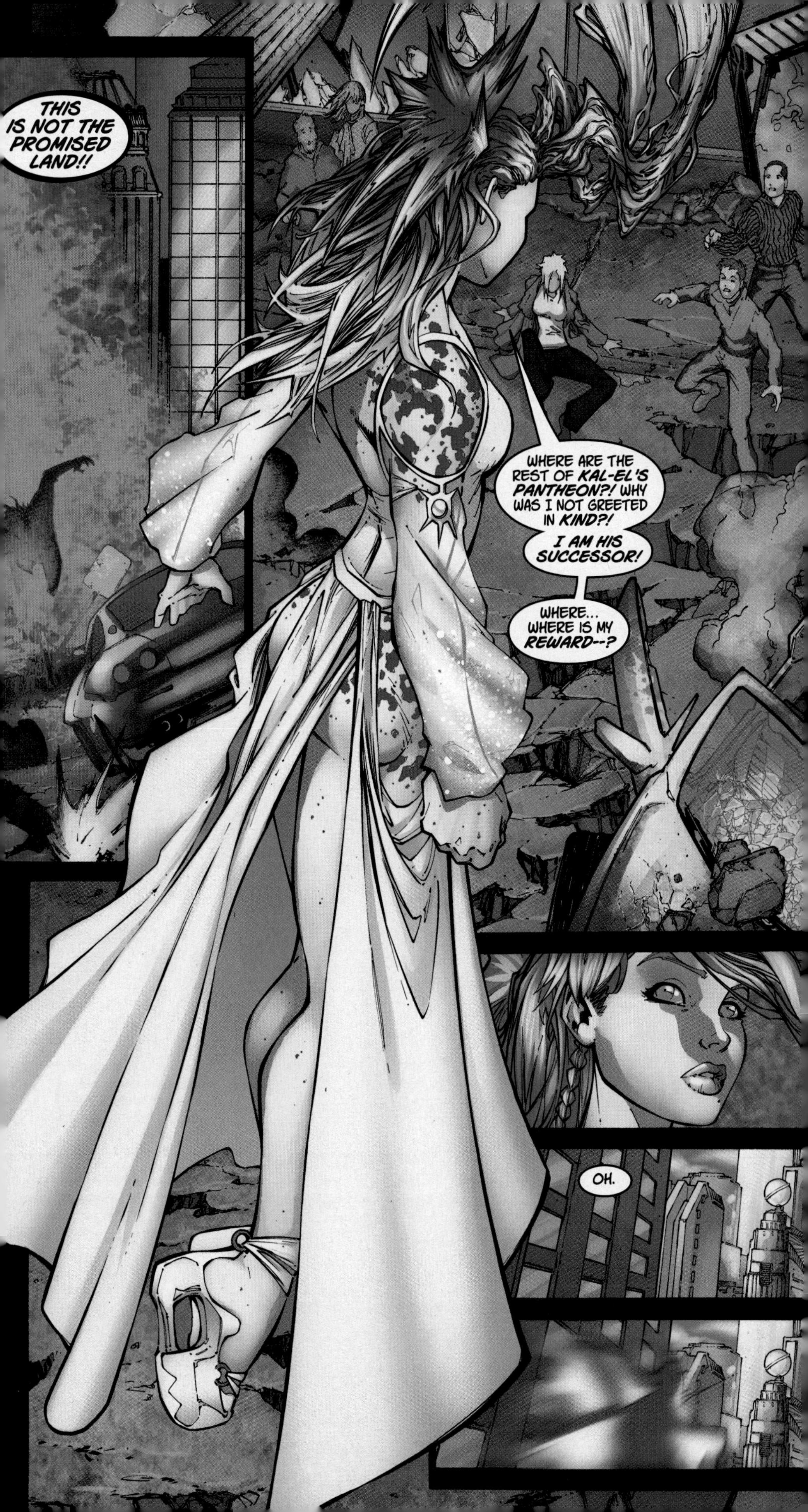
THIS IS NOT THE PROMISED LAND!!
WHERE ARE THE REST OF KAL-EL'S PANTHEON?! WHY WAS I NOT GREETED IN KIND?!
I AM HIS SUCCESSOR!
WHERE... WHERE IS MY REWARD--?
OH.

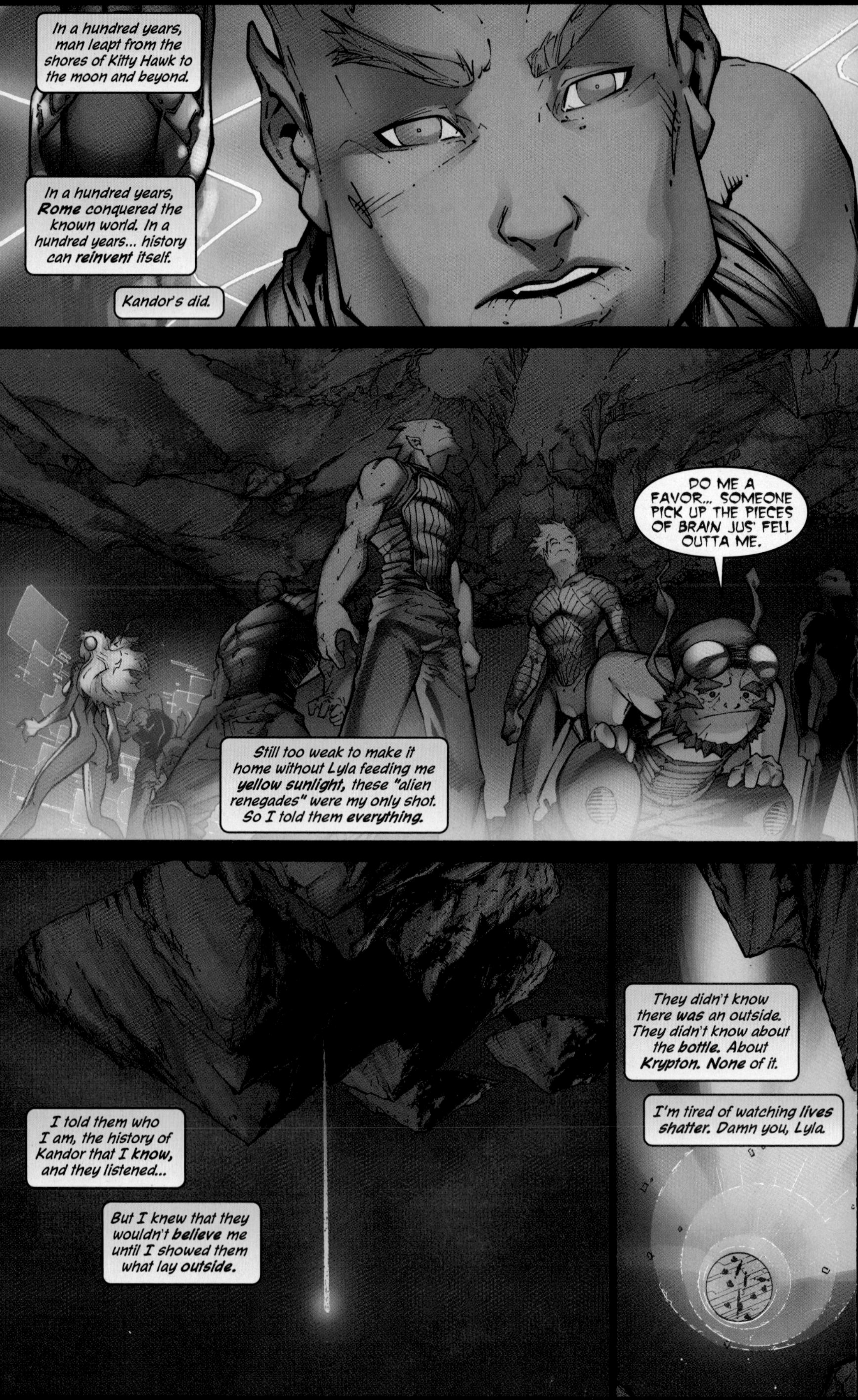
In a hundred years, man leapt from the shores of Kitty Hawk to the moon and beyond.
In a hundred years, **Rome** conquered the known world. In a hundred years... history can **reinvent** itself.
Kandor's did.
DO ME A FAVOR... SOMEONE PICK UP THE PIECES OF BRAIN JUS' FELL OUTTA ME.
Still too weak to make it home without Lyla feeding me **yellow sunlight,** these "alien renegades" were my only shot. So I told them **everything.**
I told them who I am, the history of Kandor that I **know,** and they listened...
But I knew that they wouldn't **believe** me until I showed them what lay **outside.**
They didn't know there **was** an outside. They didn't know about the **bottle.** About **Krypton. None** of it.
I'm tired of watching **lives shatter.** Damn you, Lyla.

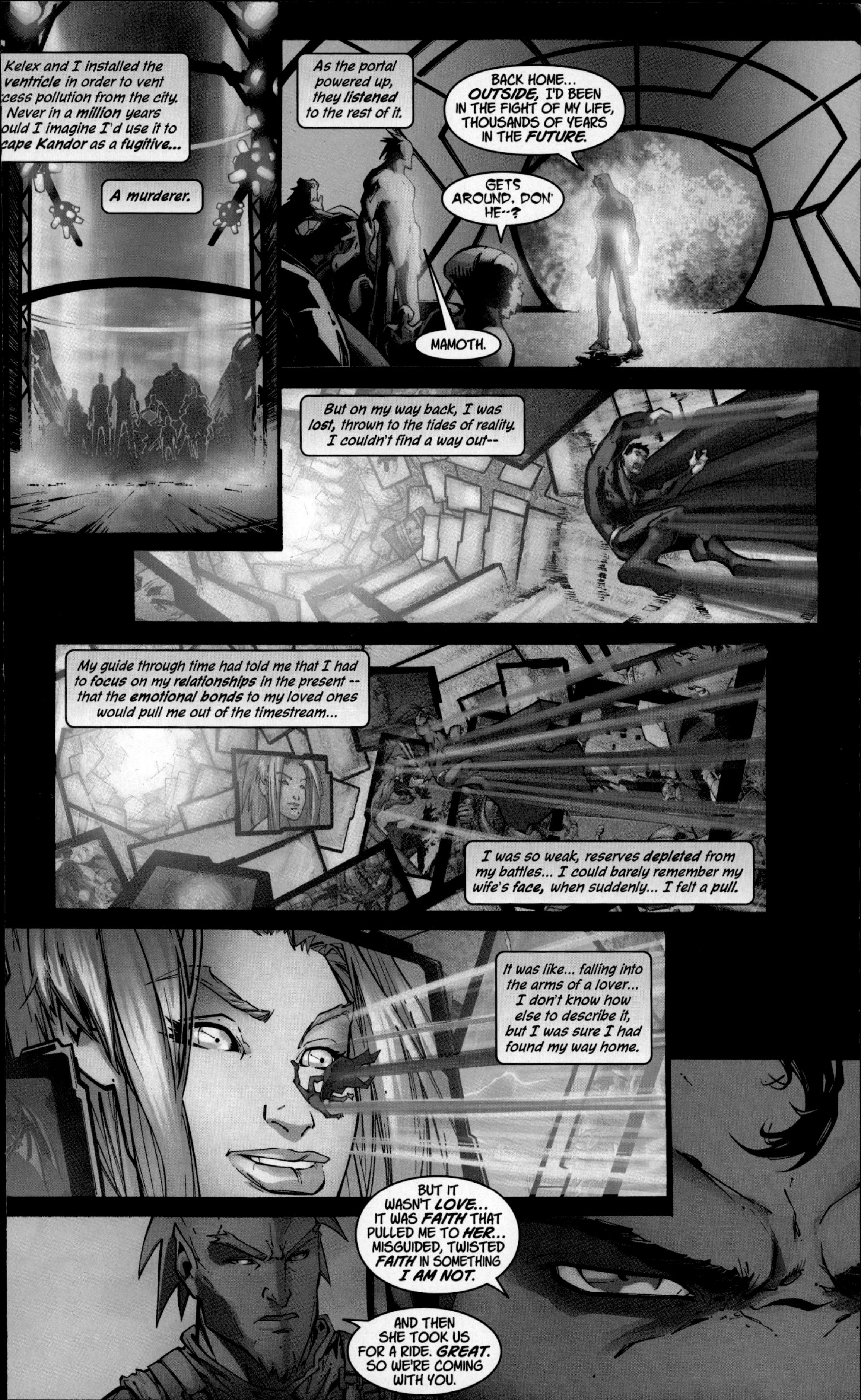
Kelex and I installed the ventricle in order to vent xcess pollution from the city. Never in a million years ould I imagine I'd use it to cape Kandor as a fugitive...
A murderer.
As the portal powered up, they listened to the rest of it.
BACK HOME... OUTSIDE, I'D BEEN IN THE FIGHT OF MY LIFE, THOUSANDS OF YEARS IN THE FUTURE.
GETS AROUND, DON' HE--?
MAMOTH.
But on my way back, I was lost, thrown to the tides of reality. I couldn't find a way out--
My guide through time had told me that I had to focus on my relationships in the present -- that the emotional bonds to my loved ones would pull me out of the timestream...
I was so weak, reserves depleted from my battles... I could barely remember my wife's face, when suddenly... I felt a pull.
It was like... falling into the arms of a lover... I don't know how else to describe it, but I was sure I had found my way home.
BUT IT WASN'T LOVE... IT WAS FAITH THAT PULLED ME TO HER... MISGUIDED, TWISTED FAITH IN SOMETHING I AM NOT.
AND THEN SHE TOOK US FOR A RIDE. GREAT. SO WE'RE COMING WITH YOU.

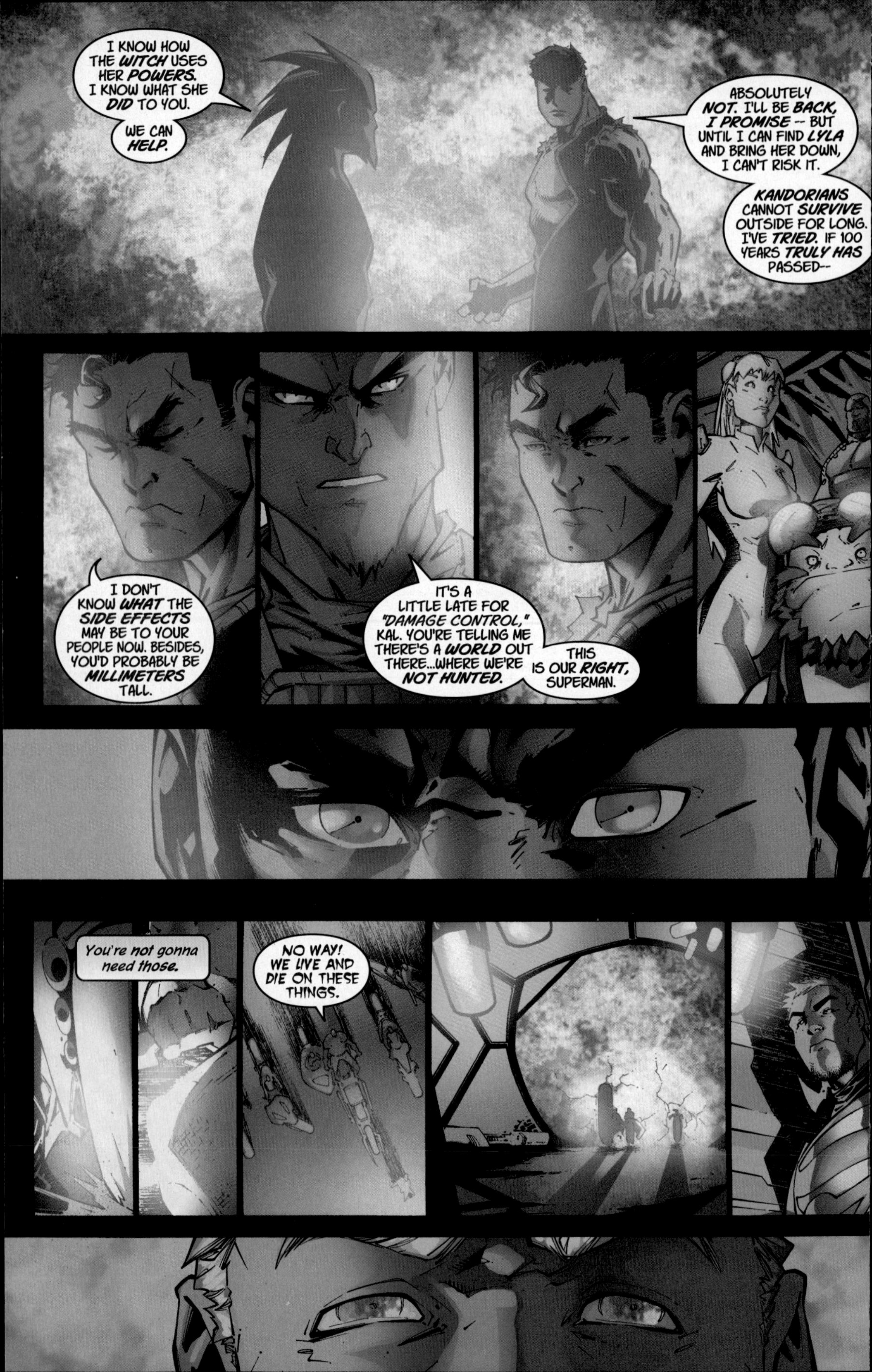
I KNOW HOW THE WITCH USES HER POWERS. I KNOW WHAT SHE DID TO YOU.
WE CAN HELP.
ABSOLUTELY NOT. I'LL BE BACK, I PROMISE -- BUT UNTIL I CAN FIND LYLA AND BRING HER DOWN, I CAN'T RISK IT.
KANDORIANS CANNOT SURVIVE OUTSIDE FOR LONG. I'VE TRIED. IF 100 YEARS TRULY HAS PASSED--
I DON'T KNOW WHAT THE SIDE EFFECTS MAY BE TO YOUR PEOPLE NOW. BESIDES, YOU'D PROBABLY BE MILLIMETERS TALL.
IT'S A LITTLE LATE FOR "DAMAGE CONTROL," KAL. YOU'RE TELLING ME THERE'S A WORLD OUT THERE...WHERE WE'RE NOT HUNTED.
THIS IS OUR RIGHT, SUPERMAN.
You're not gonna need those.
NO WAY! WE LIVE AND DIE ON THESE THINGS.

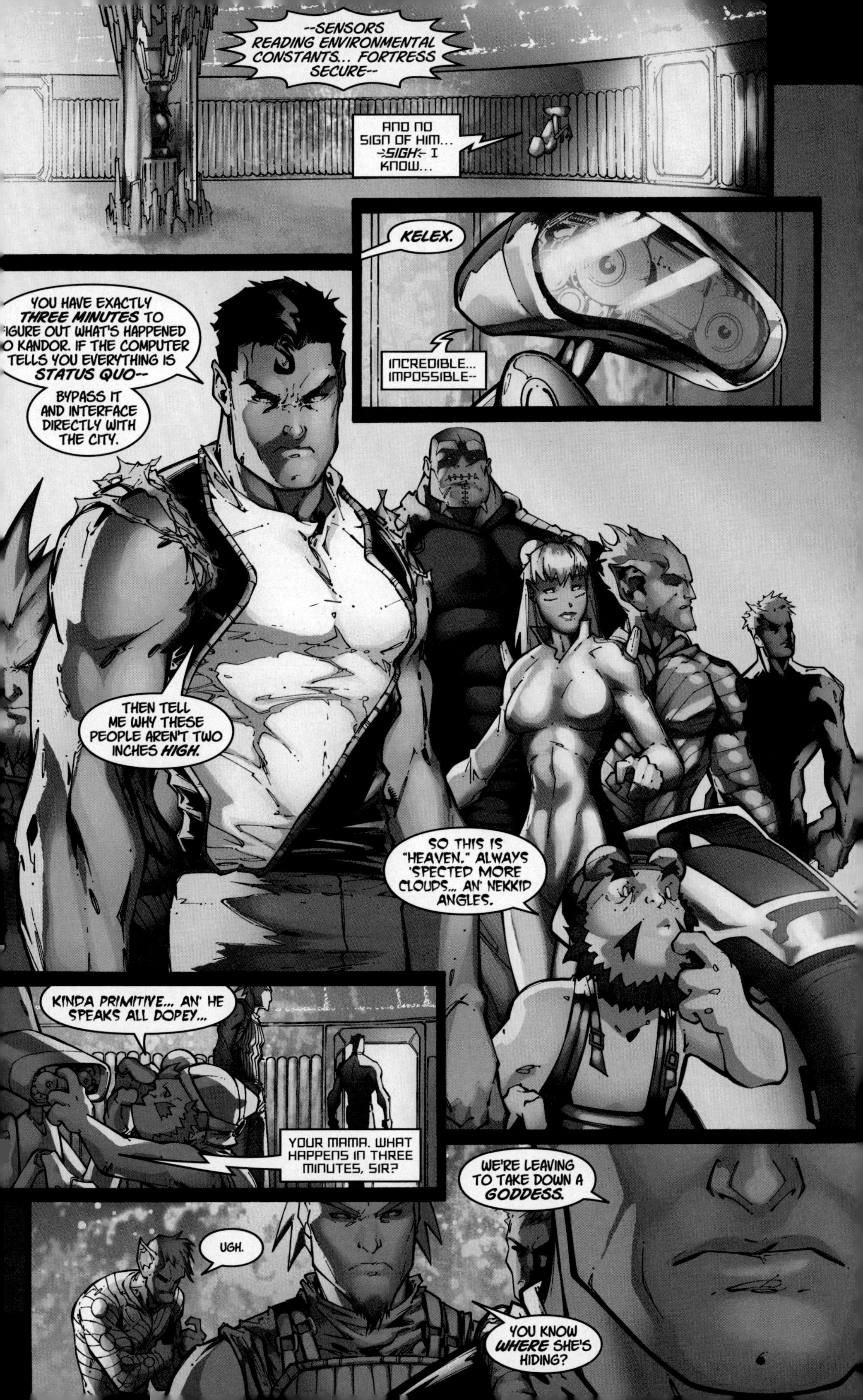
--SENSORS READING ENVIRONMENTAL CONSTANTS... FORTRESS SECURE--
AND NO SIGN OF HIM... -SIGH- I KNOW...
KELEX.
INCREDIBLE... IMPOSSIBLE--
YOU HAVE EXACTLY THREE MINUTES TO FIGURE OUT WHAT'S HAPPENED TO KANDOR. IF THE COMPUTER TELLS YOU EVERYTHING IS STATUS QUO--
BYPASS IT AND INTERFACE DIRECTLY WITH THE CITY.
THEN TELL ME WHY THESE PEOPLE AREN'T TWO INCHES HIGH.
SO THIS IS "HEAVEN." ALWAYS 'SPECTED MORE CLOUDS... AN' NEKKID ANGLES.
KINDA PRIMITIVE... AN' HE SPEAKS ALL DOPEY...
YOUR MAMA. WHAT HAPPENS IN THREE MINUTES, SIR?
WE'RE LEAVING TO TAKE DOWN A GODDESS.
UGH.
YOU KNOW WHERE SHE'S HIDING?

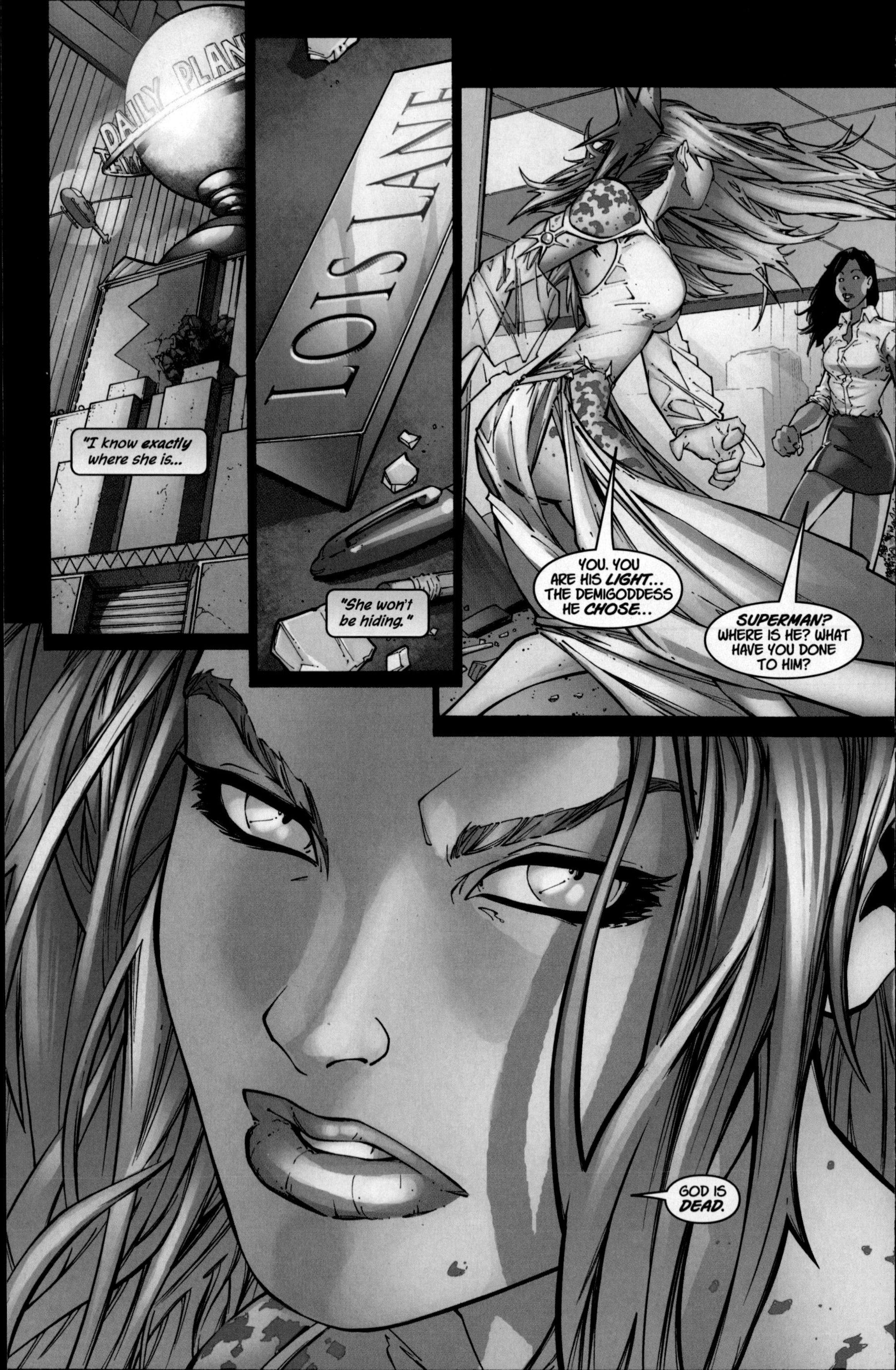
DAILY PLAN
"I know exactly where she is...
LOIS LANE
"She won't be hiding."
YOU. YOU ARE HIS LIGHT... THE DEMIGODDESS HE CHOSE...
SUPERMAN? WHERE IS HE? WHAT HAVE YOU DONE TO HIM?
GOD IS DEAD.

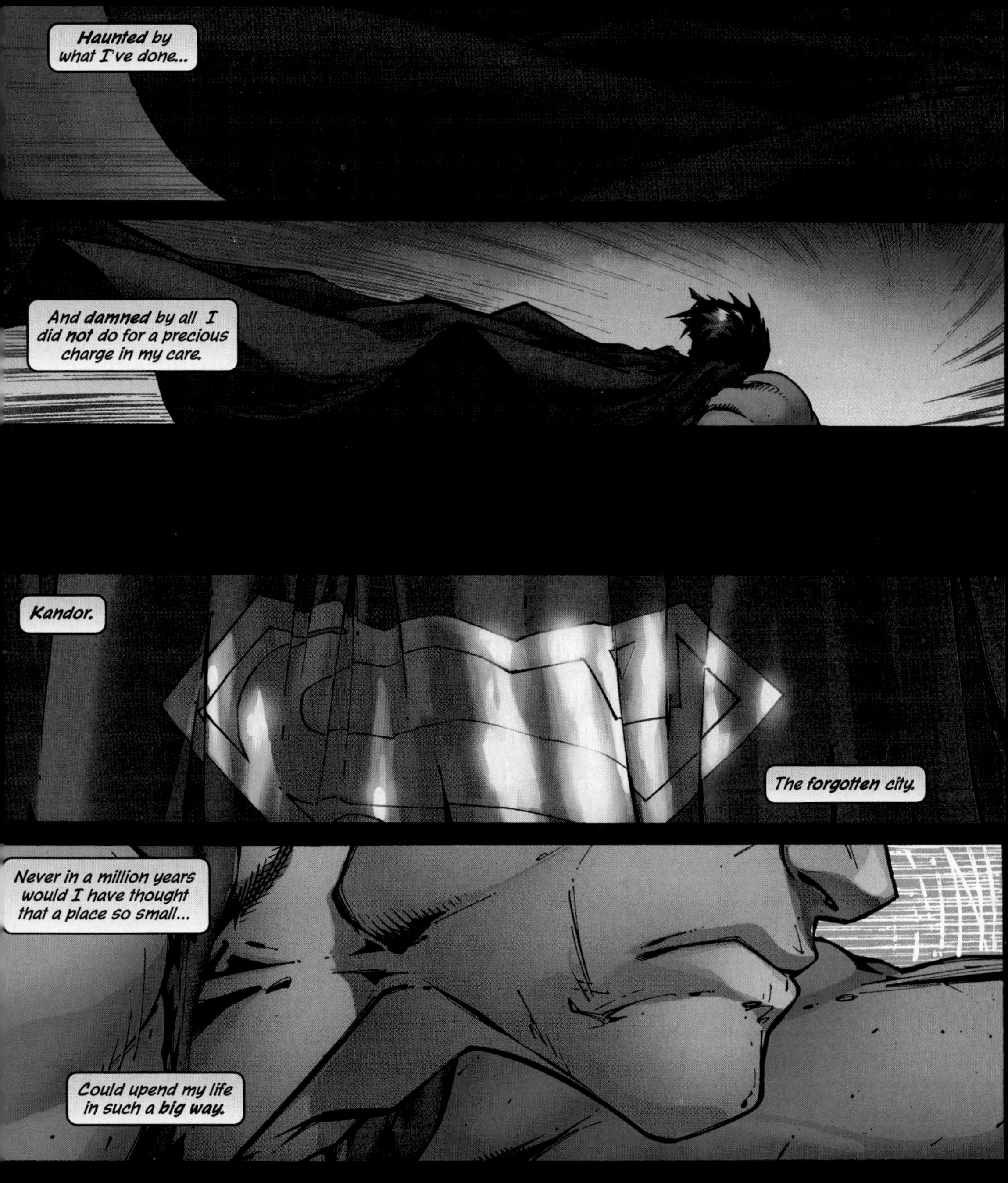
Haunted by what I've done...
And damned by all I did not do for a precious charge in my care.
Kandor.
The forgotten city.
Never in a million years would I have thought that a place so small...
Could upend my life in such a big way.

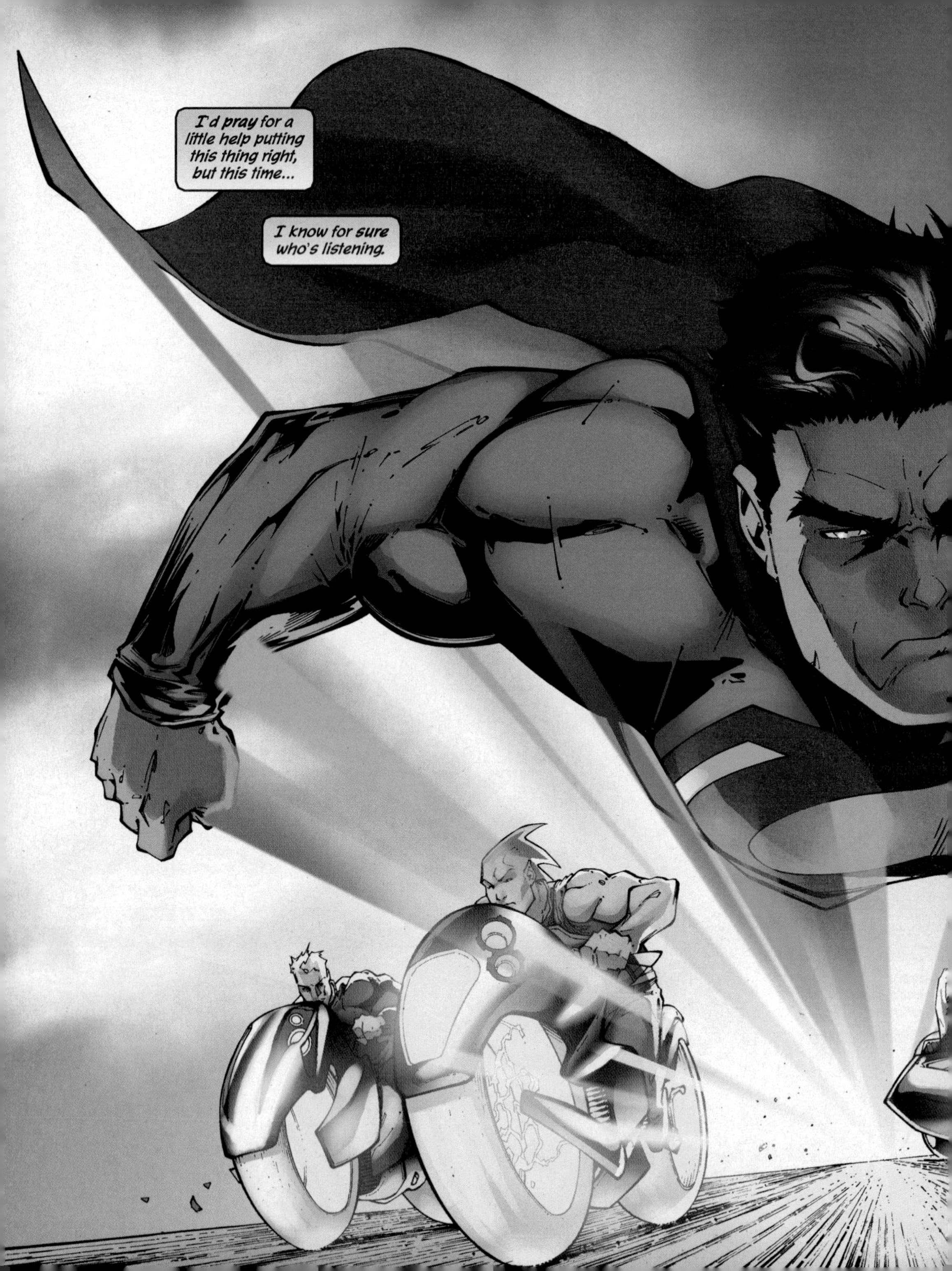
I'd pray for a little help putting this thing right, but this time...
I know for sure who's listening.

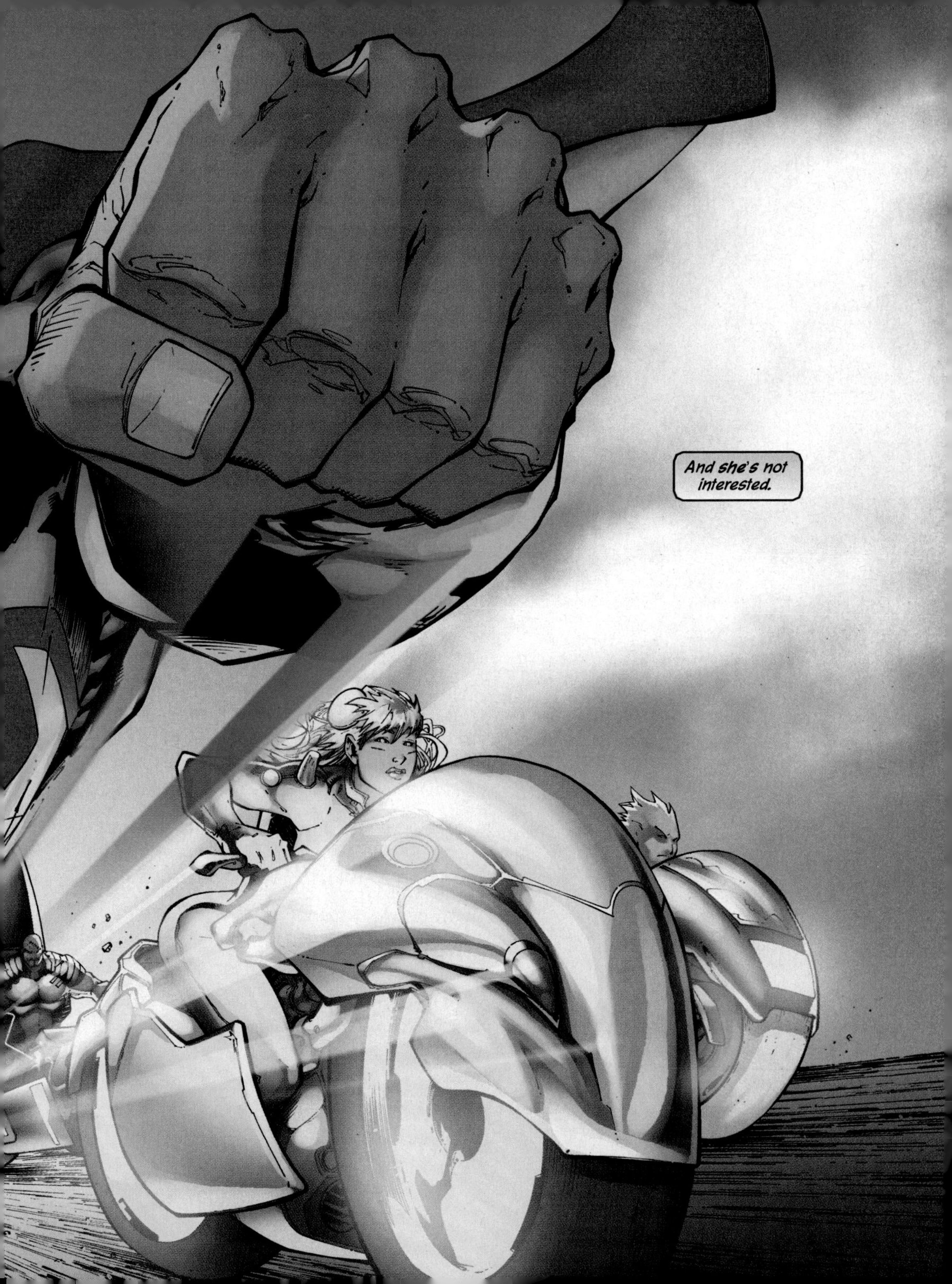
And she's not interested.

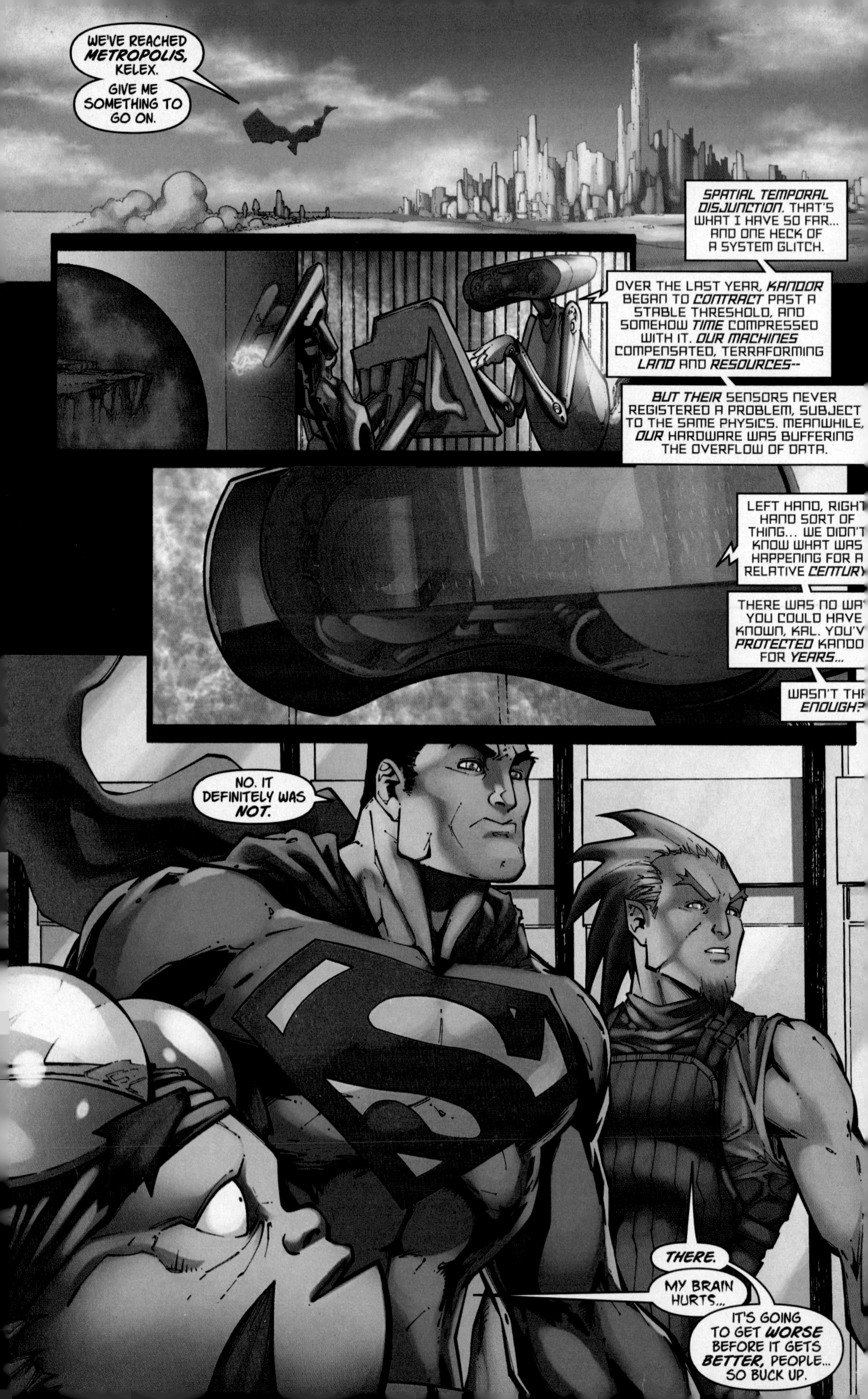
WE'VE REACHED METROPOLIS, KELEX.
GIVE ME SOMETHING TO GO ON.
SPATIAL TEMPORAL DISJUNCTION. THAT'S WHAT I HAVE SO FAR... AND ONE HECK OF A SYSTEM GLITCH.
OVER THE LAST YEAR, KANDOR BEGAN TO CONTRACT PAST A STABLE THRESHOLD, AND SOMEHOW TIME COMPRESSED WITH IT. OUR MACHINES COMPENSATED, TERRAFORMING LAND AND RESOURCES--
BUT THEIR SENSORS NEVER REGISTERED A PROBLEM, SUBJECT TO THE SAME PHYSICS. MEANWHILE, OUR HARDWARE WAS BUFFERING THE OVERFLOW OF DATA.
LEFT HAND, RIGHT HAND SORT OF THING... WE DIDN'T KNOW WHAT WAS HAPPENING FOR A RELATIVE CENTURY
THERE WAS NO WA YOU COULD HAVE KNOWN, KAL. YOU'V PROTECTED KANDO FOR YEARS...
WASN'T TH ENOUGH?
NO. IT DEFINITELY WAS NOT.
THERE.
MY BRAIN HURTS...
IT'S GOING TO GET WORSE BEFORE IT GETS BETTER, PEOPLE... SO BUCK UP.

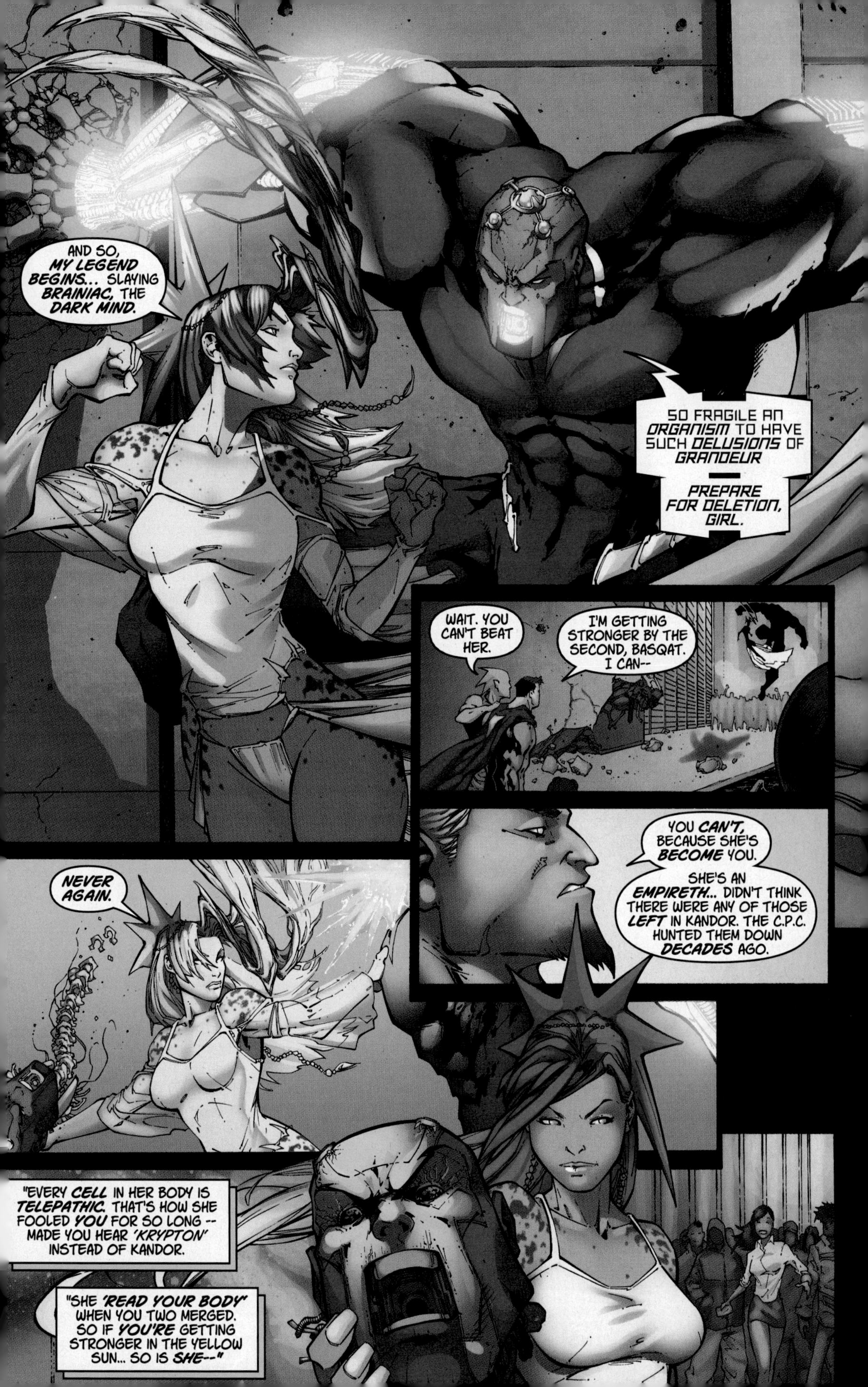
AND SO, MY LEGEND BEGINS... SLAYING BRAINIAC, THE DARK MIND.
SO FRAGILE AN ORGANISM TO HAVE SUCH DELUSIONS OF GRANDEUR — PREPARE FOR DELETION, GIRL.
WAIT. YOU CAN'T BEAT HER.
I'M GETTING STRONGER BY THE SECOND, BASQAT. I CAN--
YOU CAN'T, BECAUSE SHE'S BECOME YOU.
SHE'S AN EMPIRETH... DIDN'T THINK THERE WERE ANY OF THOSE LEFT IN KANDOR. THE C.P.C. HUNTED THEM DOWN DECADES AGO.
NEVER AGAIN.
"EVERY CELL IN HER BODY IS TELEPATHIC. THAT'S HOW SHE FOOLED YOU FOR SO LONG -- MADE YOU HEAR 'KRYPTON' INSTEAD OF KANDOR.
"SHE 'READ YOUR BODY" WHEN YOU TWO MERGED. SO IF YOU'RE GETTING STRONGER IN THE YELLOW SUN... SO IS SHE--"

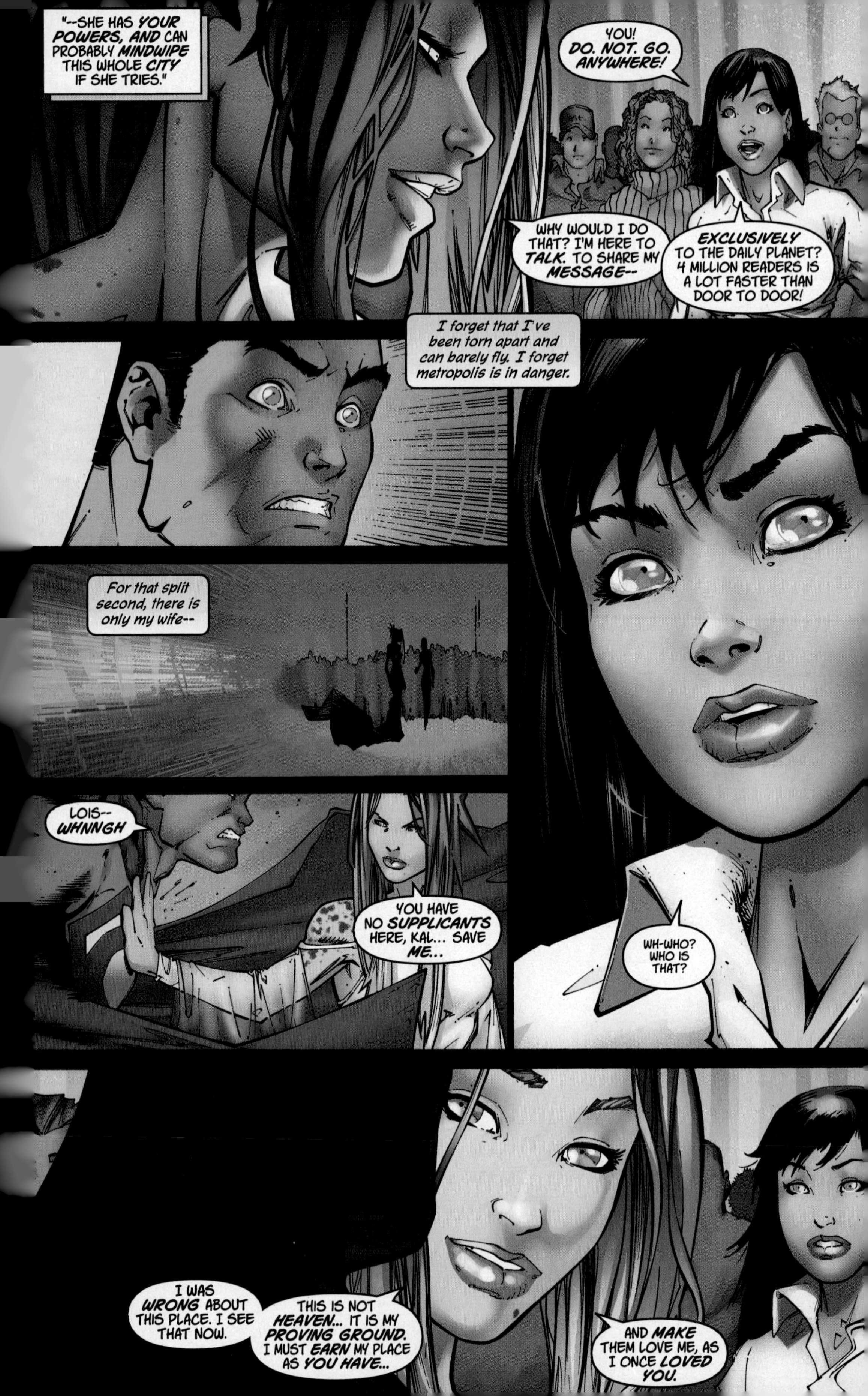

"--SHE HAS YOUR POWERS, AND CAN PROBABLY MINDWIPE THIS WHOLE CITY IF SHE TRIES."
YOU! DO. NOT. GO. ANYWHERE!
WHY WOULD I DO THAT? I'M HERE TO TALK. TO SHARE MY MESSAGE--
EXCLUSIVELY TO THE DAILY PLANET? 4 MILLION READERS IS A LOT FASTER THAN DOOR TO DOOR!
I forget that I've been torn apart and can barely fly. I forget metropolis is in danger.
For that split second, there is only my wife--
LOIS-- WHNNGH
YOU HAVE NO SUPPLICANTS HERE, KAL... SAVE ME...
WH-WHO? WHO IS THAT?
I WAS WRONG ABOUT THIS PLACE. I SEE THAT NOW.
THIS IS NOT HEAVEN... IT IS MY PROVING GROUND. I MUST EARN MY PLACE AS YOU HAVE...
AND MAKE THEM LOVE ME, AS I ONCE LOVED YOU.

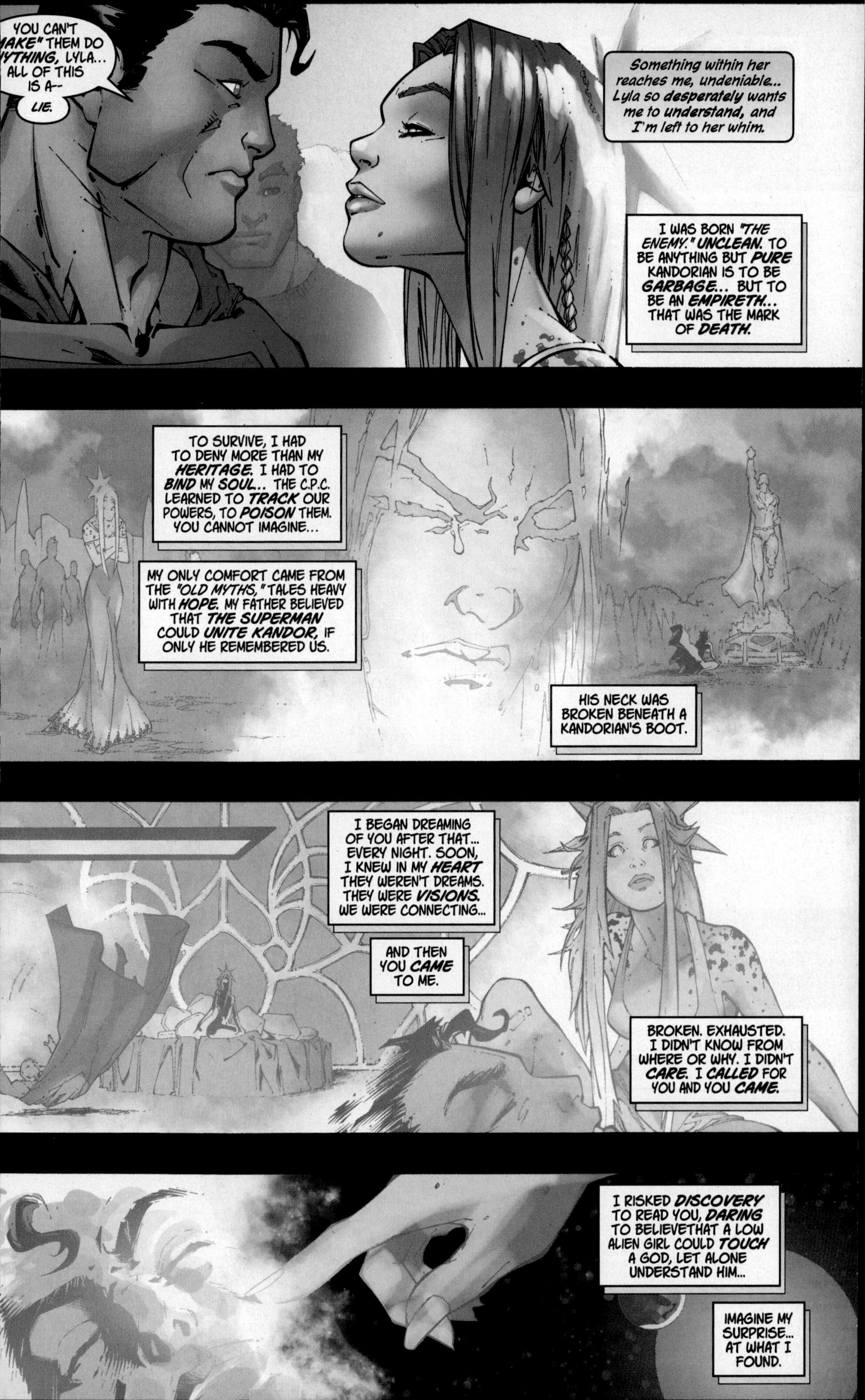

YOU CAN'T MAKE" THEM DO YTHING, LYLA... ALL OF THIS IS A-- LIE.
Something within her reaches me, undeniable... Lyla so desperately wants me to understand, and I'm left to her whim.
I WAS BORN "THE ENEMY." UNCLEAN. TO BE ANYTHING BUT PURE KANDORIAN IS TO BE GARBAGE... BUT TO BE AN EMPIRETH... THAT WAS THE MARK OF DEATH.
TO SURVIVE, I HAD TO DENY MORE THAN MY HERITAGE. I HAD TO BIND MY SOUL... THE C.P.C. LEARNED TO TRACK OUR POWERS, TO POISON THEM. YOU CANNOT IMAGINE...
MY ONLY COMFORT CAME FROM THE "OLD MYTHS," TALES HEAVY WITH HOPE. MY FATHER BELIEVED THAT THE SUPERMAN COULD UNITE KANDOR, IF ONLY HE REMEMBERED US.
HIS NECK WAS BROKEN BENEATH A KANDORIAN'S BOOT.
I BEGAN DREAMING OF YOU AFTER THAT... EVERY NIGHT. SOON, I KNEW IN MY HEART THEY WEREN'T DREAMS. THEY WERE VISIONS. WE WERE CONNECTING...
AND THEN YOU CAME TO ME.
BROKEN. EXHAUSTED. I DIDN'T KNOW FROM WHERE OR WHY. I DIDN'T CARE. I CALLED FOR YOU AND YOU CAME.
I RISKED DISCOVERY TO READ YOU, DARING TO BELIEVETHAT A LOW ALIEN GIRL COULD TOUCH A GOD, LET ALONE UNDERSTAND HIM...
IMAGINE MY SURPRISE... AT WHAT I FOUND.

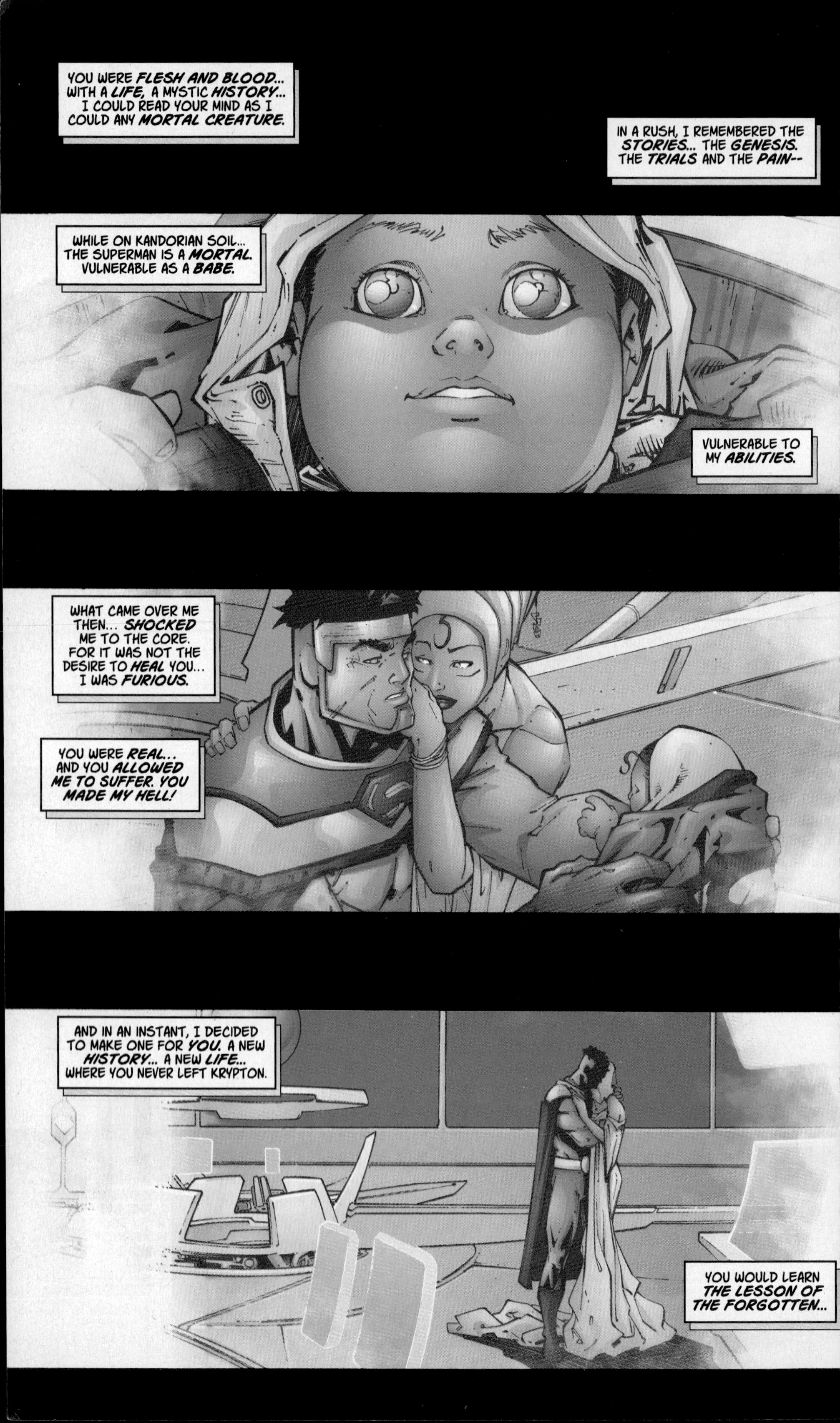
YOU WERE FLESH AND BLOOD... WITH A LIFE, A MYSTIC HISTORY... I COULD READ YOUR MIND AS I COULD ANY MORTAL CREATURE.
IN A RUSH, I REMEMBERED THE STORIES... THE GENESIS. THE TRIALS AND THE PAIN--
WHILE ON KANDORIAN SOIL... THE SUPERMAN IS A MORTAL. VULNERABLE AS A BABE.
VULNERABLE TO MY ABILITIES.
WHAT CAME OVER ME THEN... SHOCKED ME TO THE CORE. FOR IT WAS NOT THE DESIRE TO HEAL YOU... I WAS FURIOUS.
YOU WERE REAL... AND YOU ALLOWED ME TO SUFFER. YOU MADE MY HELL!
AND IN AN INSTANT, I DECIDED TO MAKE ONE FOR YOU. A NEW HISTORY... A NEW LIFE... WHERE YOU NEVER LEFT KRYPTON.
YOU WOULD LEARN THE LESSON OF THE FORGOTTEN...

AND YOU WOULD SHARE IN THE *TRAGEDY* YOUR WORLD MAKES.

I SUPPLIED A *"FAMILY"* RESEMBLING YOUR OWN, BUILT FROM *MEMORIES...*

HIRED THE REBELS TO ENSNARE YOU, TO PUSH YOU TO VIOLENCE...

SO THAT WHEN YOU LASHED OUT WITH POWERS YOU DID NOT RECOGNIZE...

YOU WOULD LOSE *EVERYTHING.*

I WOULD THEN TAKE THE *REST,* USING THE GREATEST *GIFT* OF MY KIND, THE *CISTERN...*

AND *ASCEND.*

KON-LAR? WHAT DO YOU MEAN YOU *"SUPPLIED"* A FAMILY?

EVEN *WITHOUT* THE POWER I TOOK FROM YOU THROUGH THE *CISTERN,* I HAVE *GIFTS* OF MY OWN...

BUT *WITH* DIVINE POWER?

EVERYTHING IS POSSIBLE.

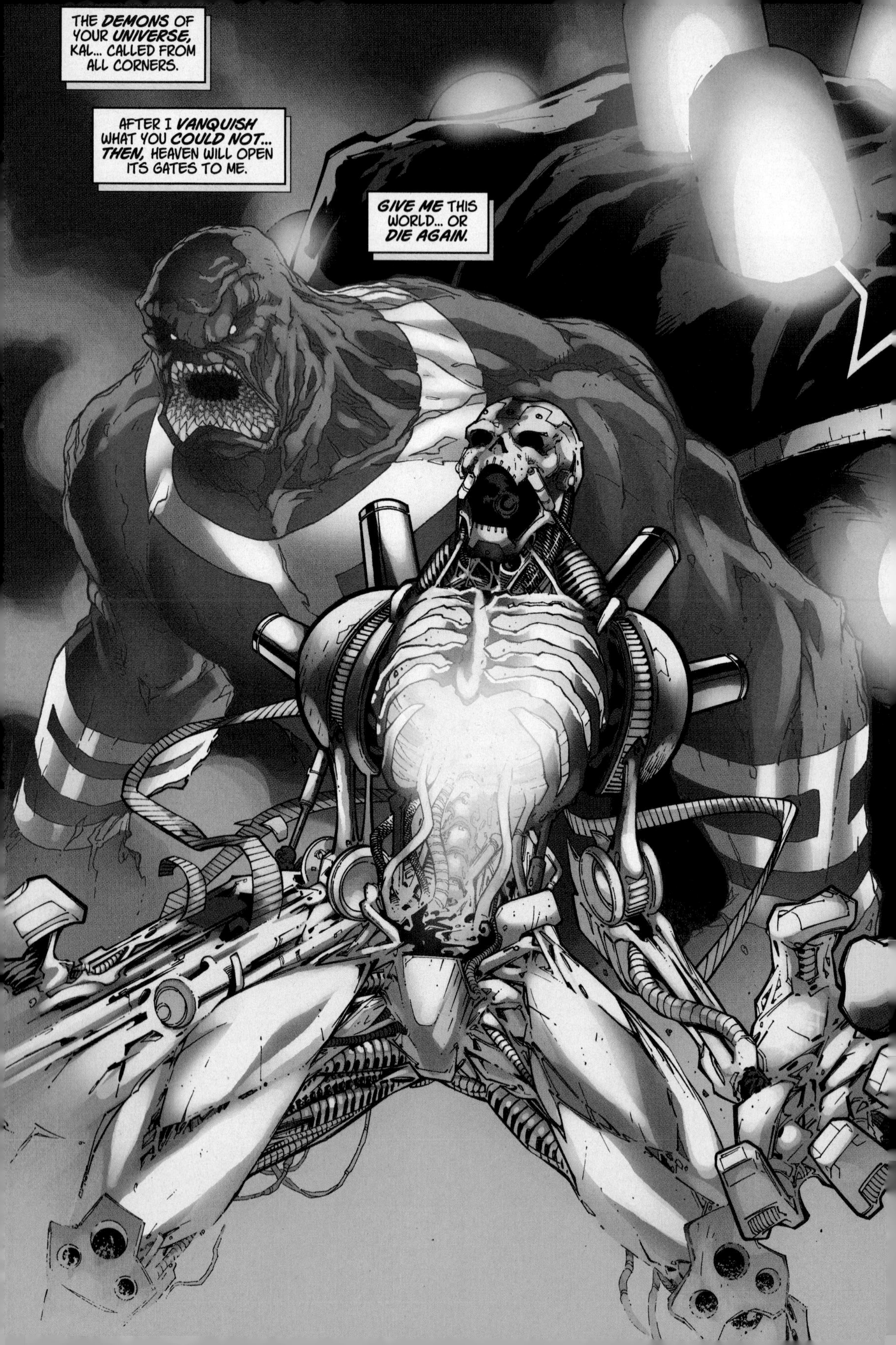
THE DEMONS OF YOUR UNIVERSE, KAL... CALLED FROM ALL CORNERS.
AFTER I VANQUISH WHAT YOU COULD NOT... THEN, HEAVEN WILL OPEN ITS GATES TO ME.
GIVE ME THIS WORLD... OR DIE AGAIN.

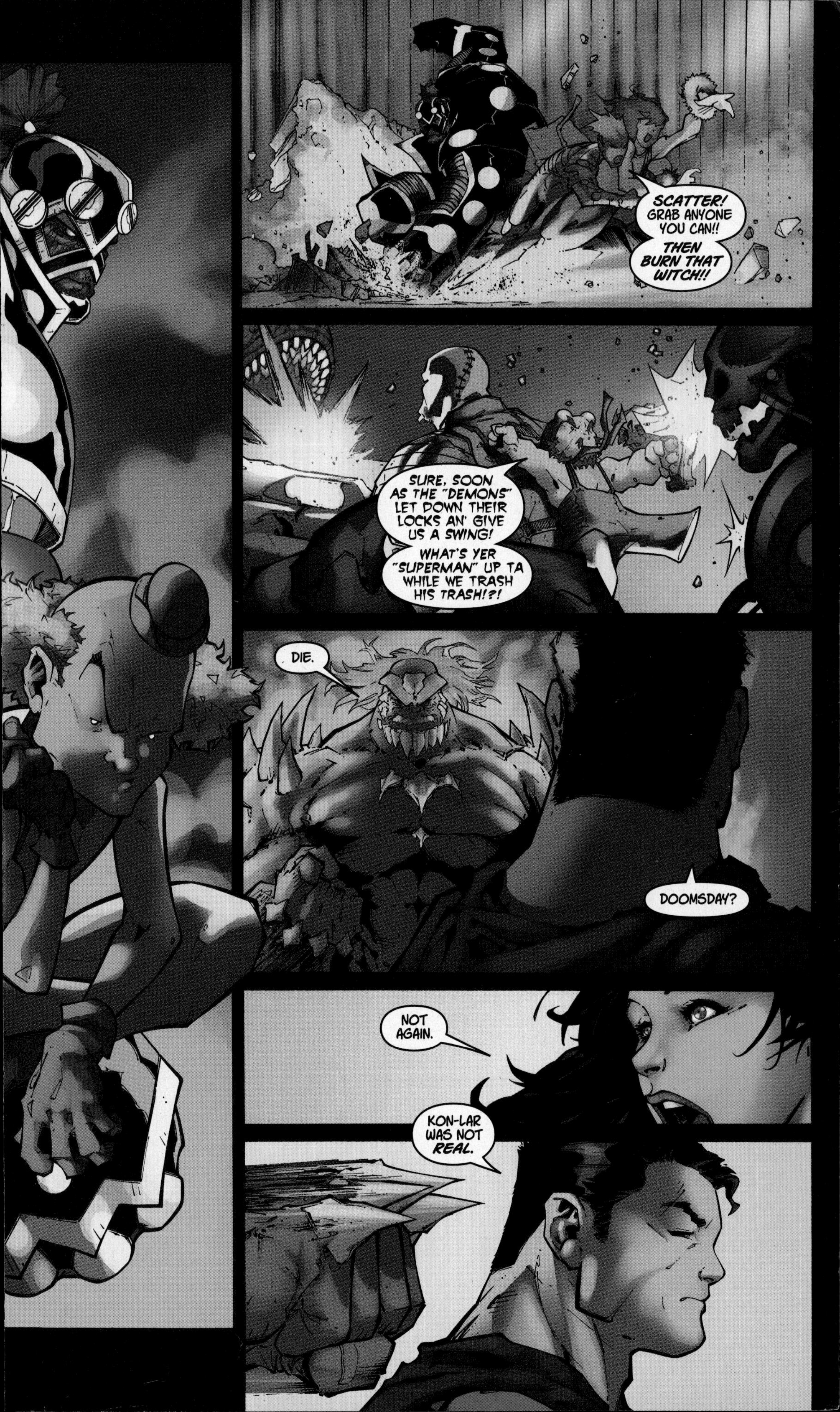
SCATTER! GRAB ANYONE YOU CAN!! THEN BURN THAT WITCH!!
SURE, SOON AS THE "DEMONS" LET DOWN THEIR LOCKS AN' GIVE US A SWING!
WHAT'S YER "SUPERMAN" UP TA WHILE WE TRASH HIS TRASH!?!
DIE.
DOOMSDAY?
NOT AGAIN.
KON-LAR WAS NOT REAL.

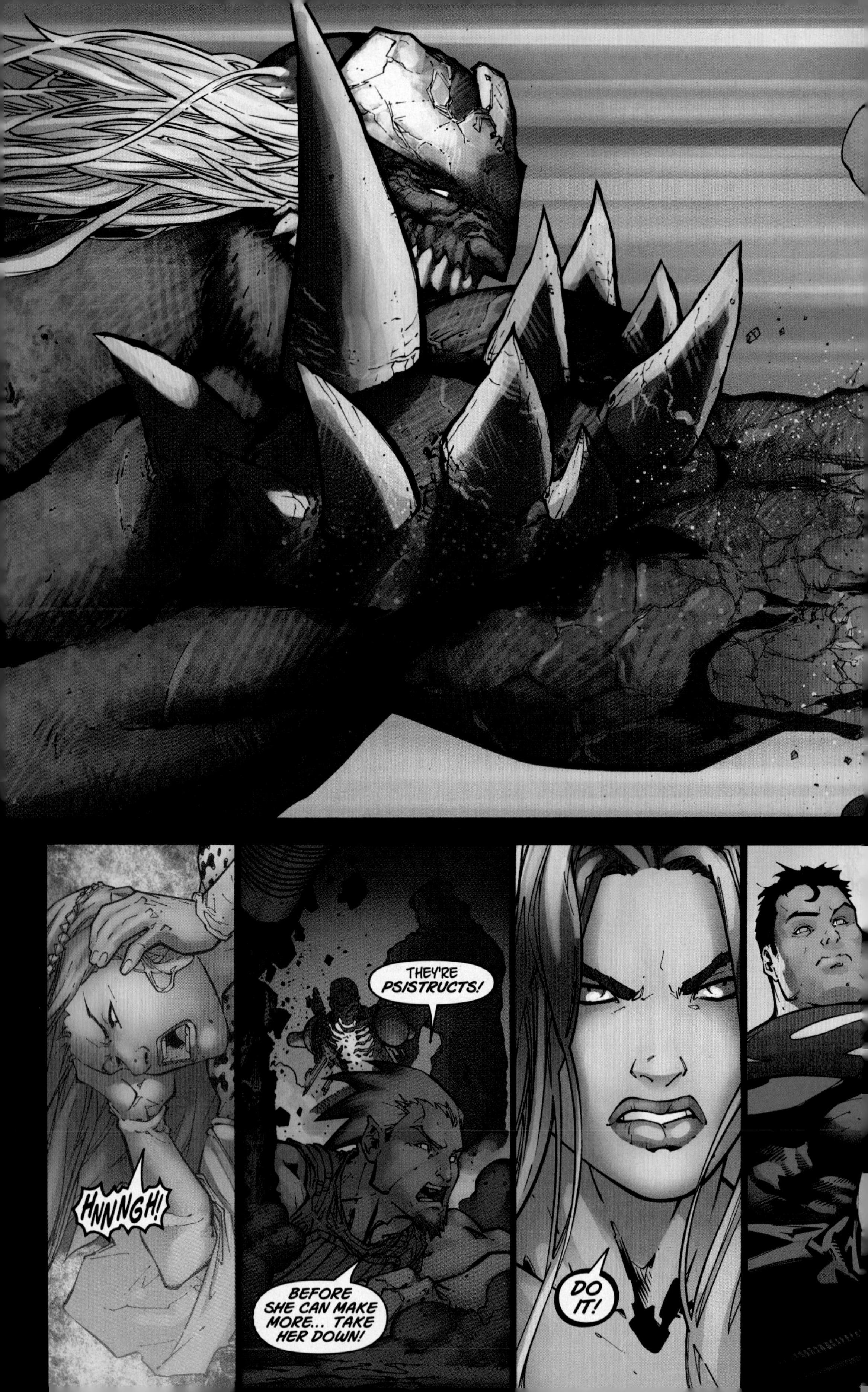
HNNNGH!
THEY'RE PSISTRUCTS!
BEFORE SHE CAN MAKE MORE... TAKE HER DOWN!
DO IT!

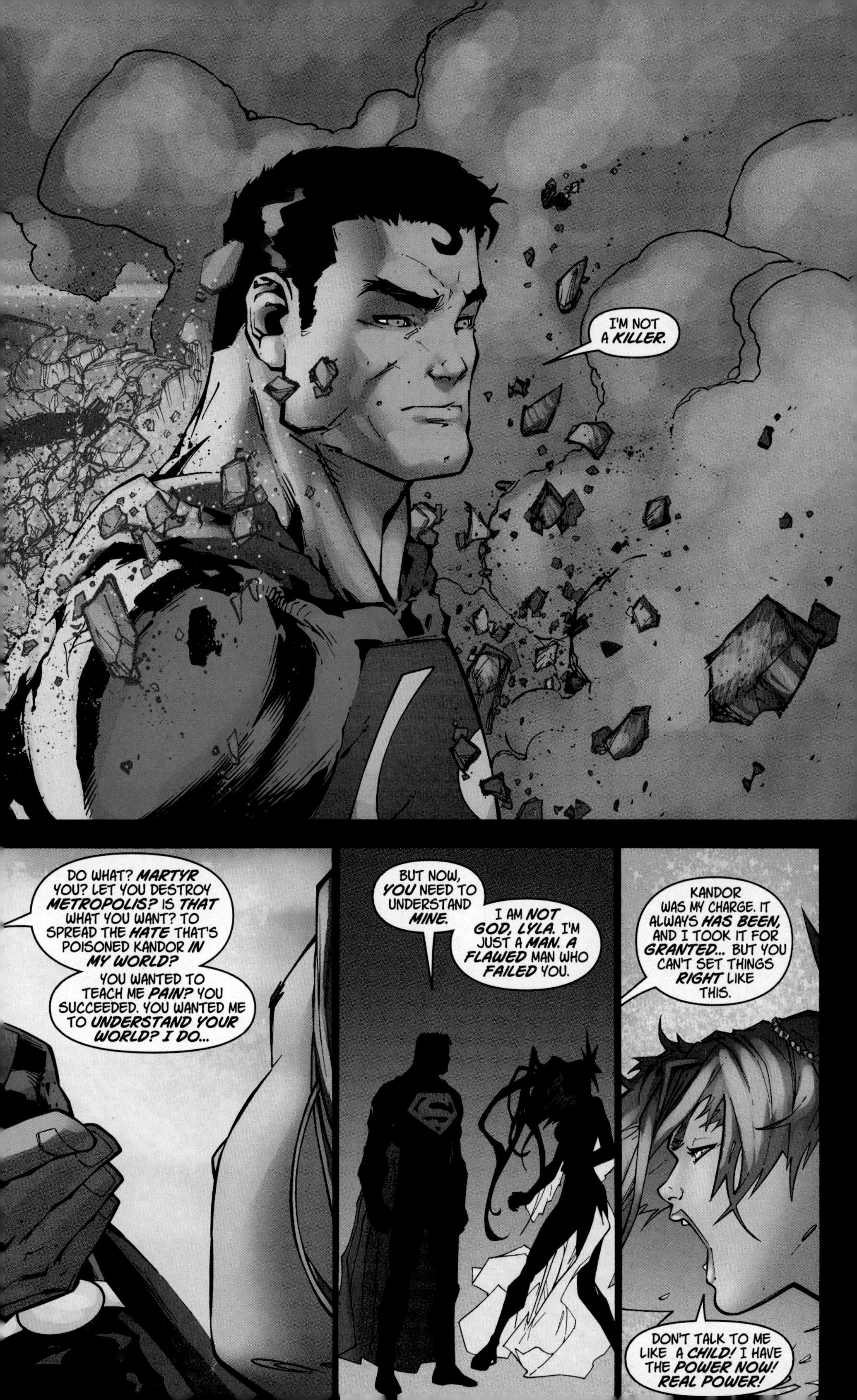
I'M NOT A KILLER.
DO WHAT? MARTYR YOU? LET YOU DESTROY METROPOLIS? IS THAT WHAT YOU WANT? TO SPREAD THE HATE THAT'S POISONED KANDOR IN MY WORLD?
YOU WANTED TO TEACH ME PAIN? YOU SUCCEEDED. YOU WANTED ME TO UNDERSTAND YOUR WORLD? I DO...
BUT NOW, YOU NEED TO UNDERSTAND MINE.
I AM NOT GOD, LYLA. I'M JUST A MAN. A FLAWED MAN WHO FAILED YOU.
KANDOR WAS MY CHARGE. IT ALWAYS HAS BEEN, AND I TOOK IT FOR GRANTED... BUT YOU CAN'T SET THINGS RIGHT LIKE THIS.
DON'T TALK TO ME LIKE A CHILD! I HAVE THE POWER NOW! REAL POWER!

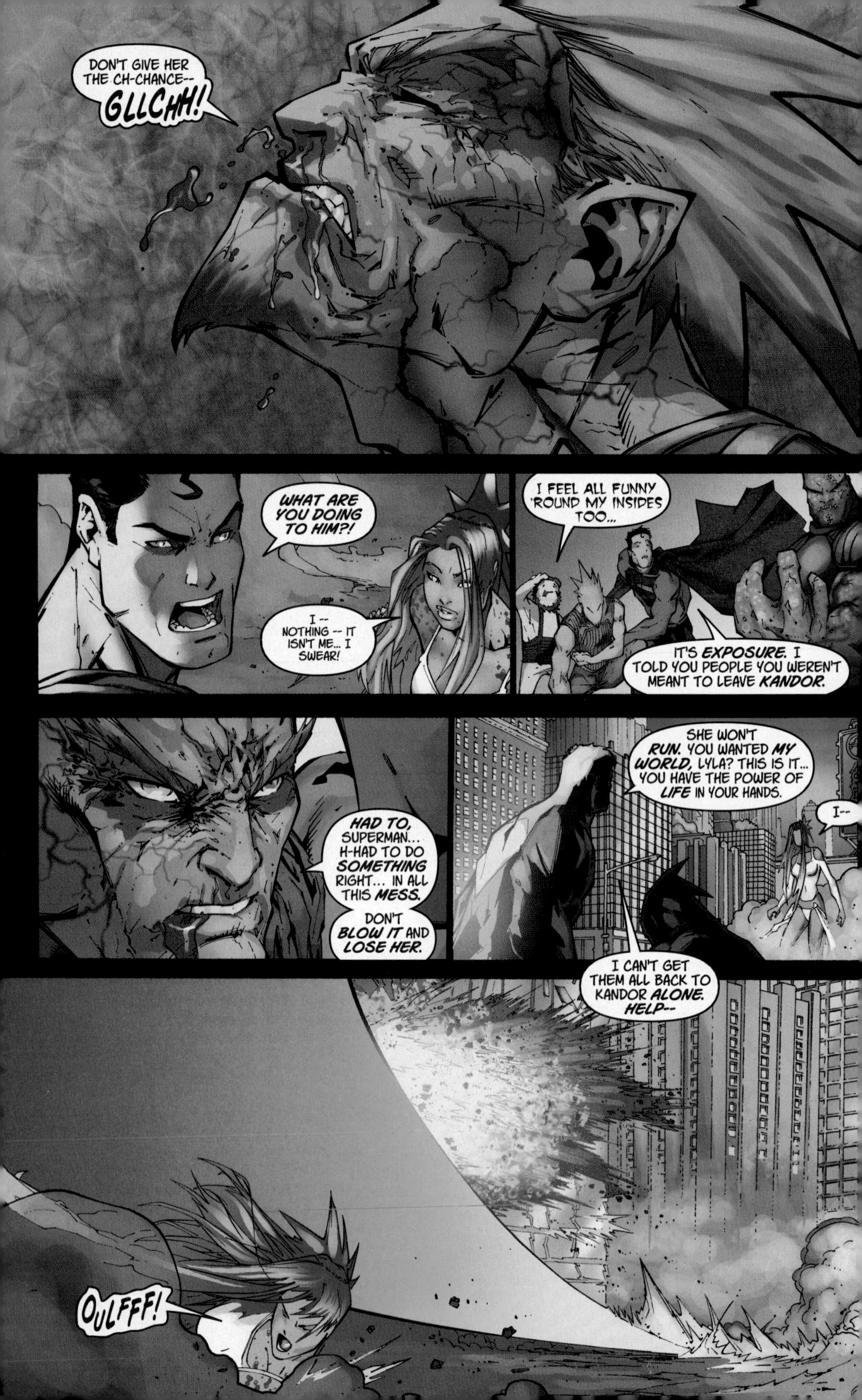
DON'T GIVE HER THE CH-CHANCE-- GLLCHH!
WHAT ARE YOU DOING TO HIM?!
I -- NOTHING -- IT ISN'T ME... I SWEAR!
I FEEL ALL FUNNY 'ROUND MY INSIDES TOO...
IT'S EXPOSURE. I TOLD YOU PEOPLE YOU WEREN'T MEANT TO LEAVE KANDOR.
HAD TO, SUPERMAN... H-HAD TO DO SOMETHING RIGHT... IN ALL THIS MESS.
DON'T BLOW IT AND LOSE HER.
SHE WON'T RUN. YOU WANTED MY WORLD, LYLA? THIS IS IT... YOU HAVE THE POWER OF LIFE IN YOUR HANDS.
I--
I CAN'T GET THEM ALL BACK TO KANDOR ALONE. HELP--
OULFFF!

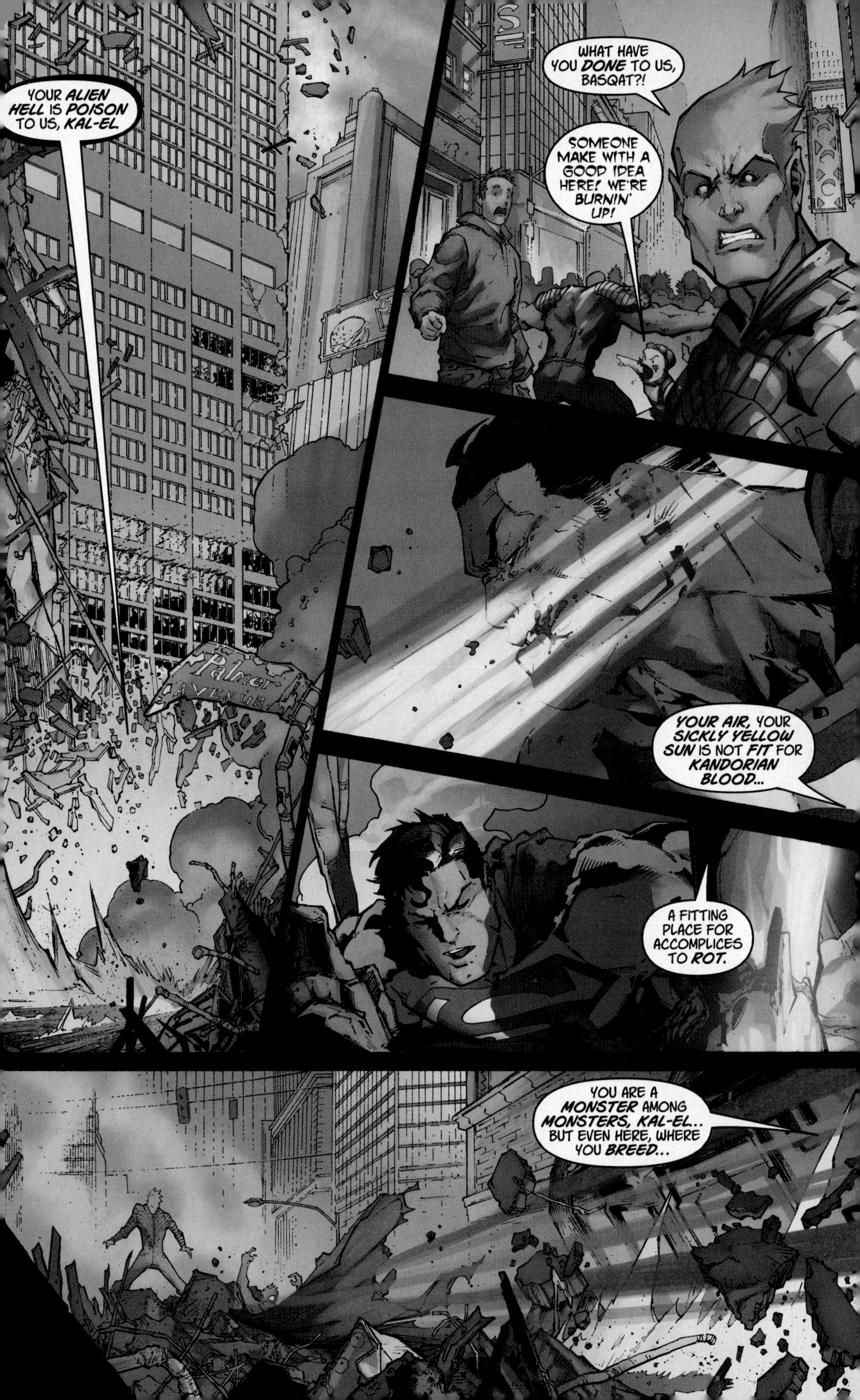
YOUR ALIEN HELL IS POISON TO US, KAL-EL.
WHAT HAVE YOU DONE TO US, BASQAT?!
SOMEONE MAKE WITH A GOOD IDEA HERE! WE'RE BURNIN' UP!
YOUR AIR, YOUR SICKLY YELLOW SUN IS NOT FIT FOR KANDORIAN BLOOD...
A FITTING PLACE FOR ACCOMPLICES TO ROT.
YOU ARE A MONSTER AMONG MONSTERS, KAL-EL... BUT EVEN HERE, WHERE YOU BREED...
Palmer AVENUE

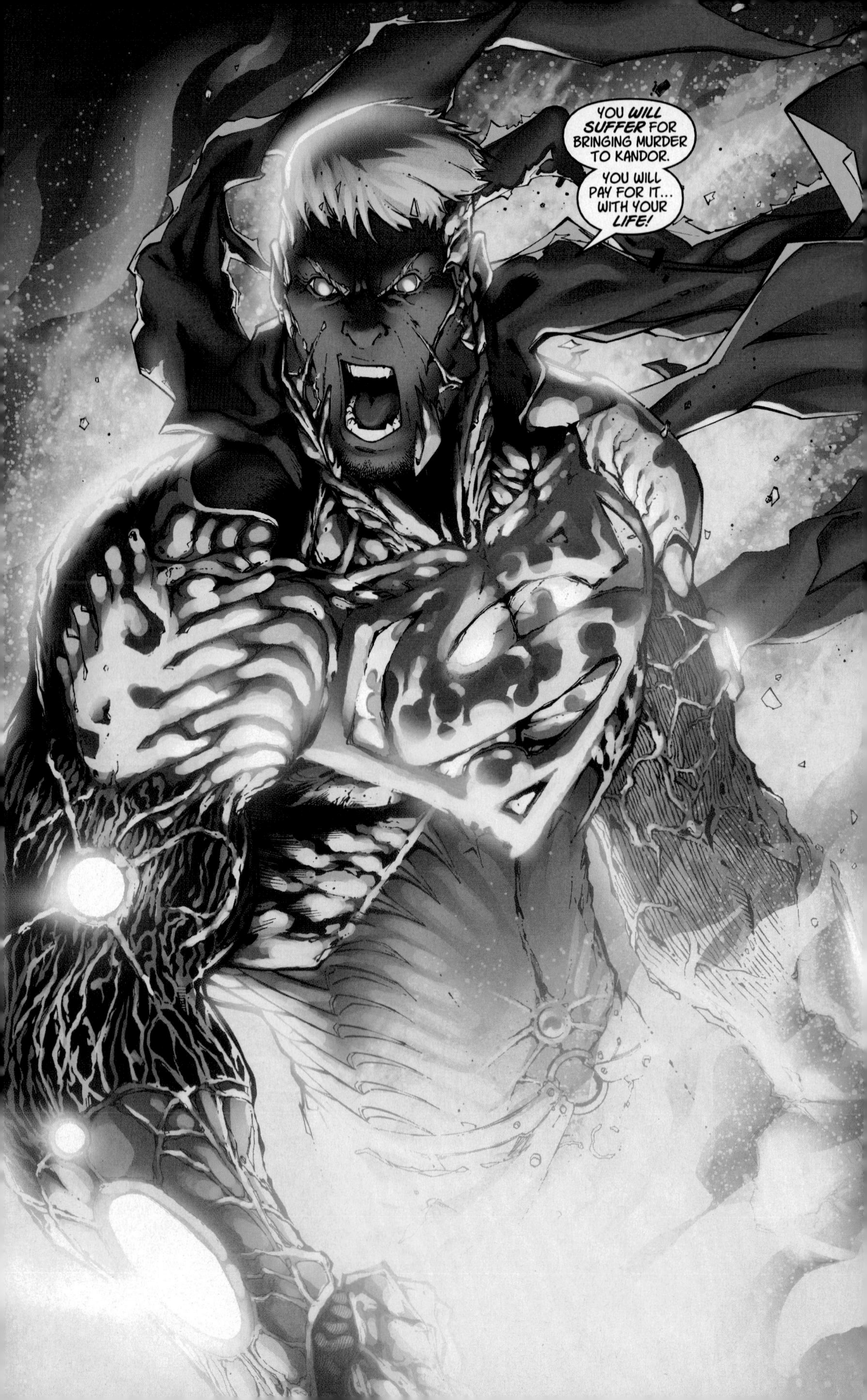
YOU WILL SUFFER FOR BRINGING MURDER TO KANDOR.
YOU WILL PAY FOR IT... WITH YOUR LIFE!

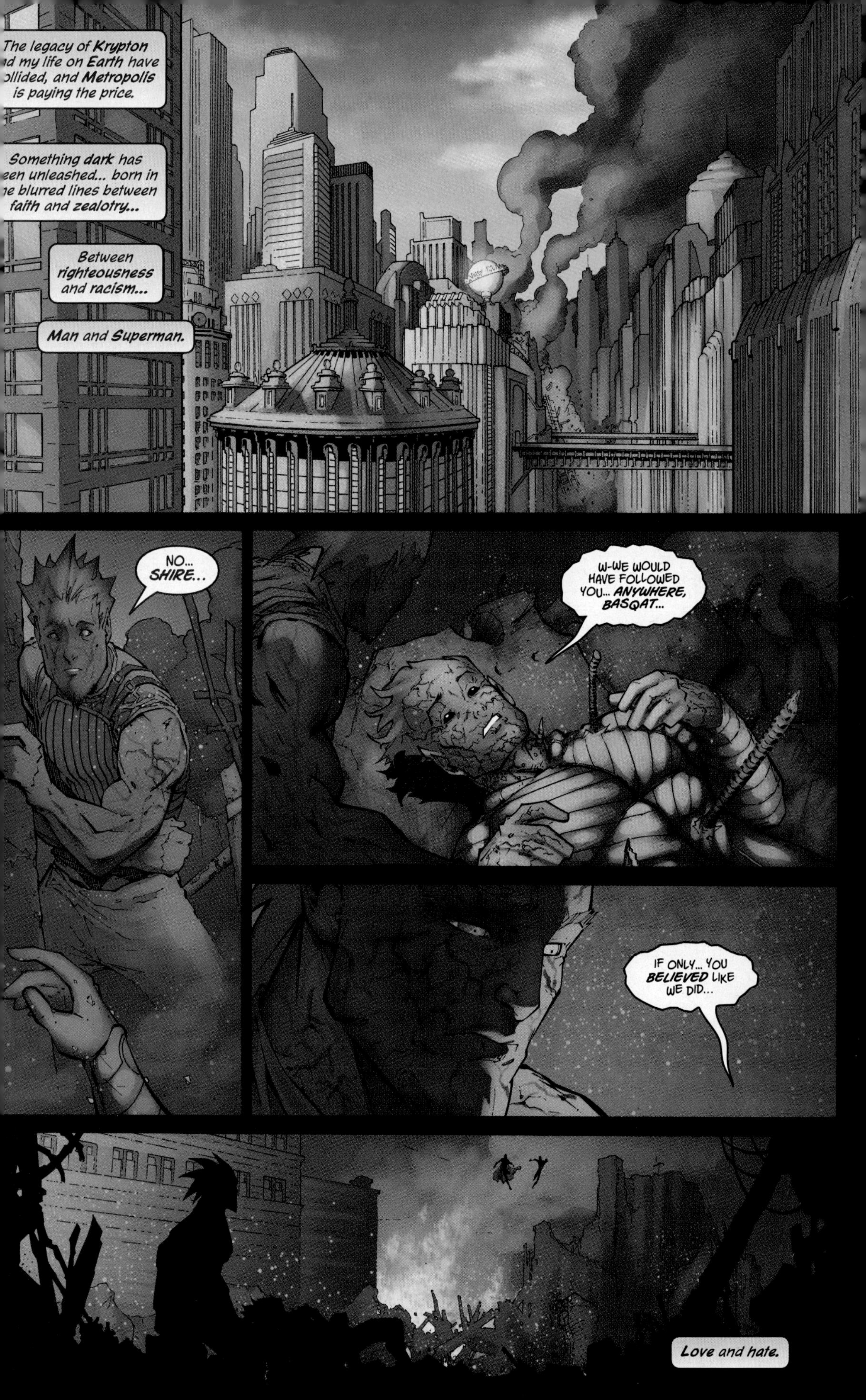
The legacy of Krypton d my life on Earth have ollided, and Metropolis is paying the price.
Something dark has een unleashed... born in e blurred lines between faith and zealotry...
Between righteousness and racism...
Man and Superman.
NO... SHIRE...
W-WE WOULD HAVE FOLLOWED YOU... ANYWHERE, BASQAT...
IF ONLY... YOU BELIEVED LIKE WE DID...
Love and hate.

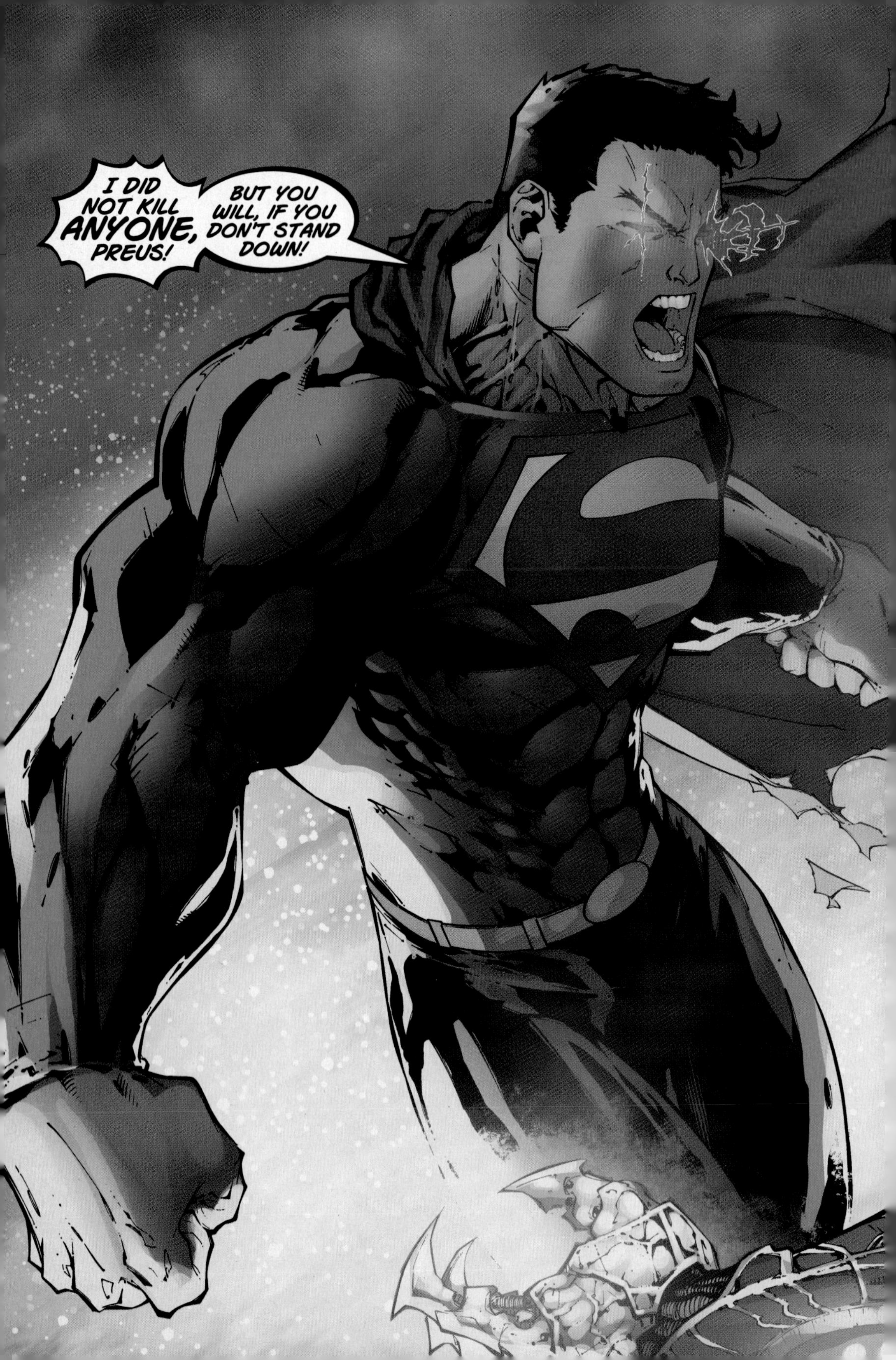
I DID NOT KILL ANYONE, PREUS!
BUT YOU WILL, IF YOU DON'T STAND DOWN!

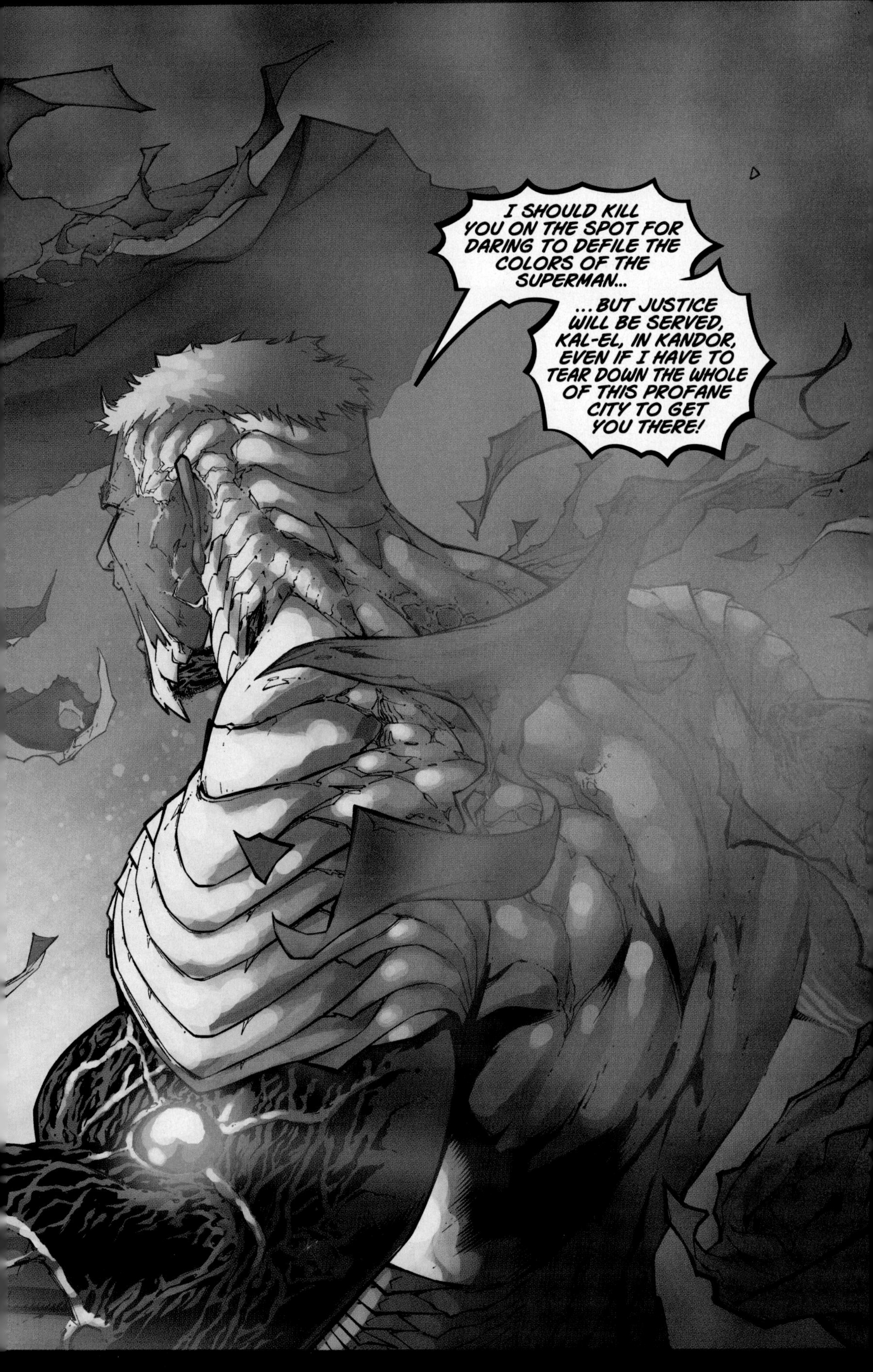
I SHOULD KILL YOU ON THE SPOT FOR DARING TO DEFILE THE COLORS OF THE SUPERMAN...
...BUT JUSTICE WILL BE SERVED, KAL-EL, IN KANDOR, EVEN IF I HAVE TO TEAR DOWN THE WHOLE OF THIS PROFANE CITY TO GET YOU THERE!

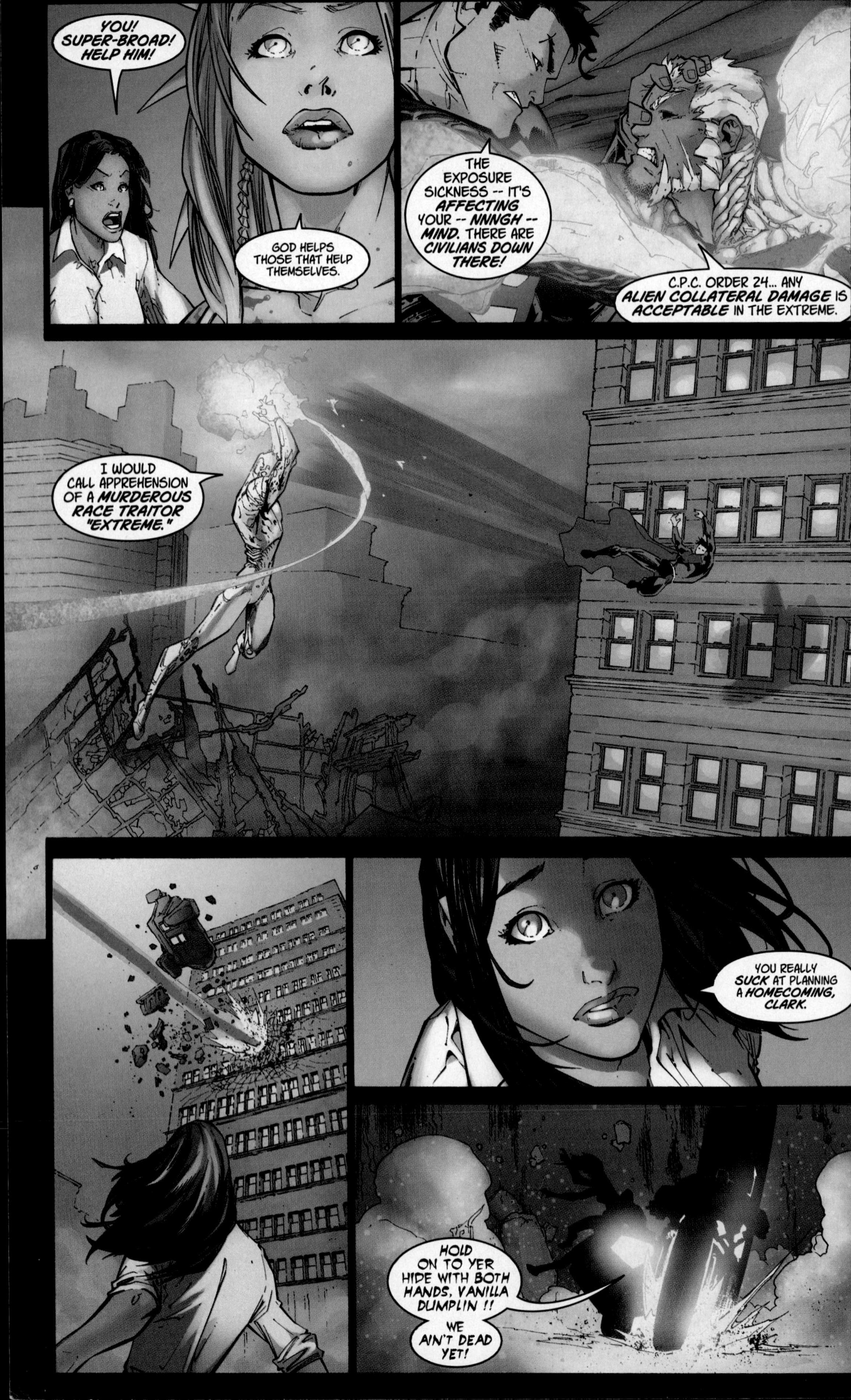
YOU! SUPER-BROAD! HELP HIM!
GOD HELPS THOSE THAT HELP THEMSELVES.
THE EXPOSURE SICKNESS -- IT'S AFFECTING YOUR -- NNNGH -- MIND. THERE ARE CIVILIANS DOWN THERE!
C.P.C. ORDER 24... ANY ALIEN COLLATERAL DAMAGE IS ACCEPTABLE IN THE EXTREME.
I WOULD CALL APPREHENSION OF A MURDEROUS RACE TRAITOR "EXTREME."
YOU REALLY SUCK AT PLANNING A HOMECOMING, CLARK.
HOLD ON TO YER HIDE WITH BOTH HANDS, VANILLA DUMPLIN !!
WE AIN'T DEAD YET!

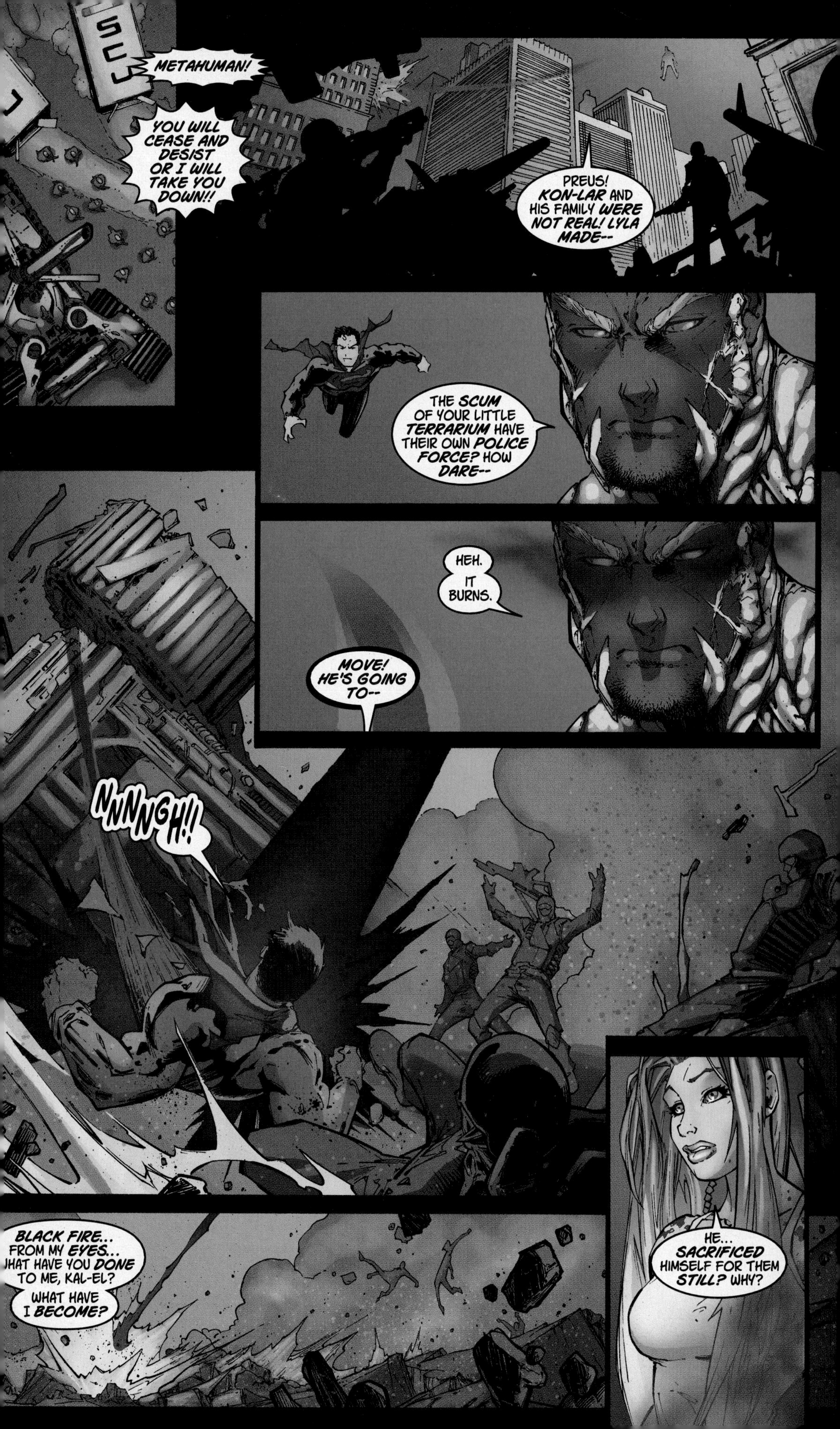
METAHUMAN!
YOU WILL CEASE AND DESIST OR I WILL TAKE YOU DOWN!!
PREUS! KON-LAR AND HIS FAMILY WERE NOT REAL! LYLA MADE--
THE SCUM OF YOUR LITTLE TERRARIUM HAVE THEIR OWN POLICE FORCE? HOW DARE--
HEH. IT BURNS.
MOVE! HE'S GOING TO--
NNNNGH!!
BLACK FIRE... FROM MY EYES... WHAT HAVE YOU DONE TO ME, KAL-EL?
WHAT HAVE I BECOME?
HE... SACRIFICED HIMSELF FOR THEM STILL? WHY?

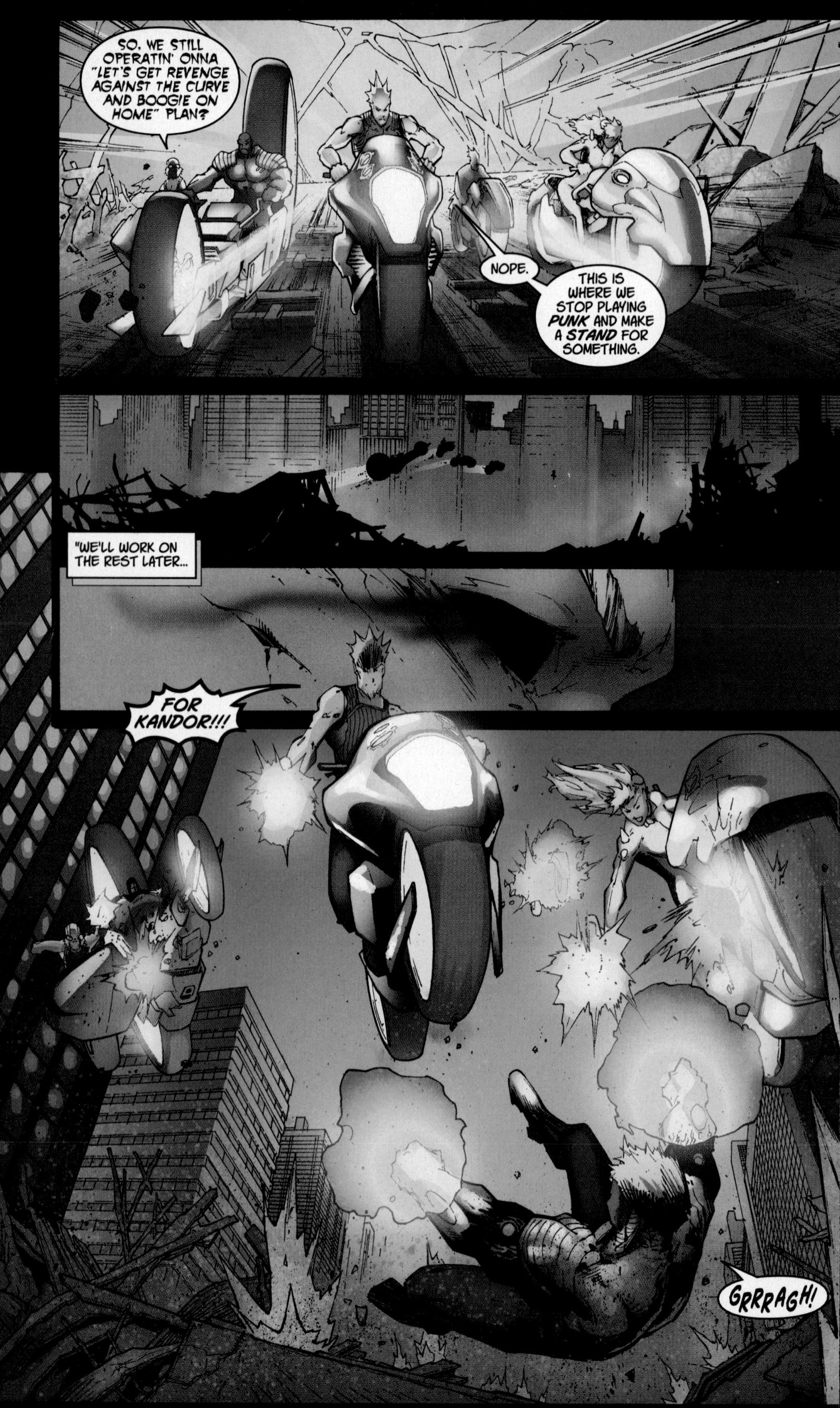
SO, WE STILL OPERATIN' ONNA "LET'S GET REVENGE AGAINST THE CURVE AND BOOGIE ON HOME" PLAN?
NOPE.
THIS IS WHERE WE STOP PLAYING PUNK AND MAKE A STAND FOR SOMETHING.
"WE'LL WORK ON THE REST LATER...
FOR KANDOR!!!
GRRRAGH!

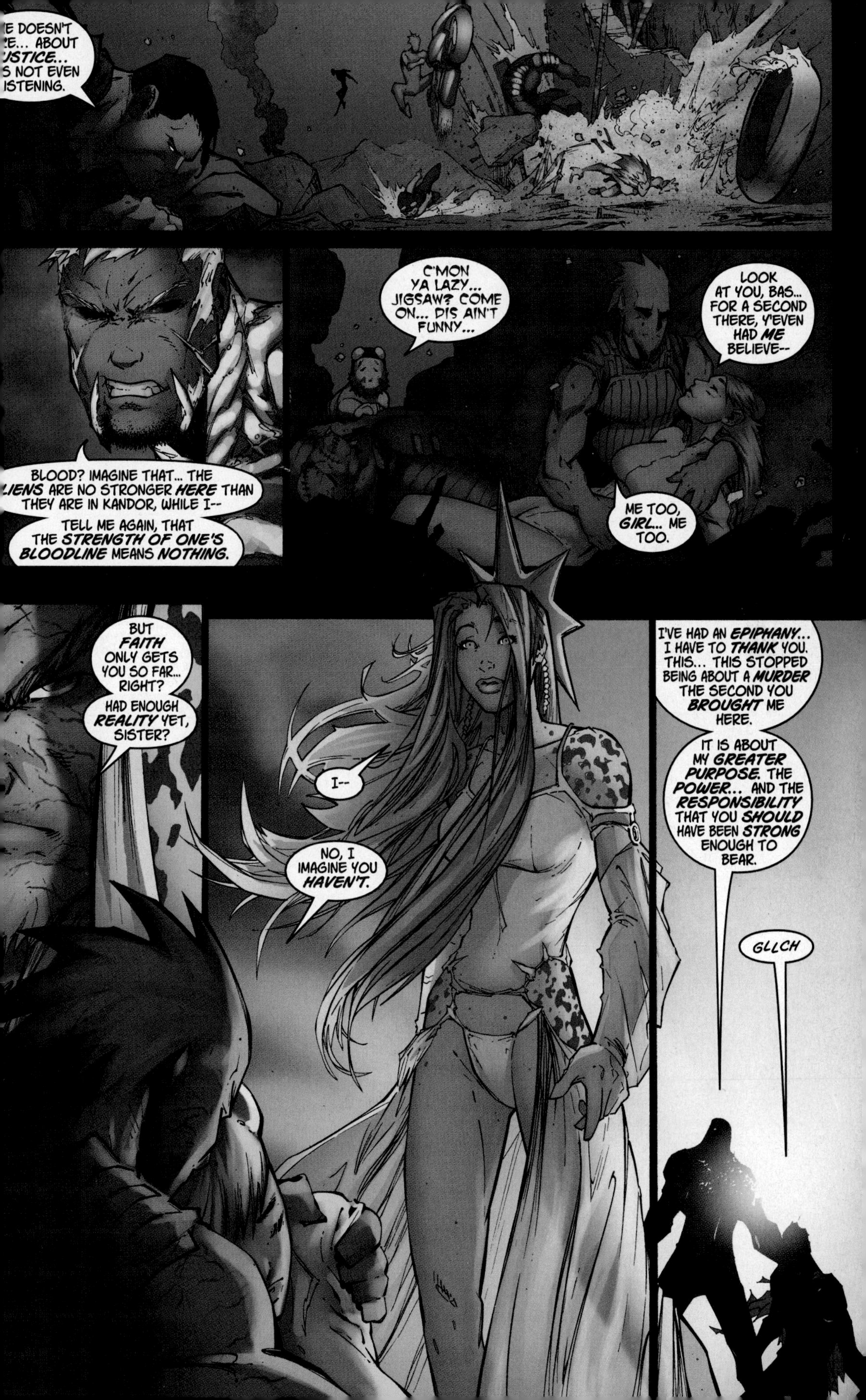

E DOESN'T E... ABOUT USTICE... S NOT EVEN ISTENING.
BLOOD? IMAGINE THAT... THE LIENS ARE NO STRONGER HERE THAN THEY ARE IN KANDOR, WHILE I--
TELL ME AGAIN, THAT THE STRENGTH OF ONE'S BLOODLINE MEANS NOTHING.
C'MON YA LAZY... JIGSAW? COME ON... DIS AIN'T FUNNY...
LOOK AT YOU, BAS... FOR A SECOND THERE, Y'EVEN HAD ME BELIEVE--
ME TOO, GIRL... ME TOO.
BUT FAITH ONLY GETS YOU SO FAR... RIGHT?
HAD ENOUGH REALITY YET, SISTER?
I--
NO, I IMAGINE YOU HAVEN'T.
I'VE HAD AN EPIPHANY... I HAVE TO THANK YOU. THIS... THIS STOPPED BEING ABOUT A MURDER THE SECOND YOU BROUGHT ME HERE.
IT IS ABOUT MY GREATER PURPOSE. THE POWER... AND THE RESPONSIBILITY THAT YOU SHOULD HAVE BEEN STRONG ENOUGH TO BEAR.
GLLCH

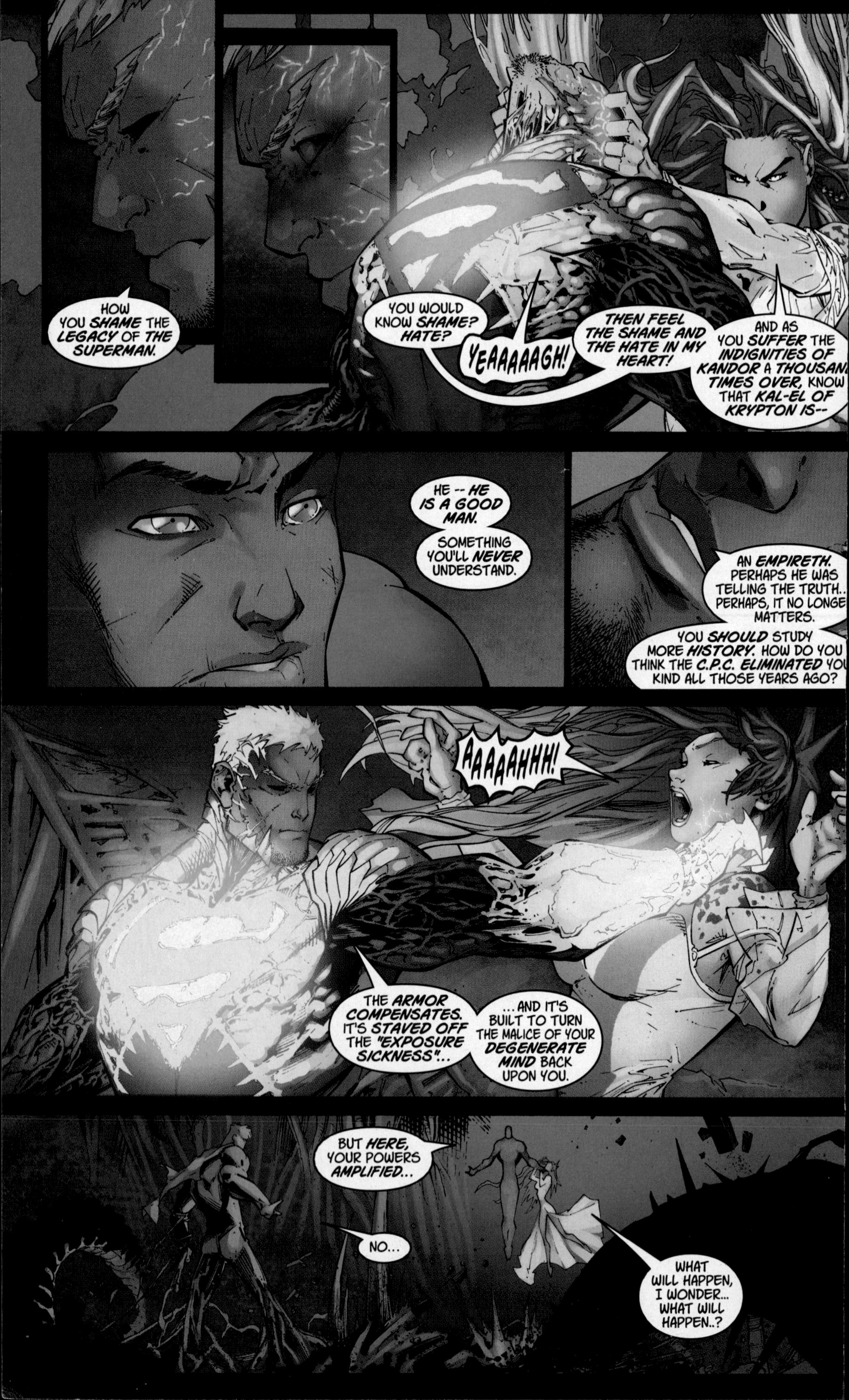

HOW YOU SHAME THE LEGACY OF THE SUPERMAN.
YOU WOULD KNOW SHAME? HATE?
YEAAAAAGH!
THEN FEEL THE SHAME AND THE HATE IN MY HEART!
AND AS YOU SUFFER THE INDIGNITIES OF KANDOR A THOUSAN TIMES OVER, KNOW THAT KAL-EL OF KRYPTON IS--
HE -- HE IS A GOOD MAN.
SOMETHING YOU'LL NEVER UNDERSTAND.
AN EMPIRETH. PERHAPS HE WAS TELLING THE TRUTH.. PERHAPS, IT NO LONGE MATTERS.
YOU SHOULD STUDY MORE HISTORY. HOW DO YOU THINK THE C.P.C. ELIMINATED YOU KIND ALL THOSE YEARS AGO?
AAAAAHHH!
THE ARMOR COMPENSATES. IT'S STAVED OFF THE "EXPOSURE SICKNESS"...
...AND IT'S BUILT TO TURN THE MALICE OF YOUR DEGENERATE MIND BACK UPON YOU.
BUT HERE, YOUR POWERS AMPLIFIED...
NO...
WHAT WILL HAPPEN, I WONDER... WHAT WILL HAPPEN..?

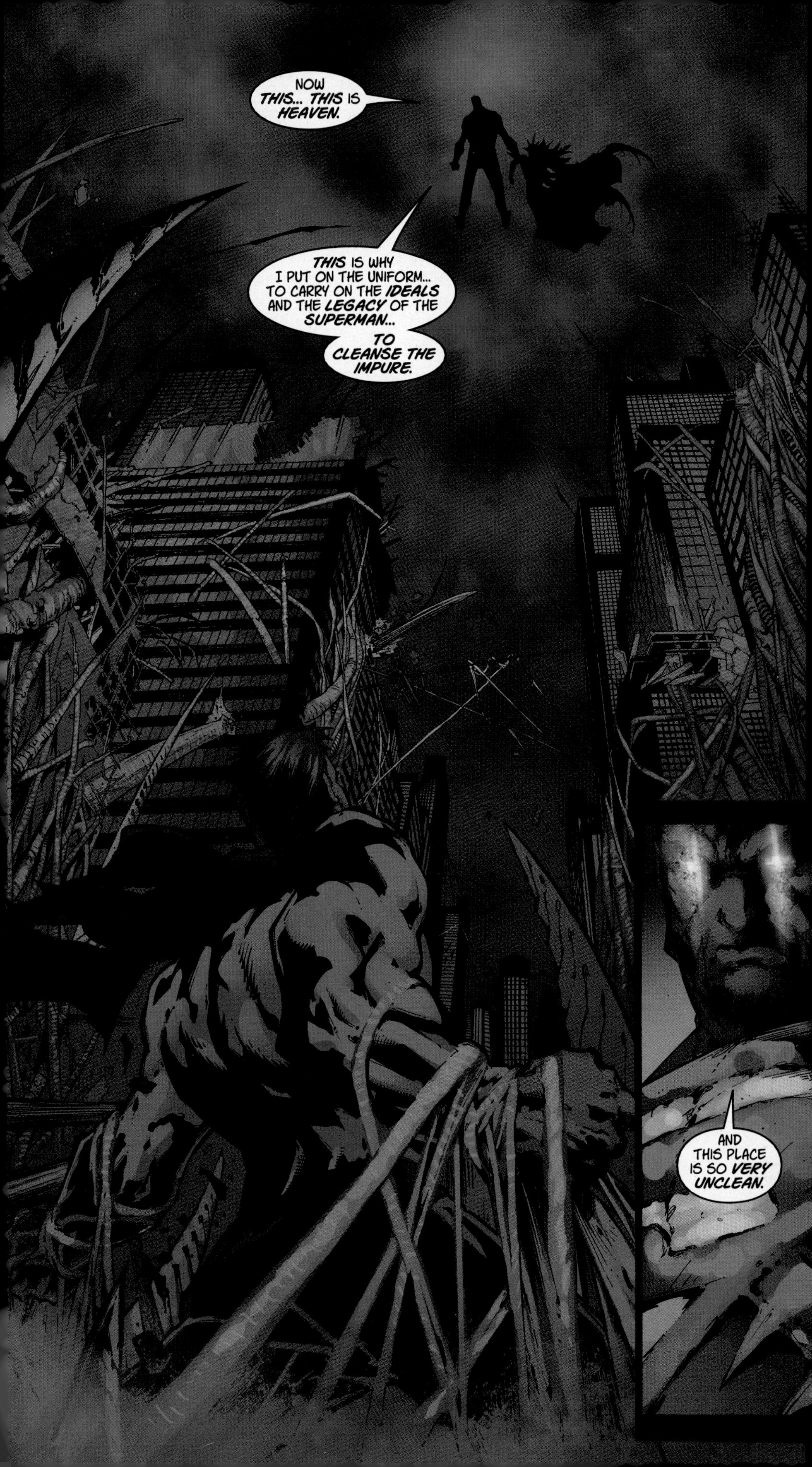
NOW *THIS... THIS* IS *HEAVEN.*
THIS IS WHY I PUT ON THE UNIFORM... TO CARRY ON THE *IDEALS* AND THE *LEGACY* OF THE *SUPERMAN...*
TO CLEANSE THE IMPURE.
AND THIS PLACE IS SO *VERY UNCLEAN.*

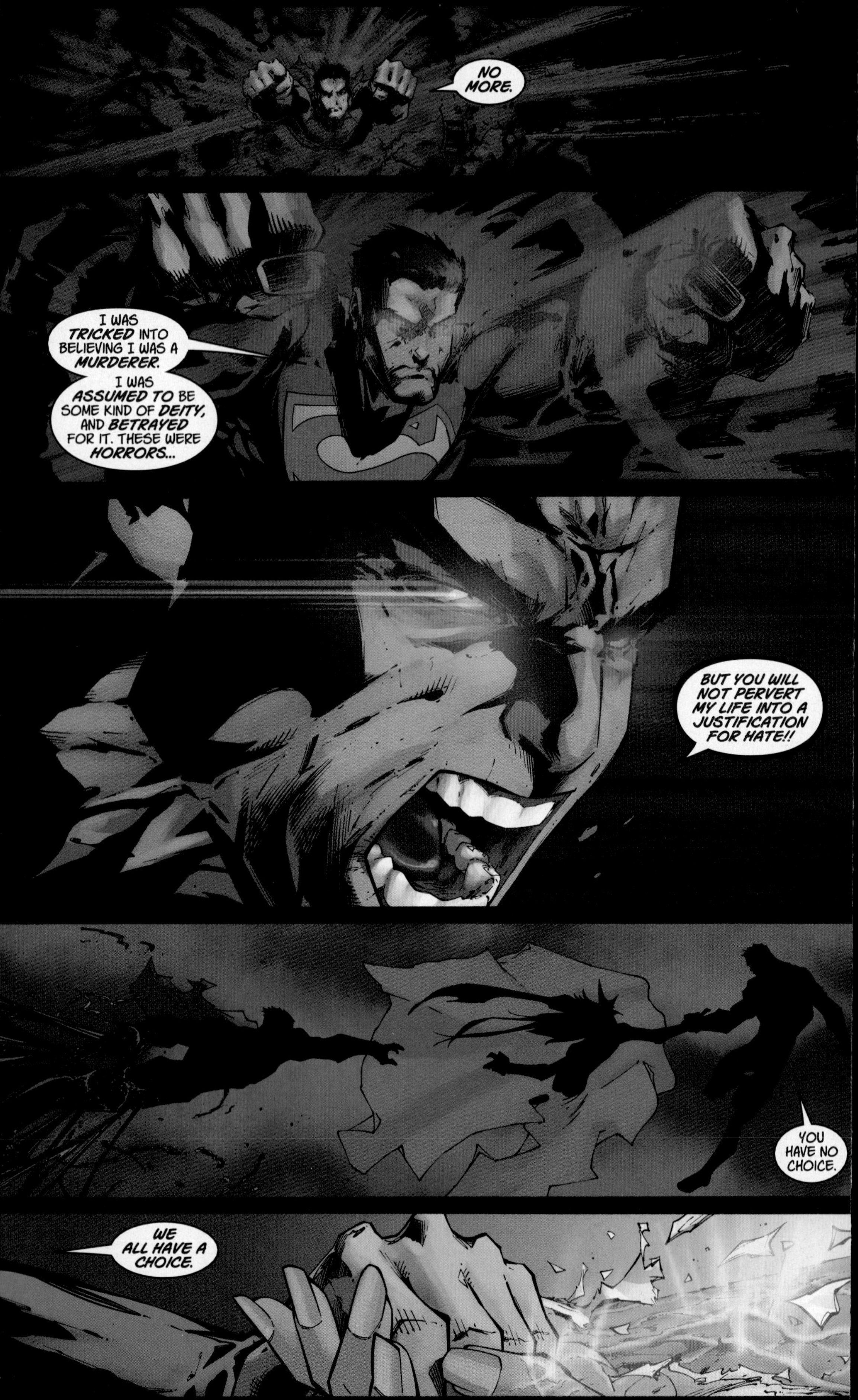
NO MORE.
I WAS TRICKED INTO BELIEVING I WAS A MURDERER.
I WAS ASSUMED TO BE SOME KIND OF DEITY, AND BETRAYED FOR IT. THESE WERE HORRORS...
BUT YOU WILL NOT PERVERT MY LIFE INTO A JUSTIFICATION FOR HATE!!
YOU HAVE NO CHOICE.
WE ALL HAVE A CHOICE.

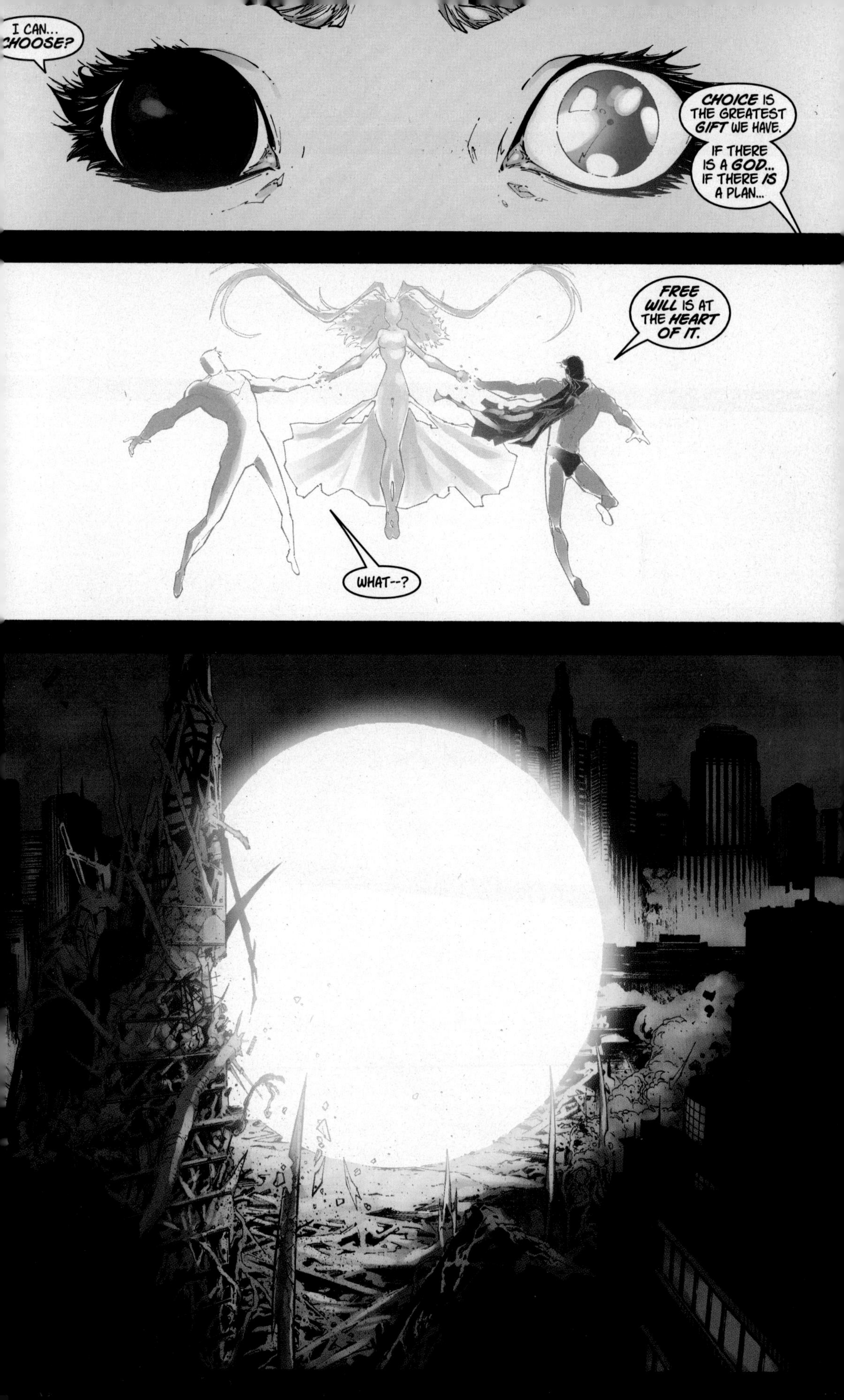
I CAN... CHOOSE?
CHOICE IS THE GREATEST GIFT WE HAVE.
IF THERE IS A GOD... IF THERE IS A PLAN...
FREE WILL IS AT THE HEART OF IT.
WHAT--?

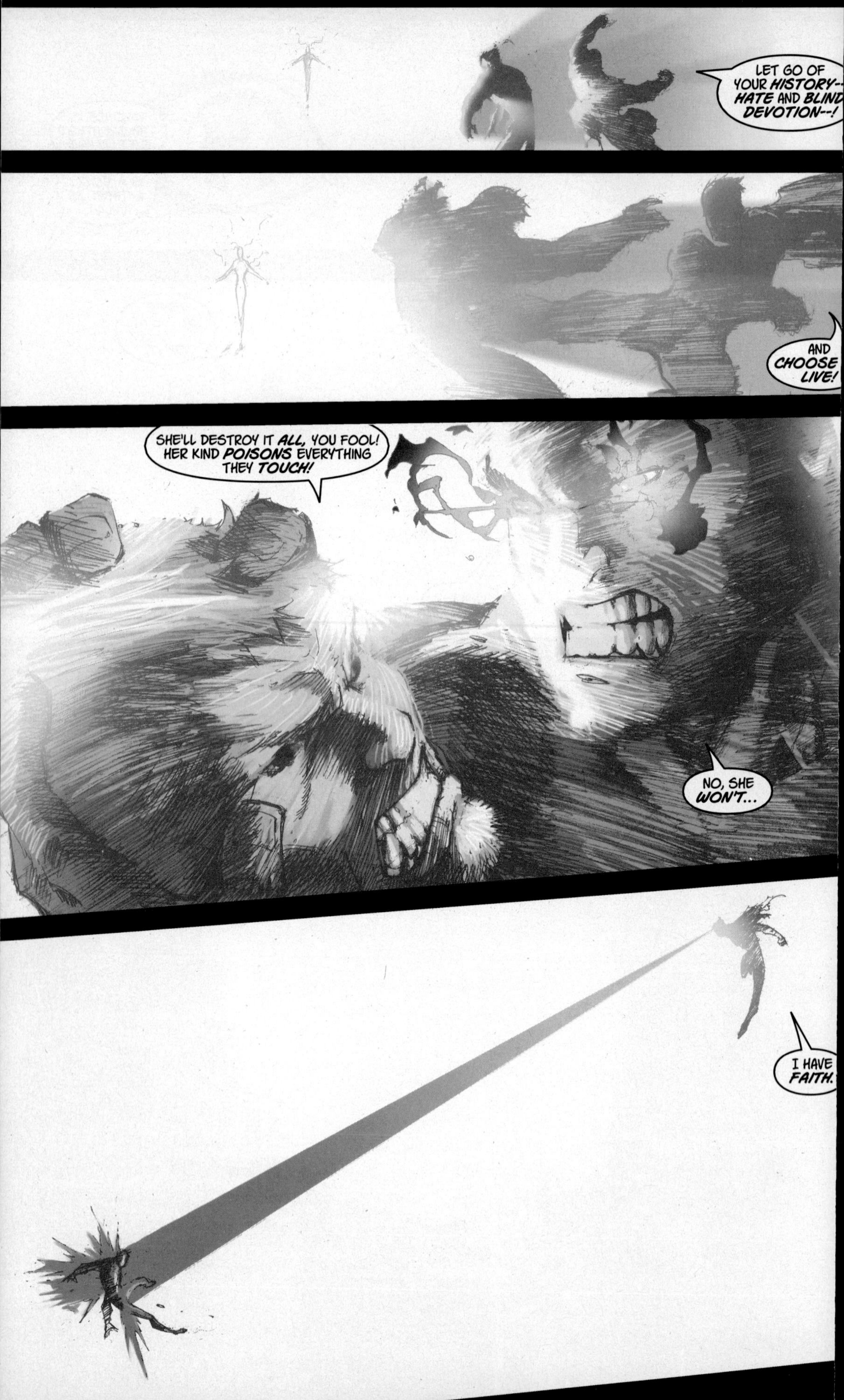
LET GO OF YOUR HISTORY--HATE AND BLIND DEVOTION--!
AND CHOOSE LIVE!
SHE'LL DESTROY IT ALL, YOU FOOL! HER KIND POISONS EVERYTHING THEY TOUCH!
NO, SHE WON'T...
I HAVE FAITH.

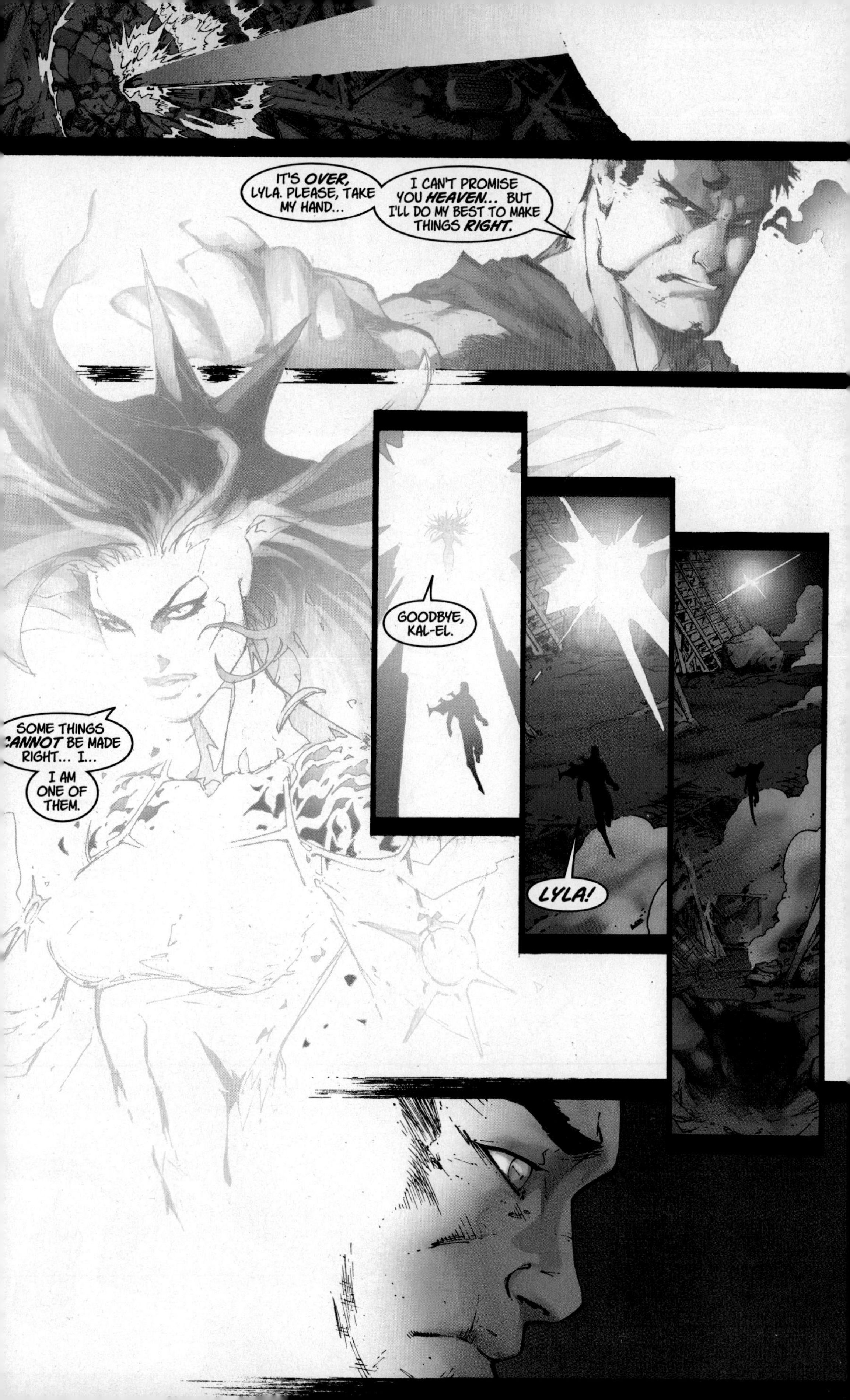
IT'S OVER, LYLA. PLEASE, TAKE MY HAND...
I CAN'T PROMISE YOU HEAVEN... BUT I'LL DO MY BEST TO MAKE THINGS RIGHT.
SOME THINGS CANNOT BE MADE RIGHT... I... I AM ONE OF THEM.
GOODBYE, KAL-EL.
LYLA!

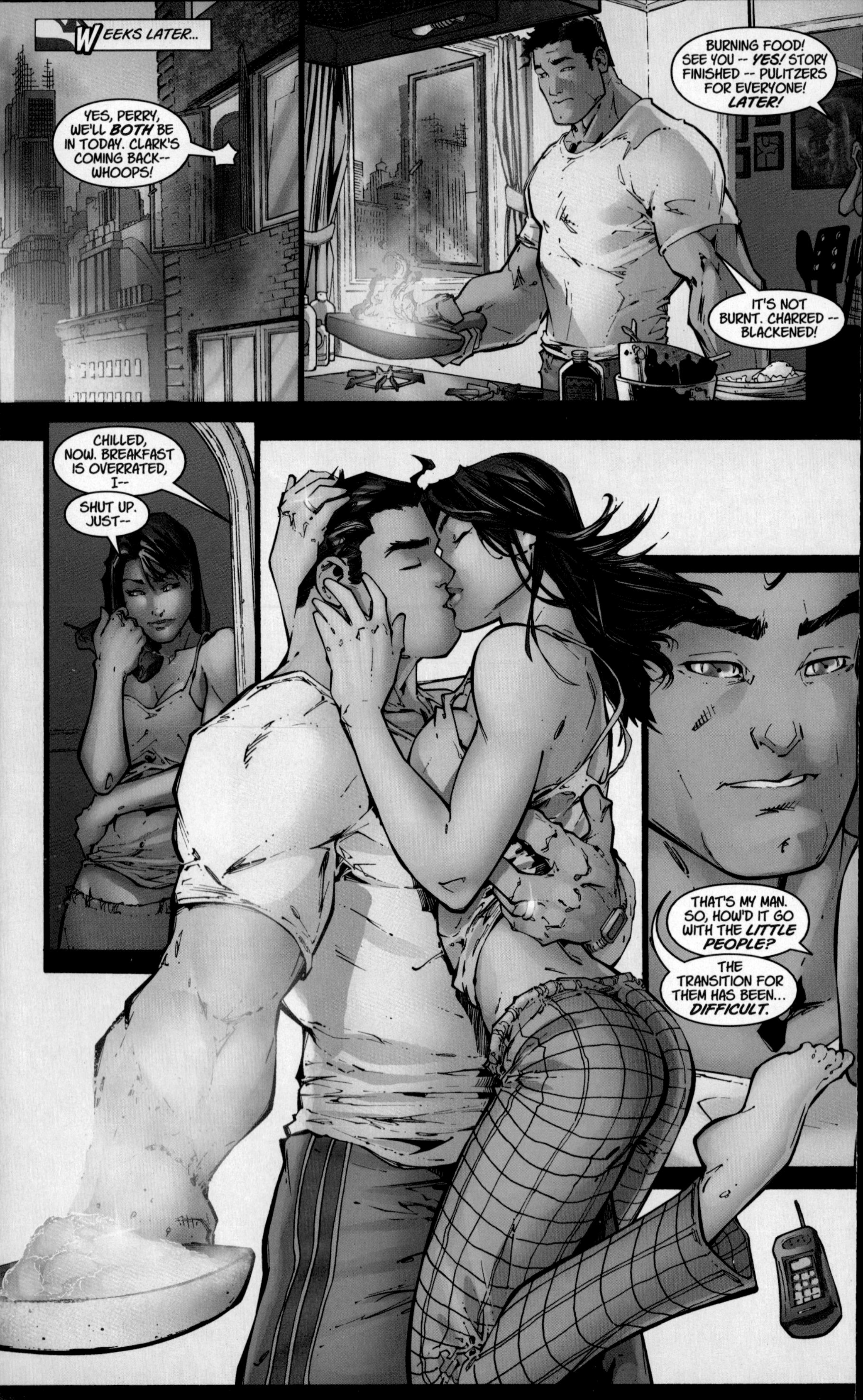
WEEKS LATER...
YES, PERRY, WE'LL BOTH BE IN TODAY. CLARK'S COMING BACK-- WHOOPS!
BURNING FOOD! SEE YOU -- YES! STORY FINISHED -- PULITZERS FOR EVERYONE! LATER!
IT'S NOT BURNT. CHARRED -- BLACKENED!
CHILLED, NOW. BREAKFAST IS OVERRATED, I--
SHUT UP. JUST--
THAT'S MY MAN. SO, HOW'D IT GO WITH THE LITTLE PEOPLE?
THE TRANSITION FOR THEM HAS BEEN... DIFFICULT.

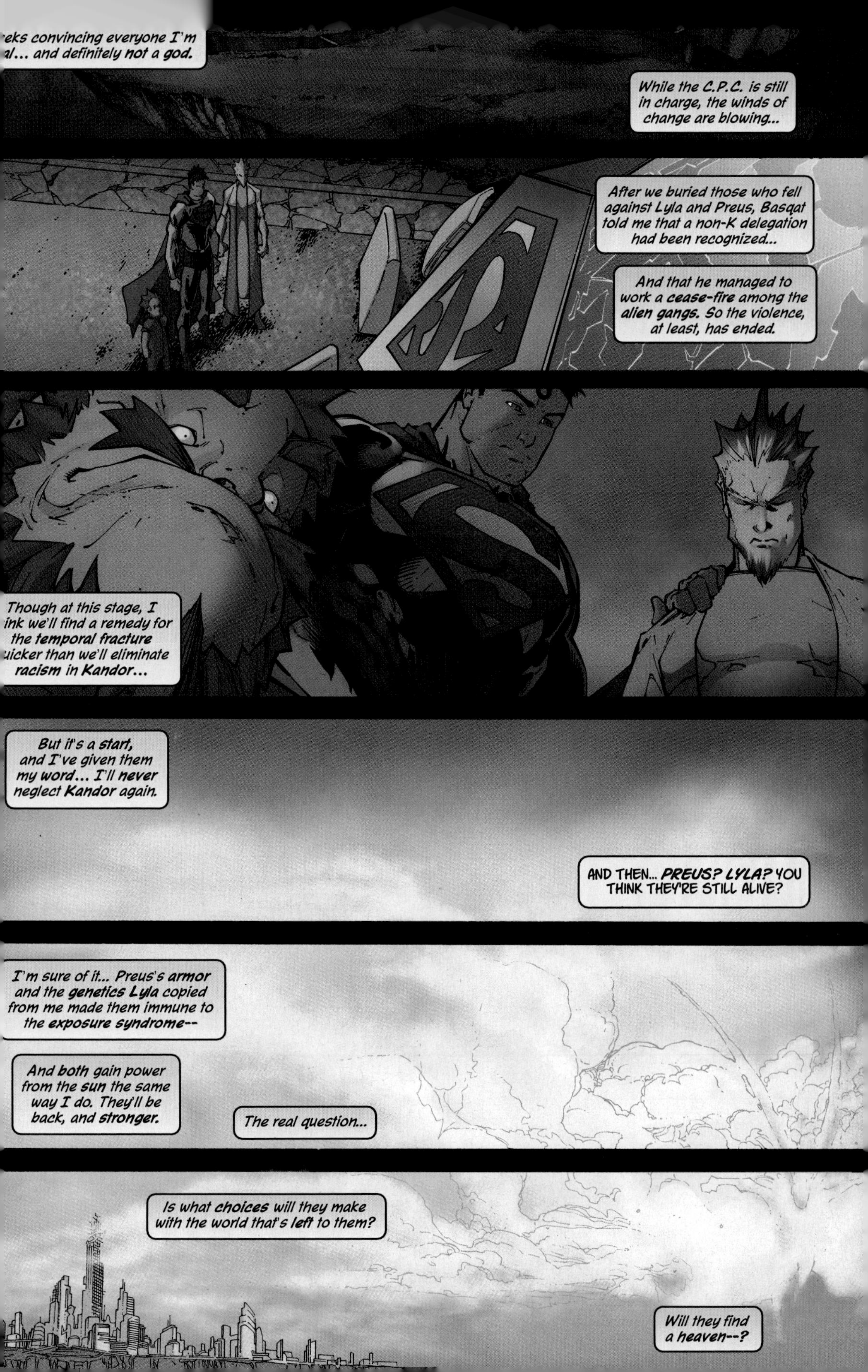
eks convincing everyone I'm
al... and definitely not a god.
While the C.P.C. is still in charge, the winds of change are blowing...
After we buried those who fell against Lyla and Preus, Basqat told me that a non-K delegation had been recognized...
And that he managed to work a cease-fire among the alien gangs. So the violence, at least, has ended.
Though at this stage, I ink we'll find a remedy for the temporal fracture uicker than we'll eliminate racism in Kandor...
But it's a start, and I've given them my word... I'll never neglect Kandor again.
AND THEN... PREUS? LYLA? YOU THINK THEY'RE STILL ALIVE?
I'm sure of it... Preus's armor and the genetics Lyla copied from me made them immune to the exposure syndrome--
And both gain power from the sun the same way I do. They'll be back, and stronger.
The real question...
Is what choices will they make with the world that's left to them?
Will they find a heaven--?

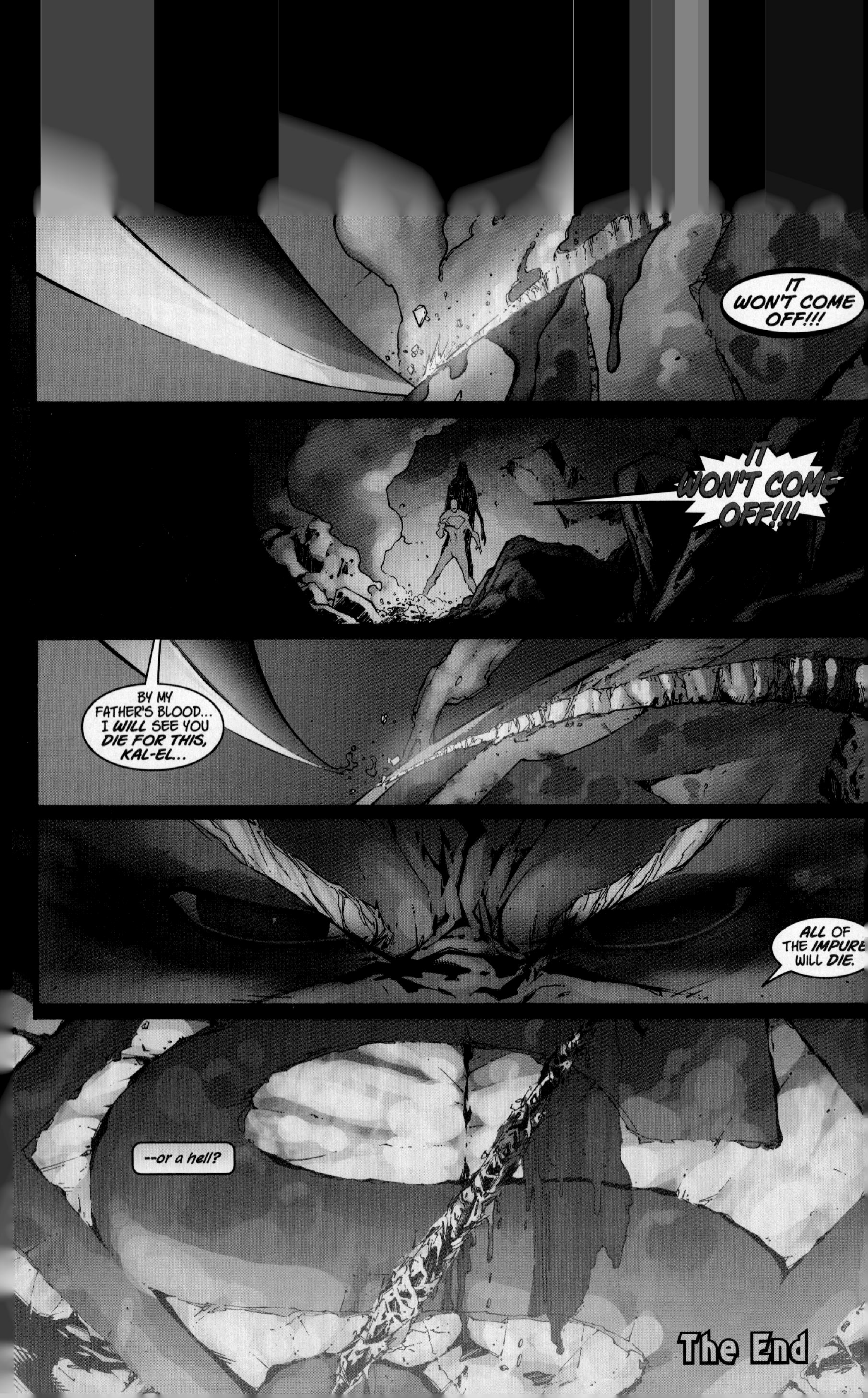
IT WON'T COME OFF!!!
IT WON'T COME OFF!!!
BY MY FATHER'S BLOOD... I WILL SEE YOU DIE FOR THIS, KAL-EL...
ALL OF THE IMPURE WILL DIE.
--or a hell?
The End

GODFALL

COVER GALLERY

Soon after the first issue of this story hit the shelves, ACTION COMICS #812 sold out. A week later, ADVENTURES OF SUPERMAN #625 sold out. Both were rushed back to press and the second printings sported variant covers, showcasing just the original pencils by Michael Turner.

On the pages that follow are all six covers in their pencilled and then finished forms, colored by Peter Steigerwald.

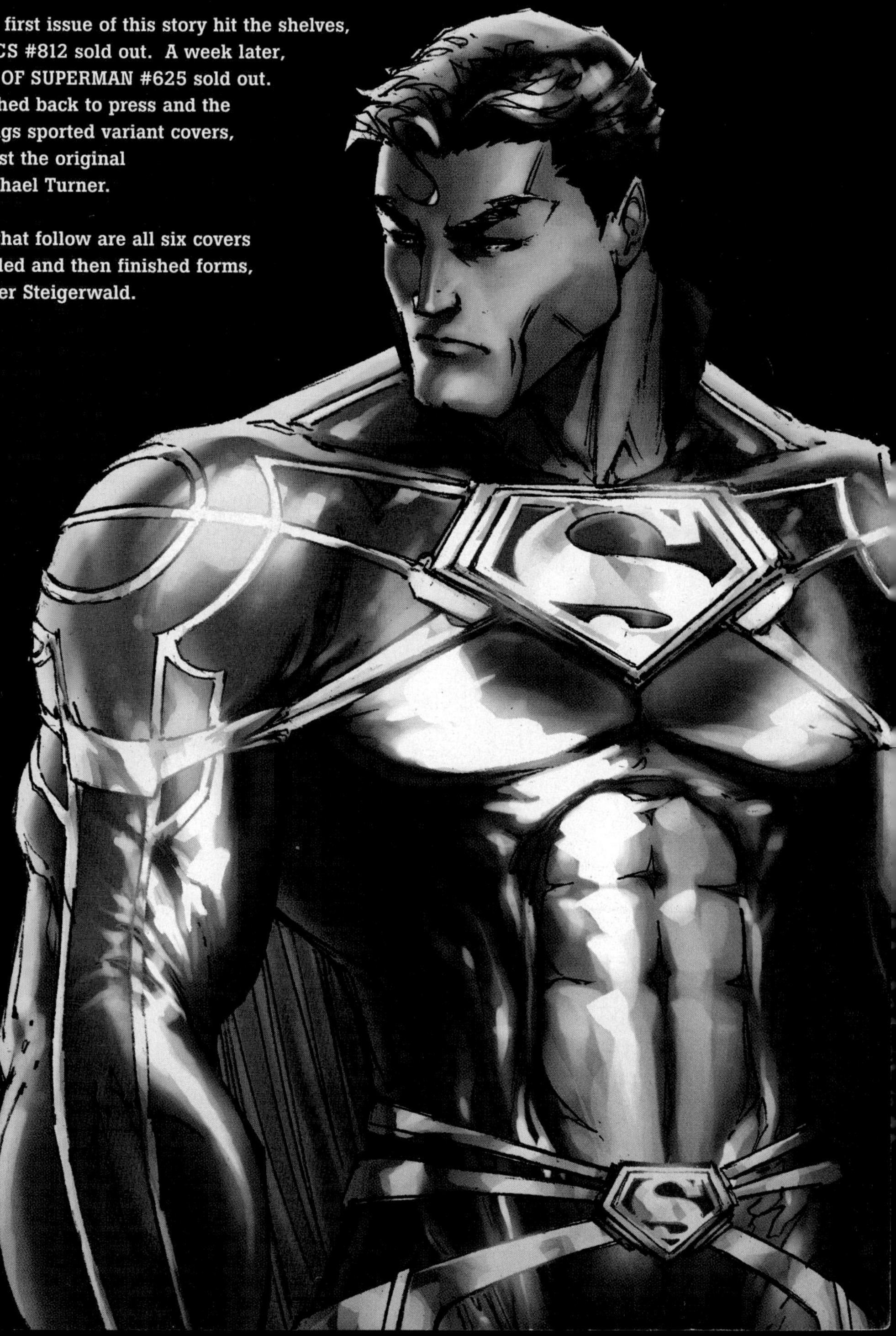

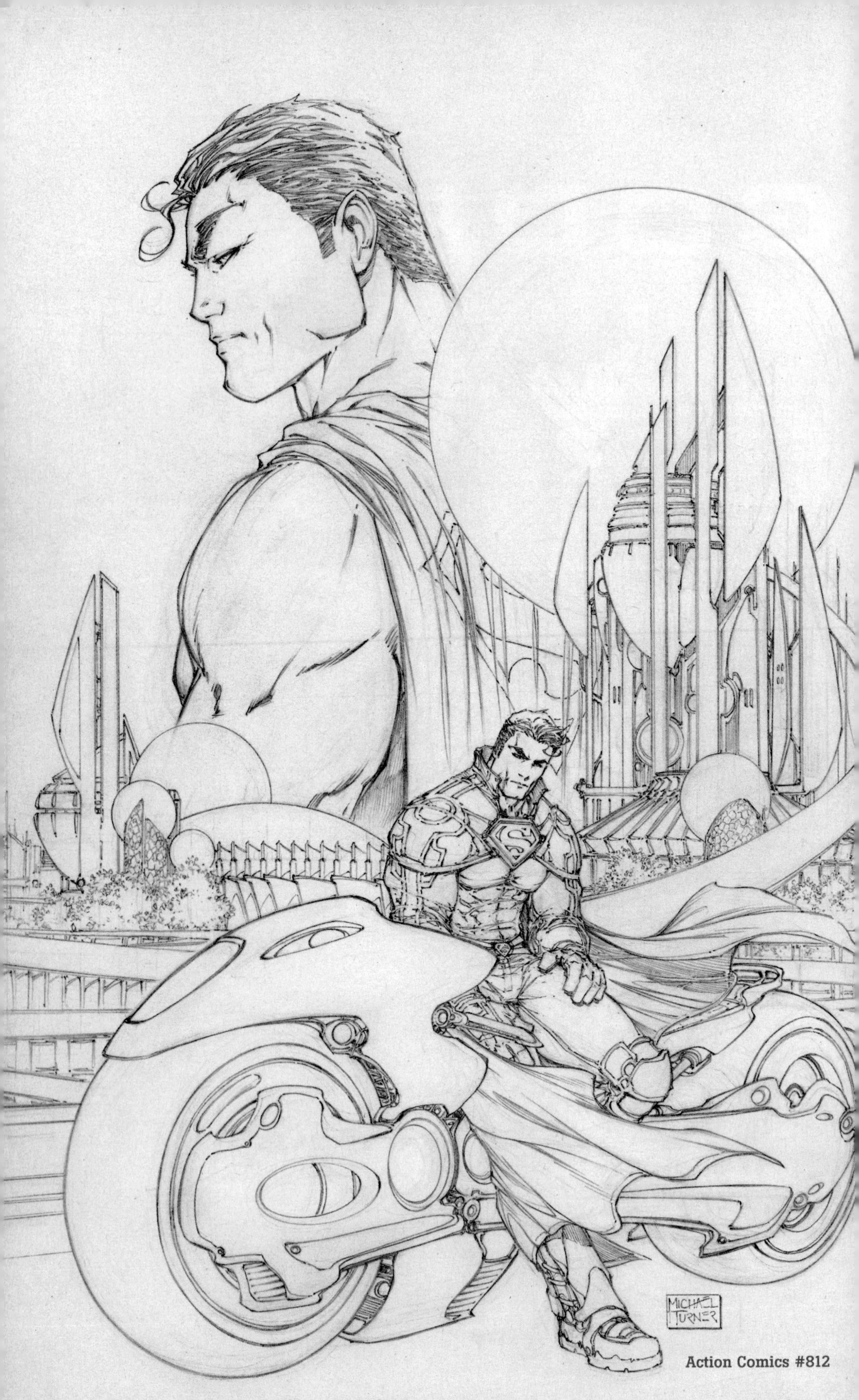
MICHAEL TURNER

Action Comics #812

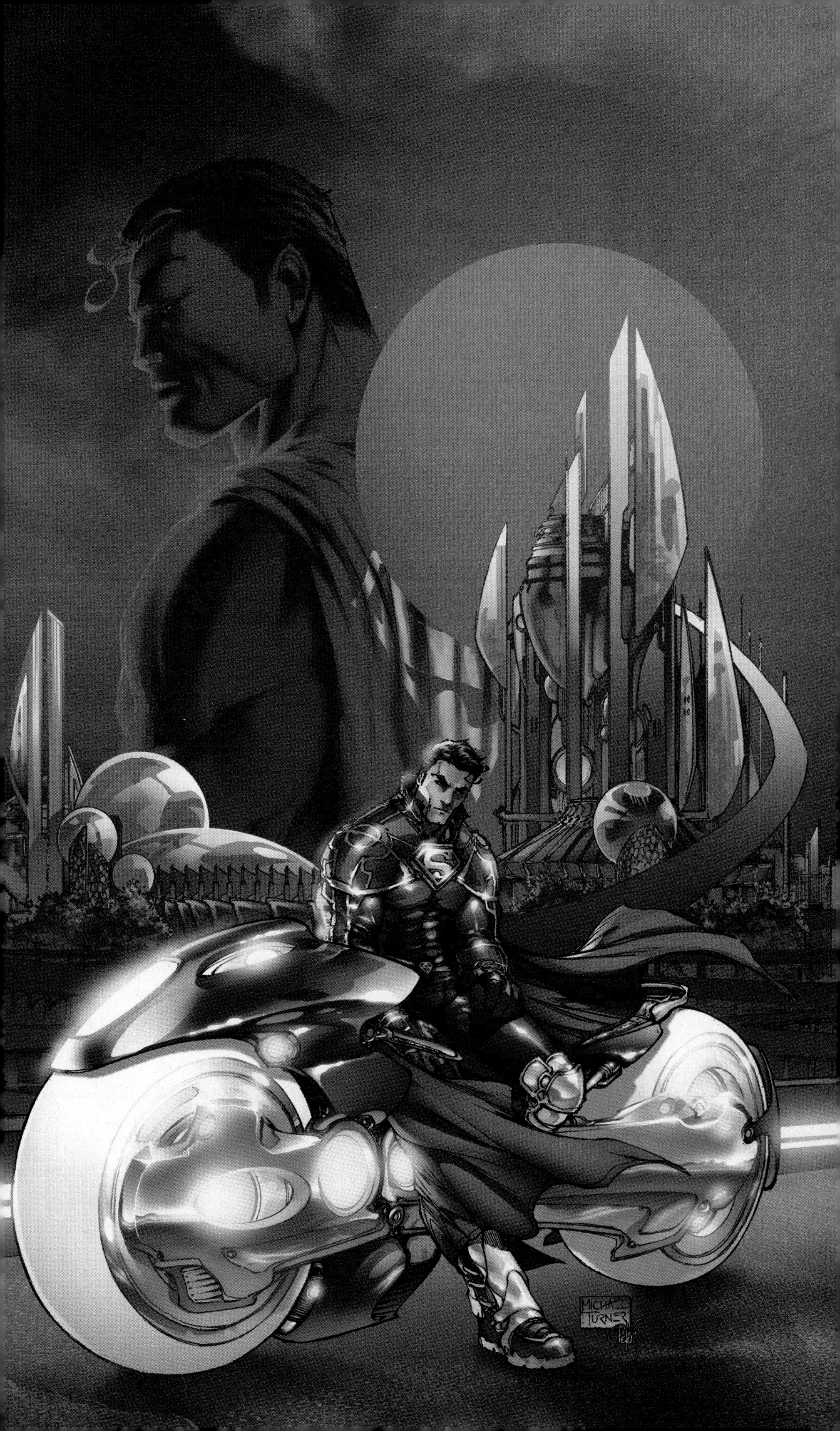

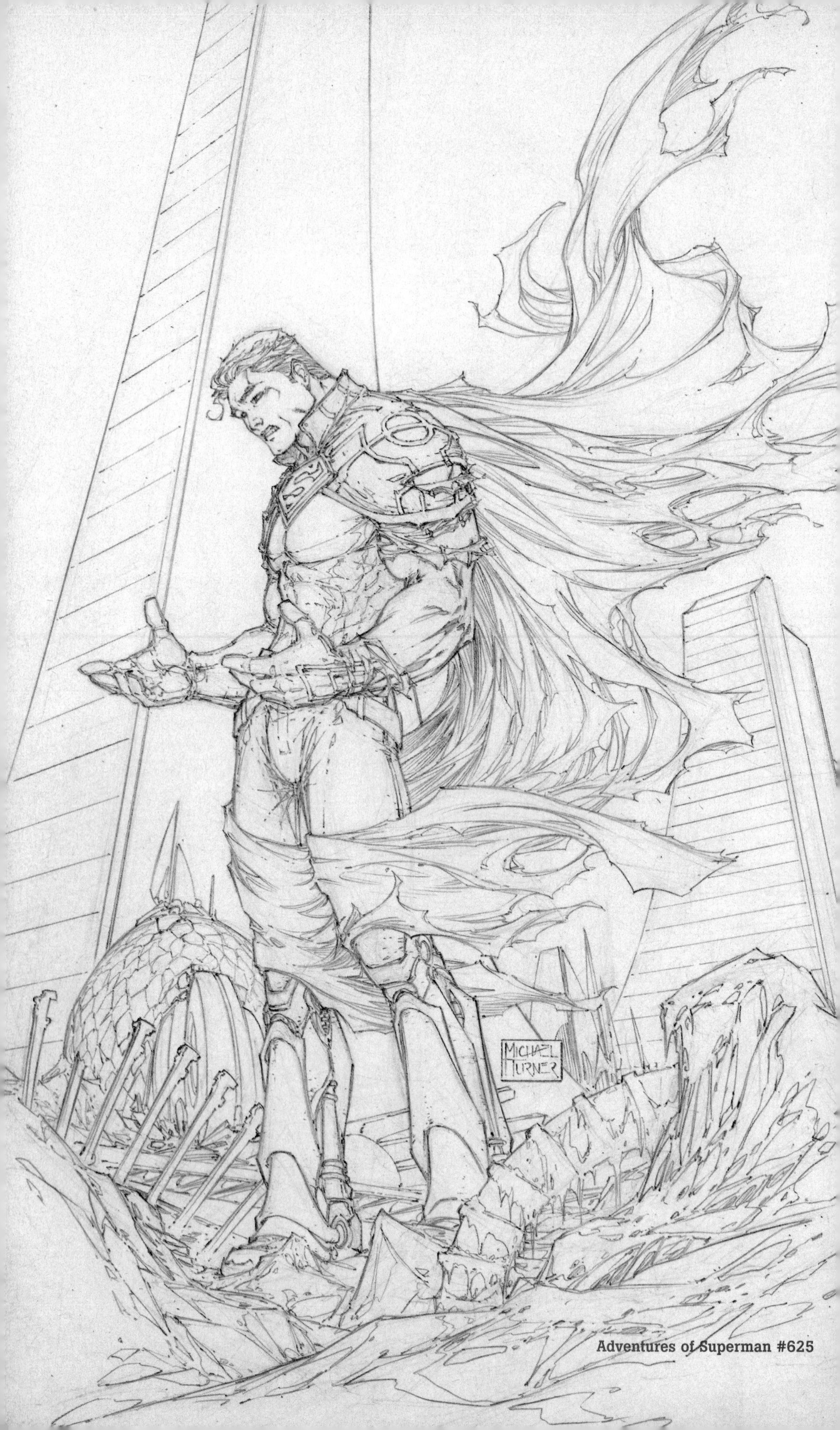
MICHAEL TURNER

Adventures of Superman #625

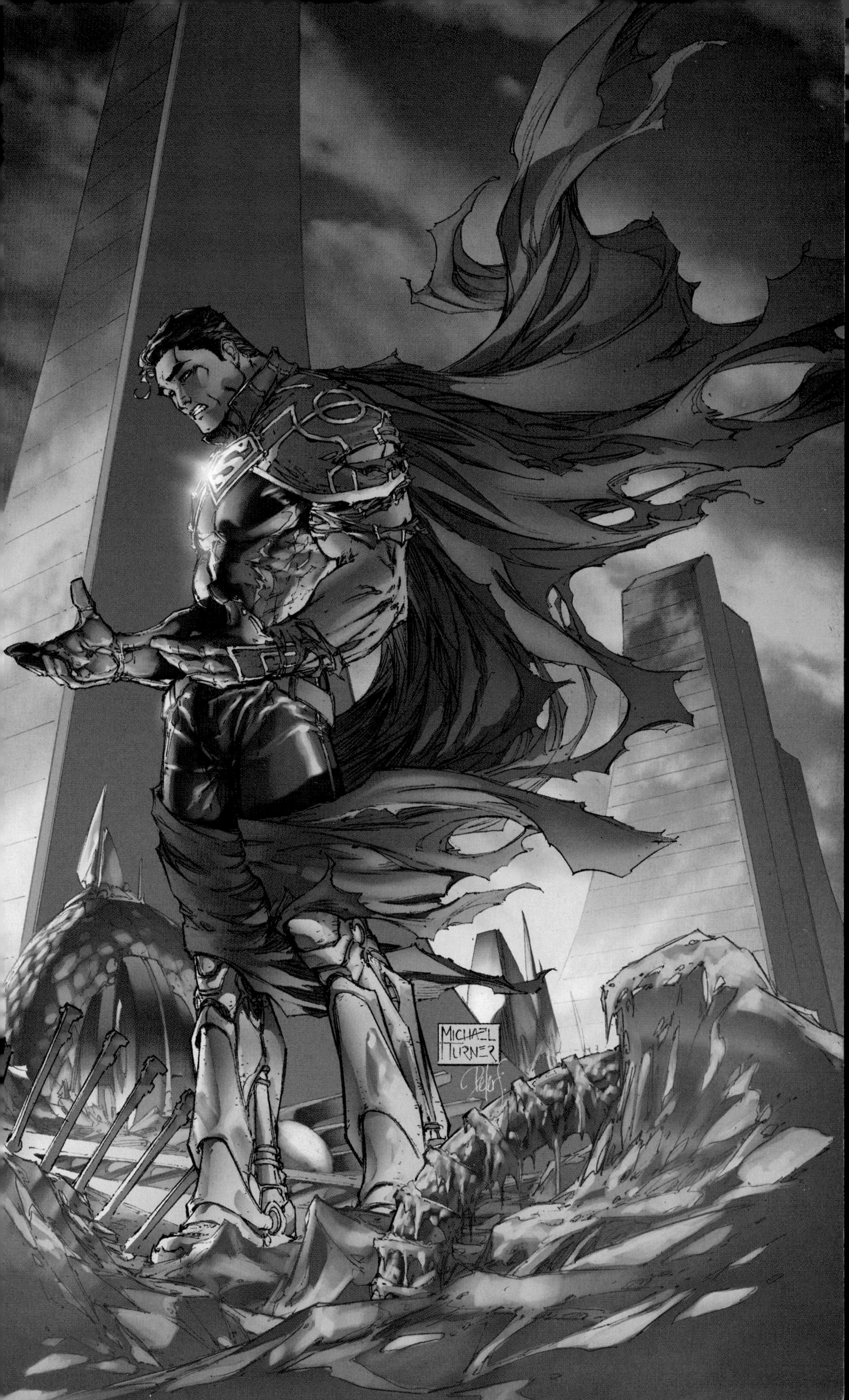
MICHAEL TURNER

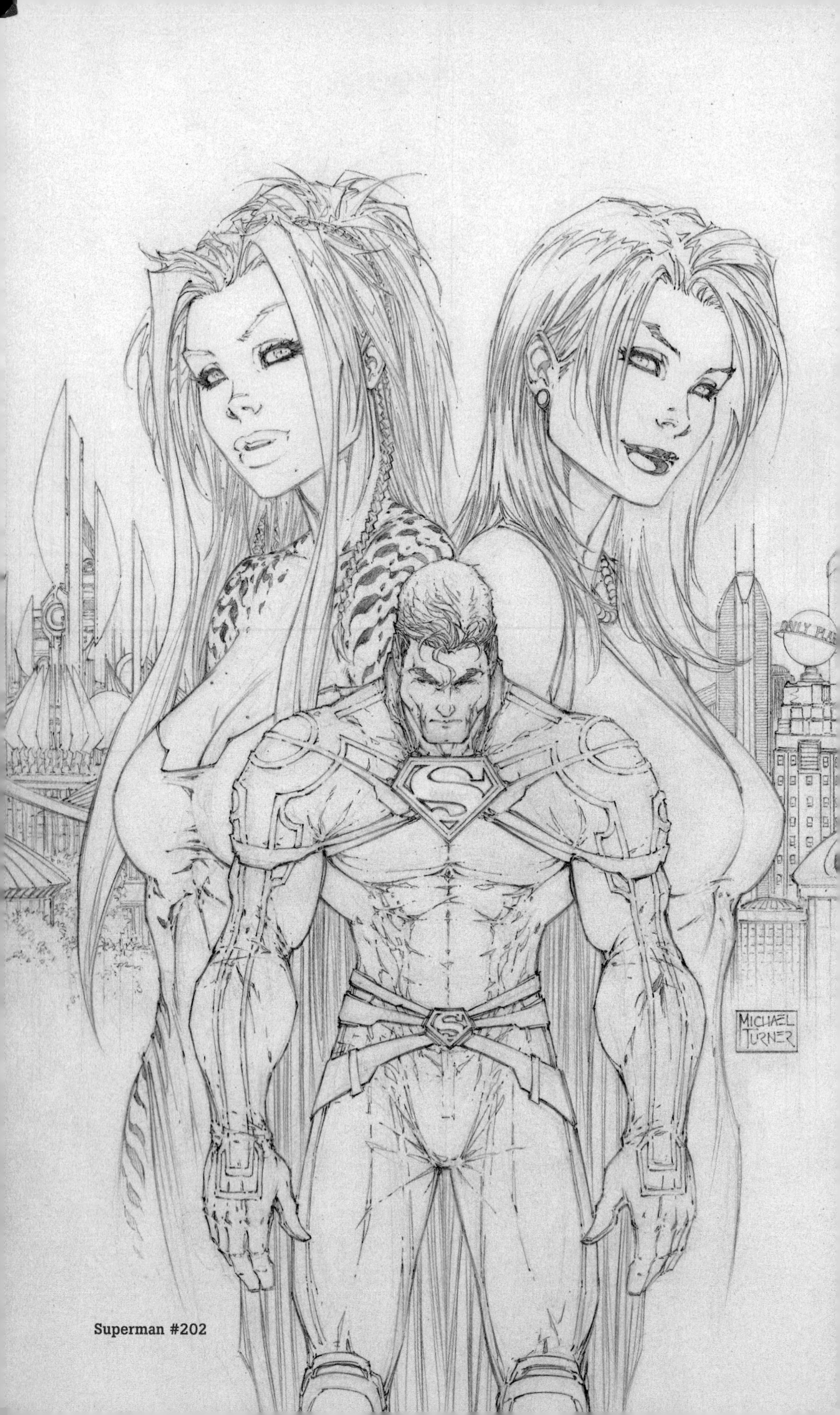
MICHAEL
TURNER

Superman #202

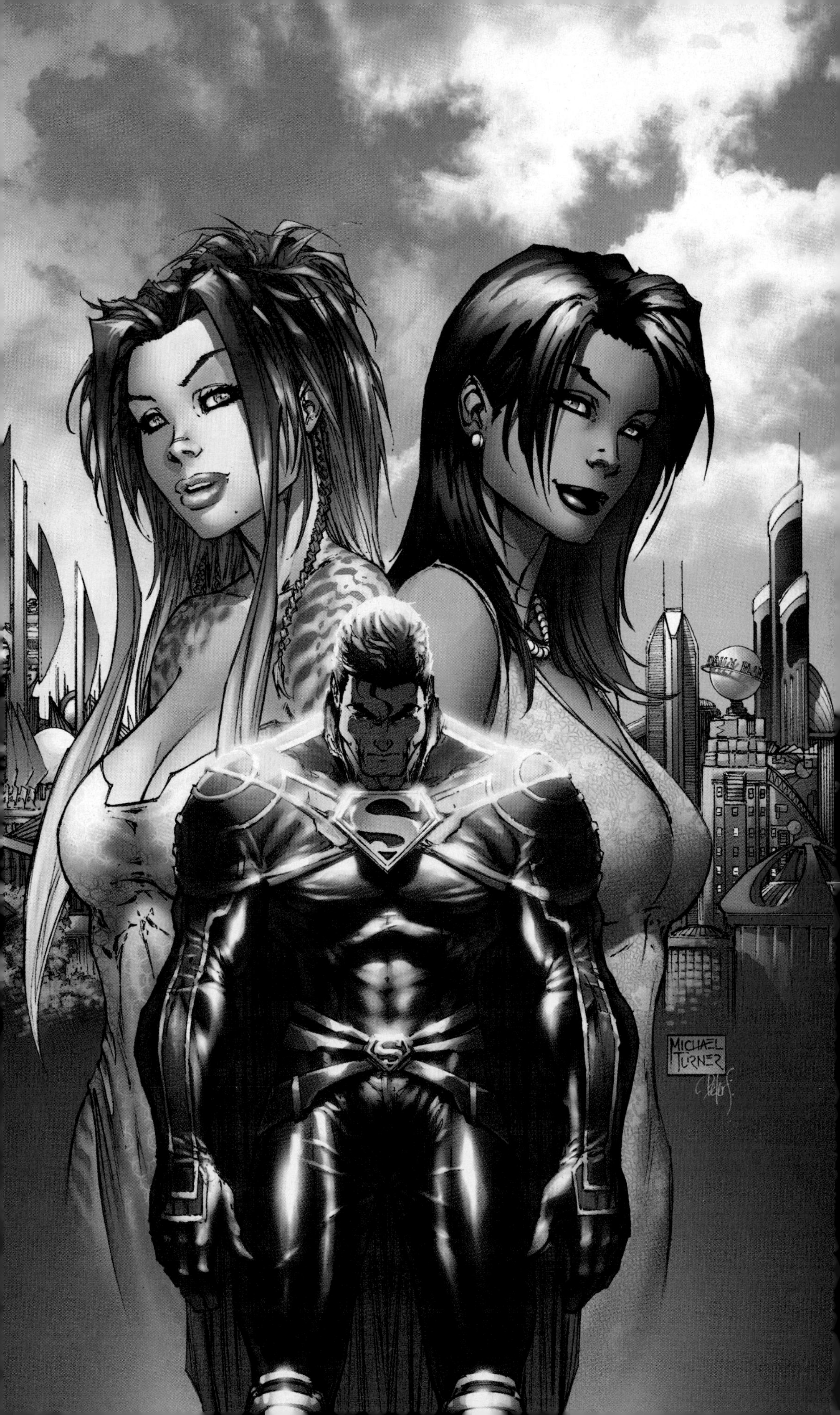
MICHAEL TURNER

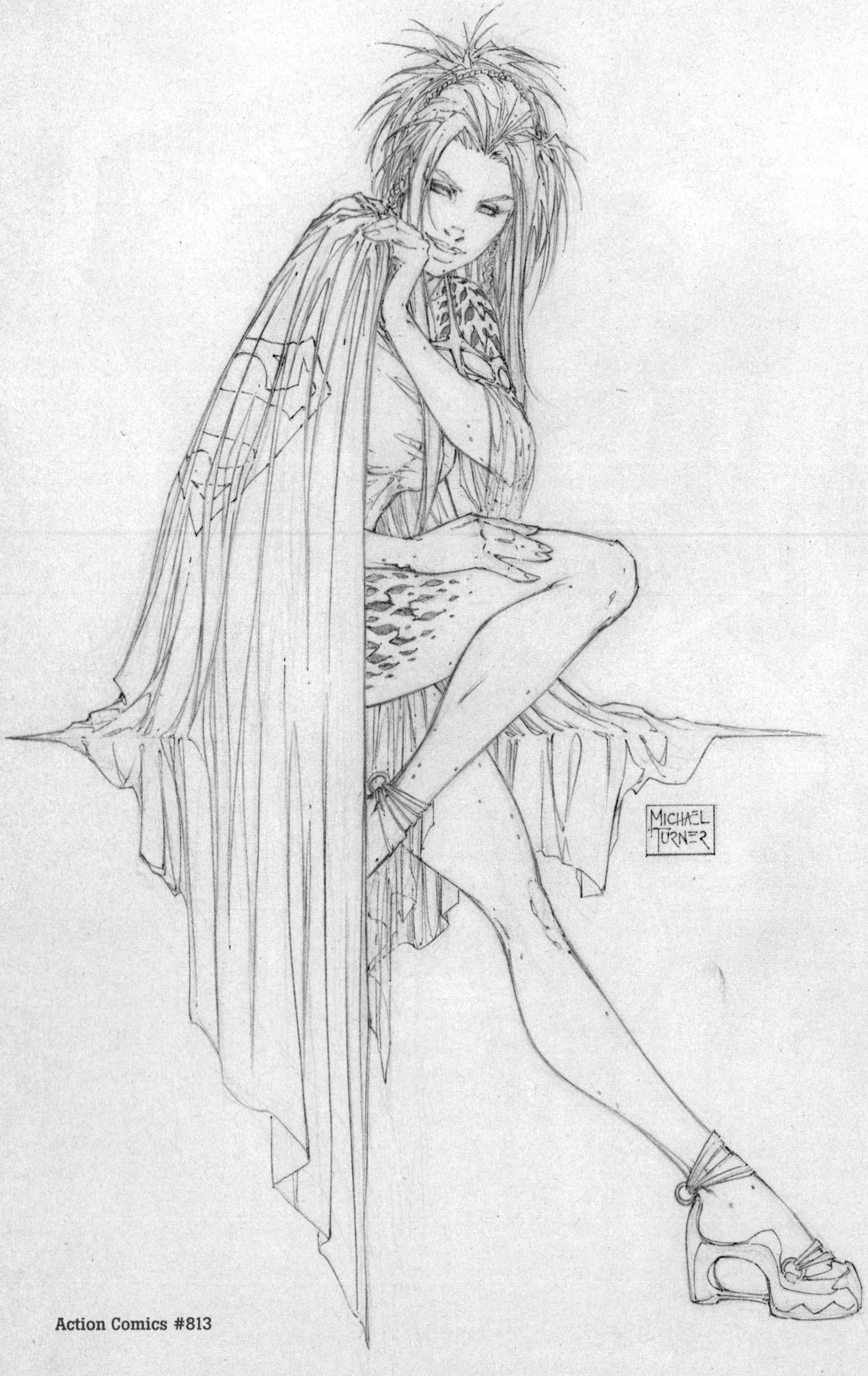
MICHAEL TURNER

Action Comics #813

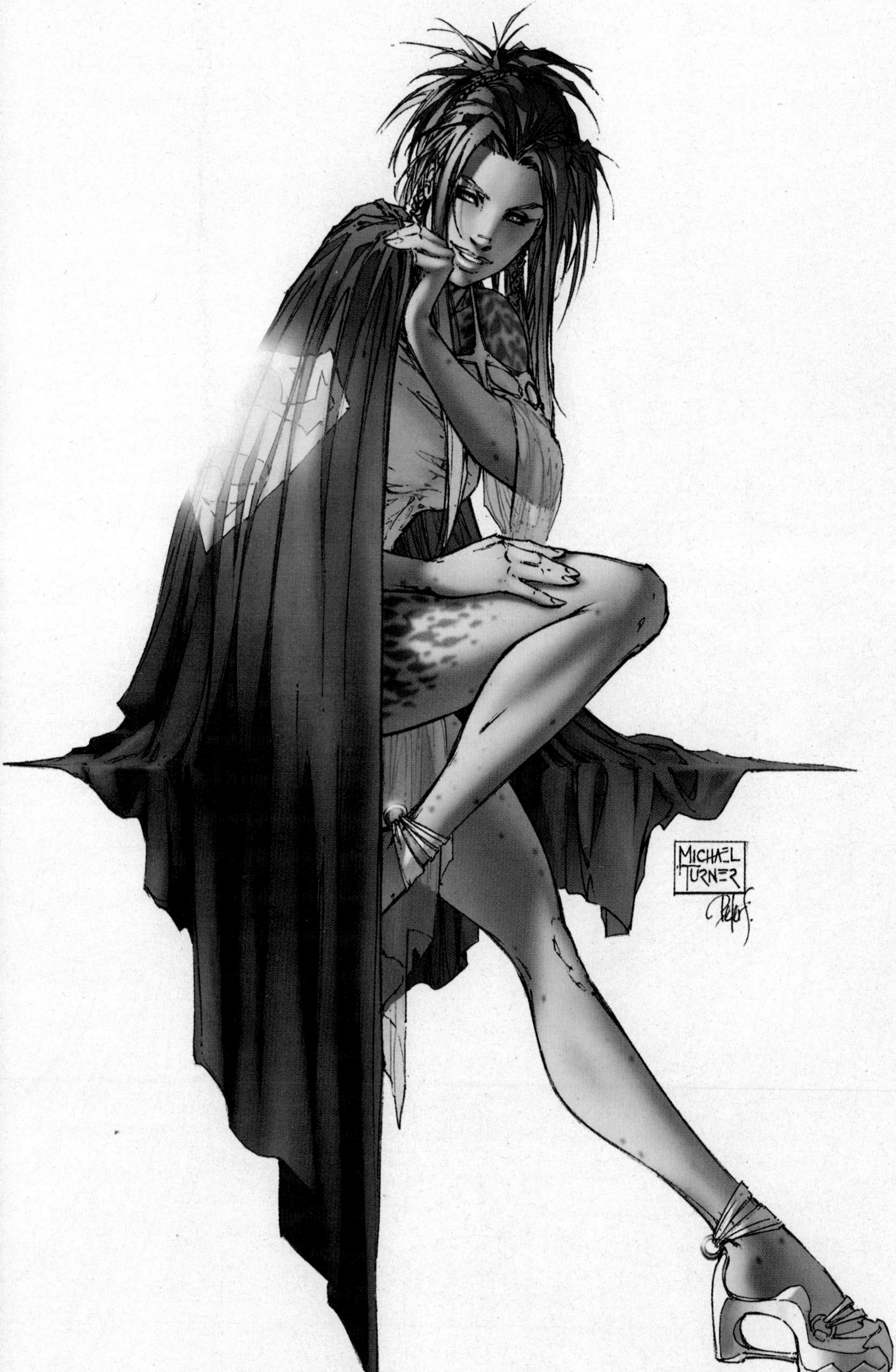
MICHAEL TURNER

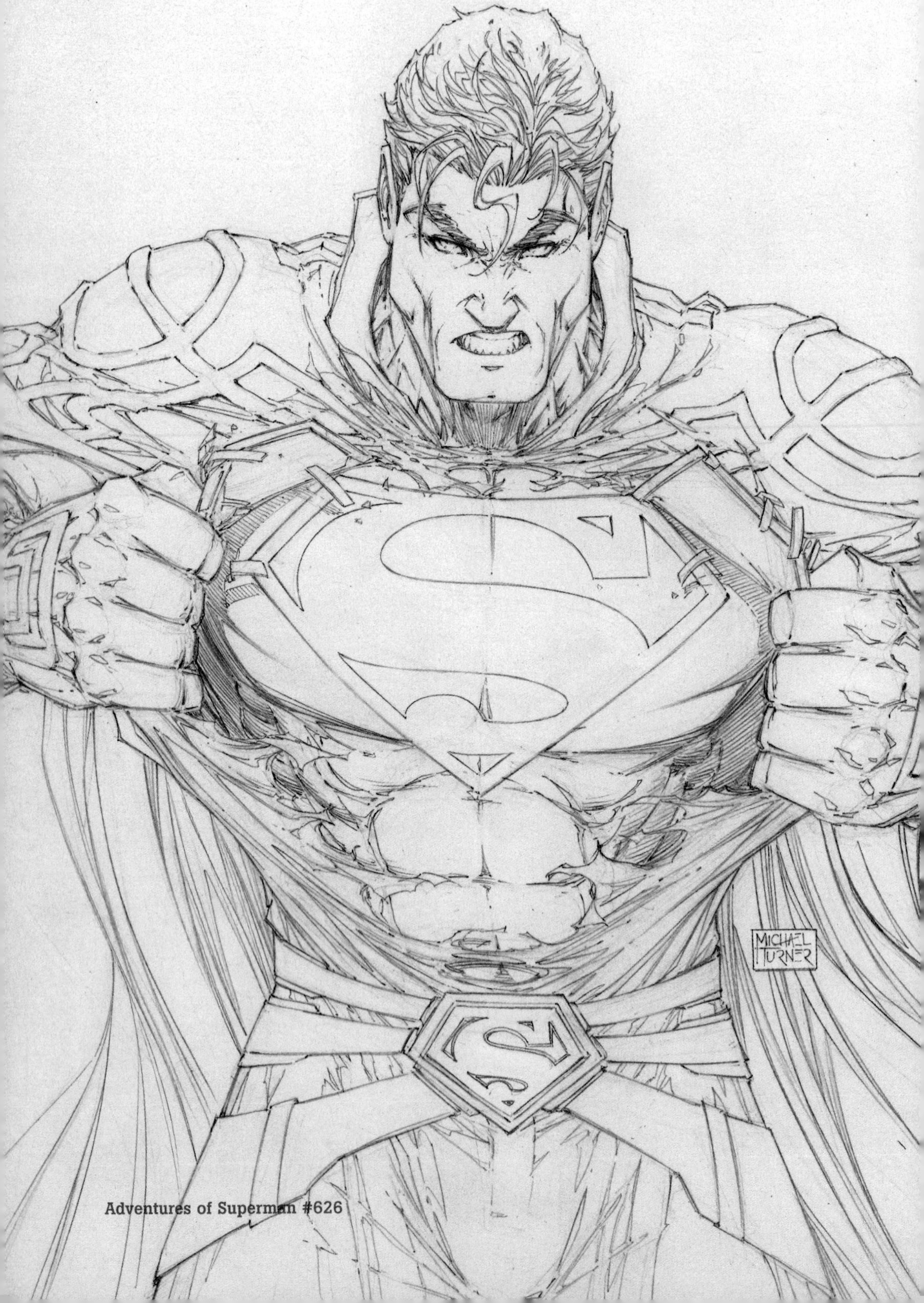
MICHAEL TURNER

Adventures of Superman #626

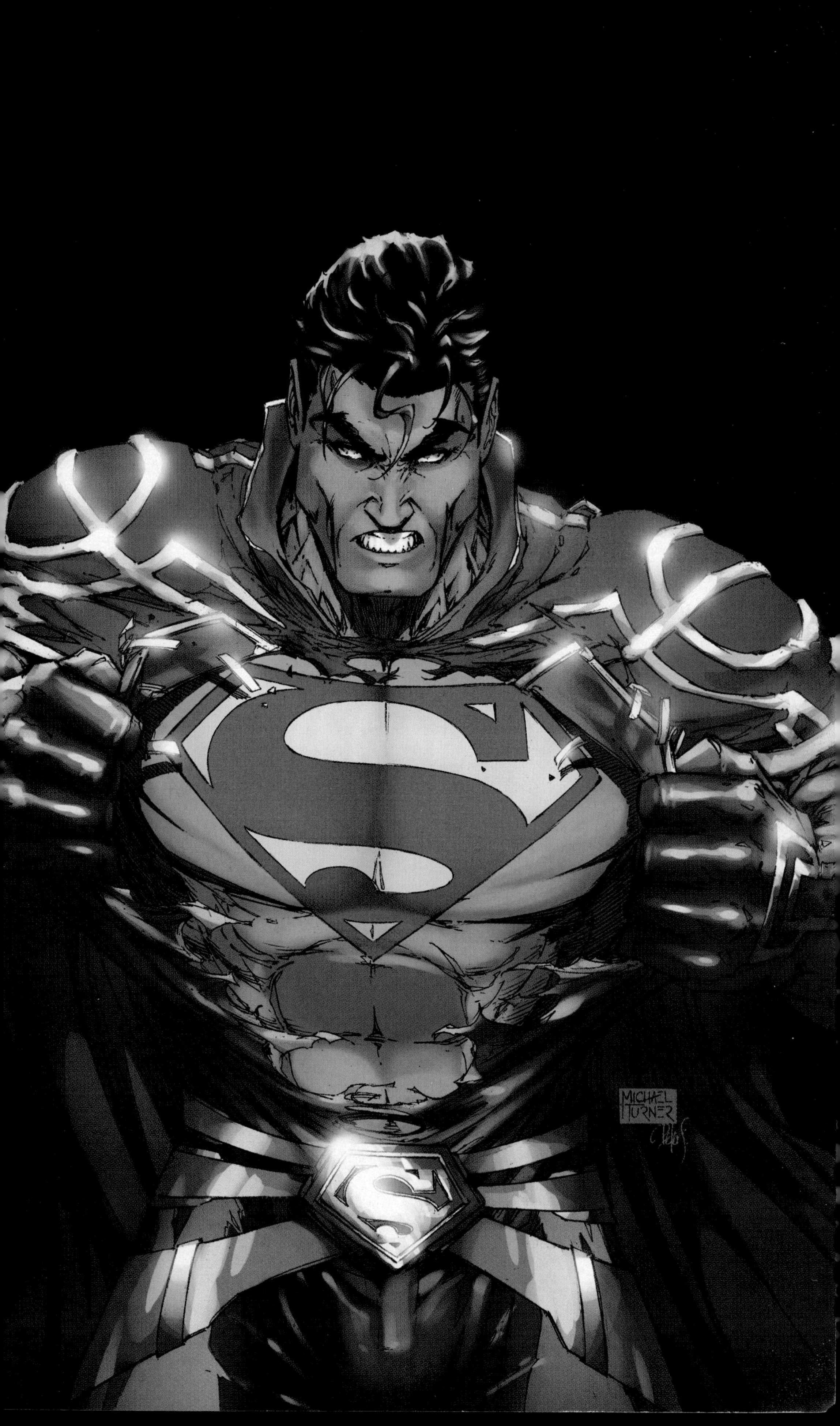
MICHAEL TURNER

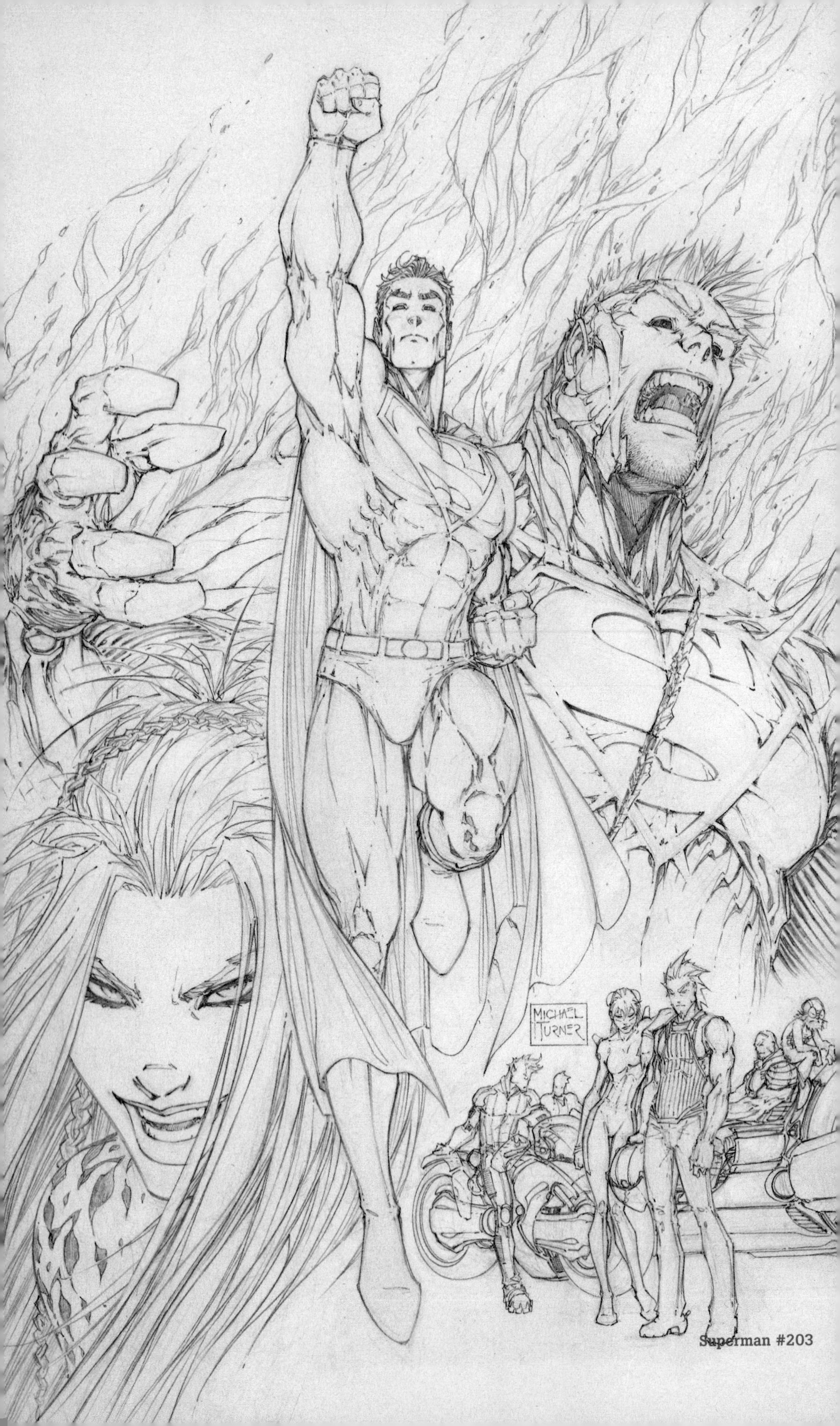
MICHAEL TURNER

Superman #203

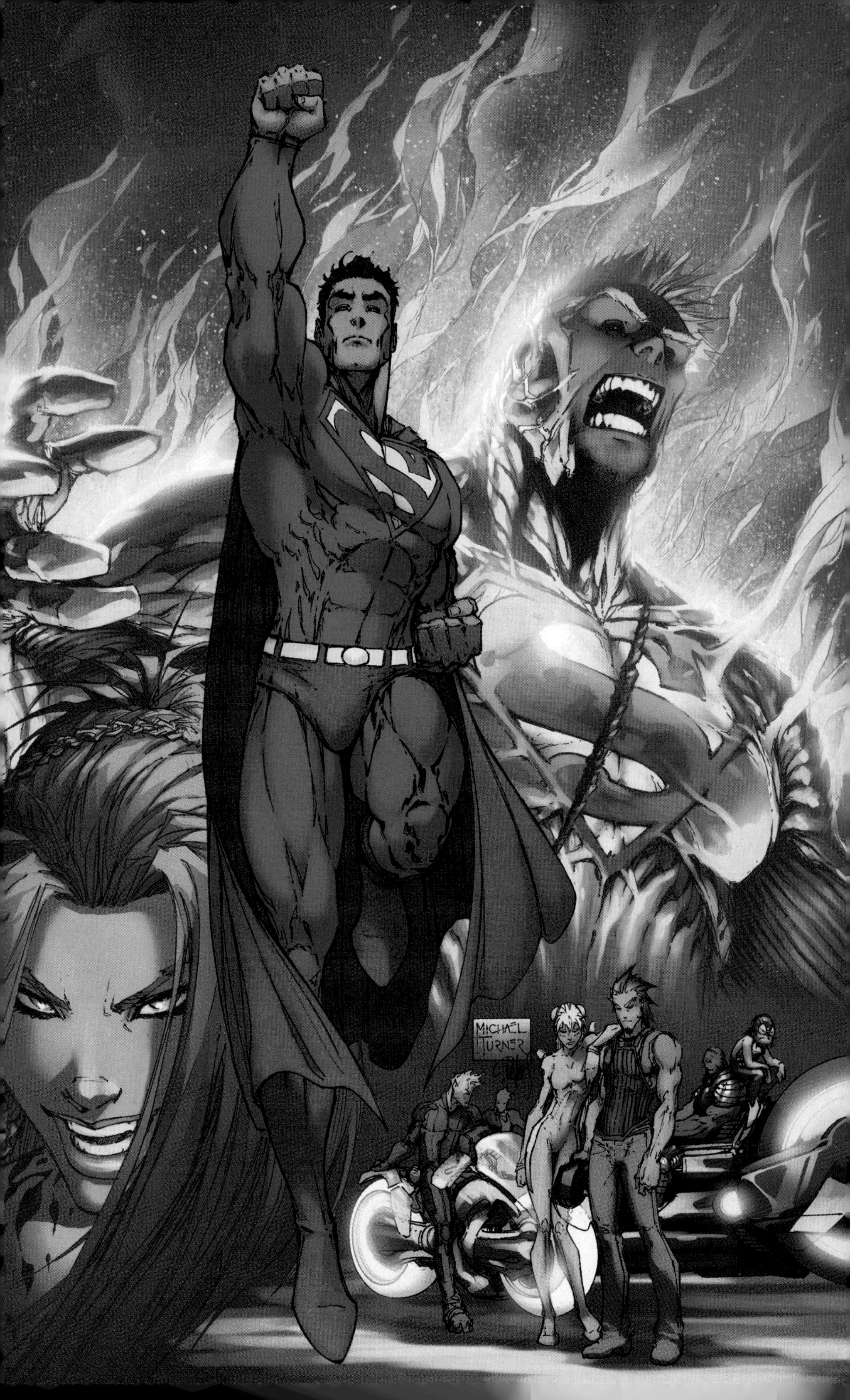
MICHAEL
TURNER

GODFALL
SKETCH GALLERY

One of Michael Turner's first attempts
at drawing the last son of Krypton.

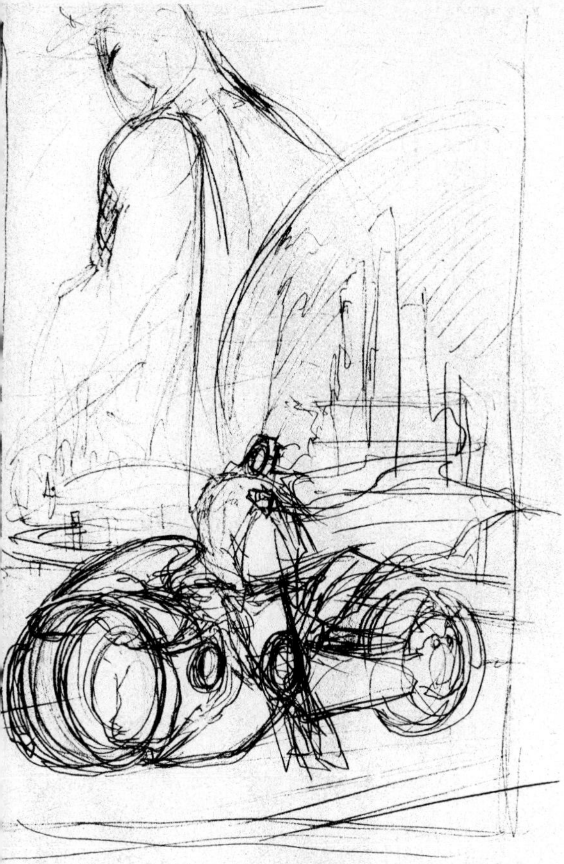

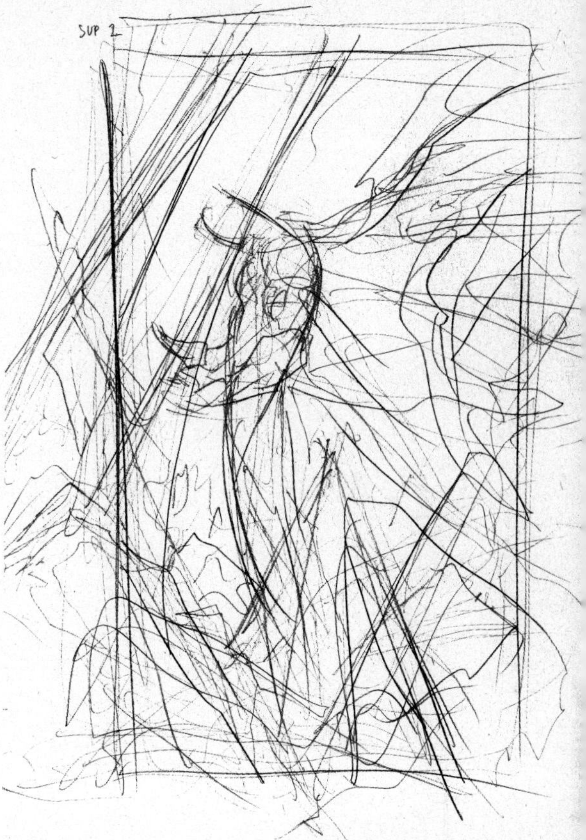
SUP 2

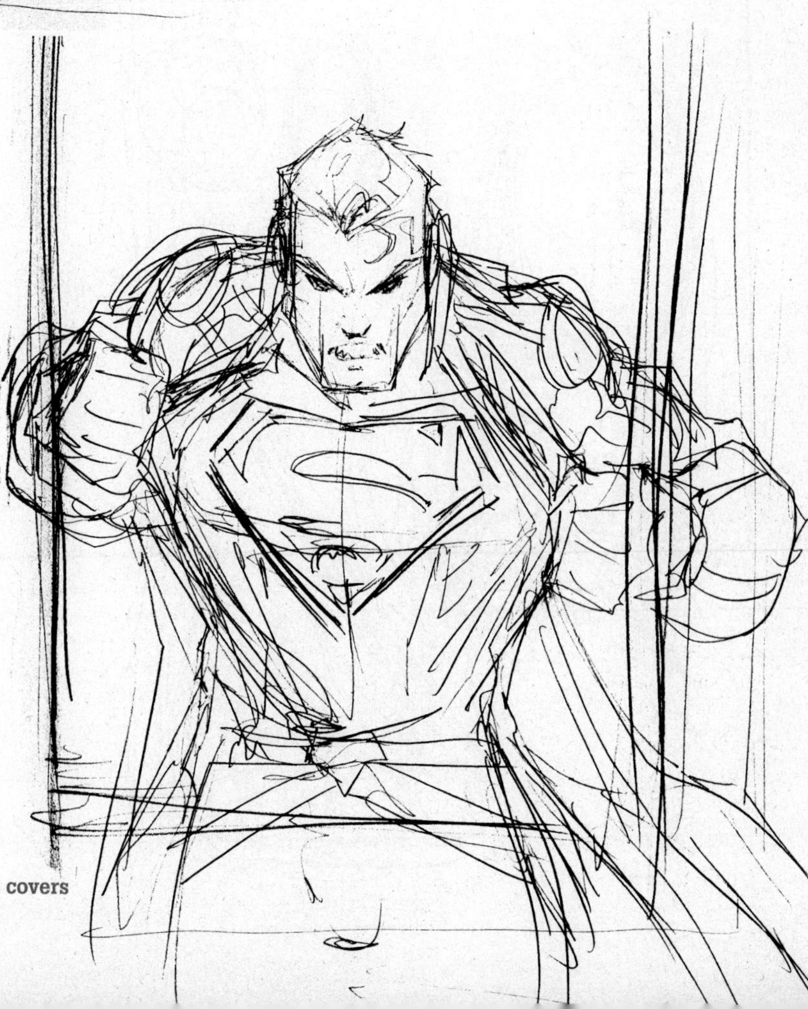

Thumbnails for various covers
by Michael Turner.

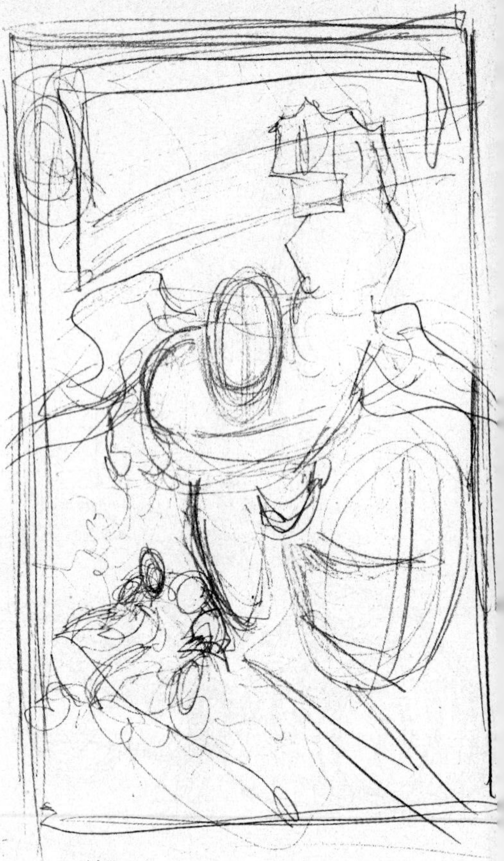

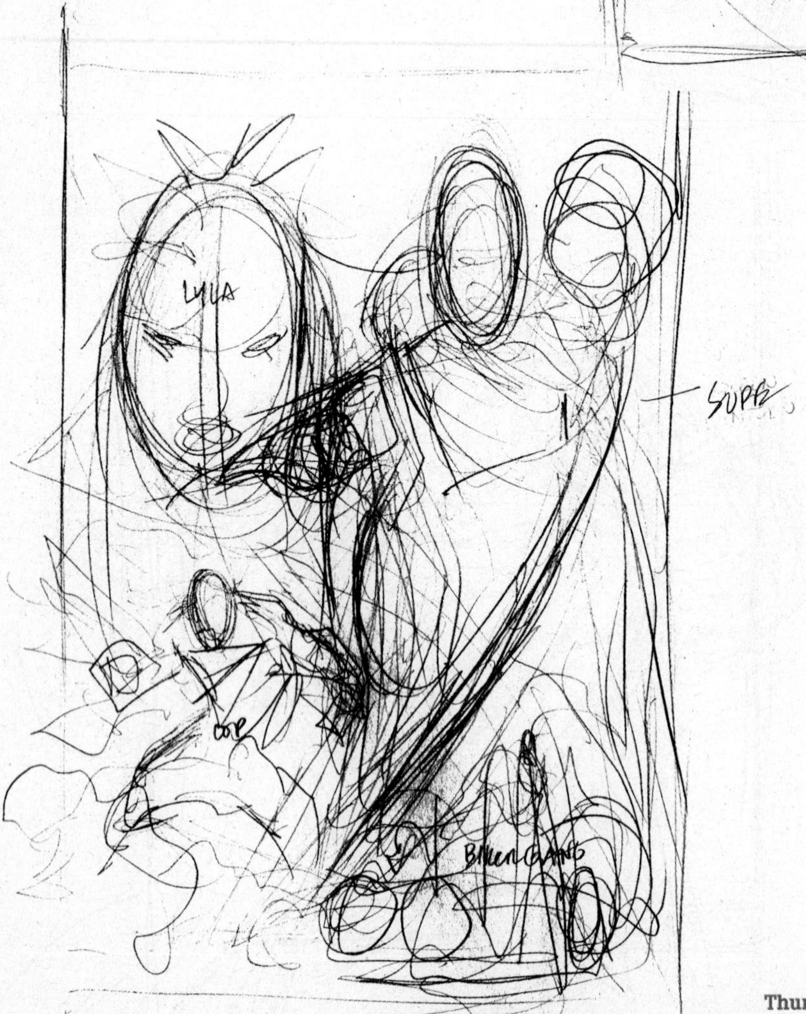
LYLA
SUPE
COP
BIKER GANG

Thumbnails for the cover of Superman #203 by Michael Turner.

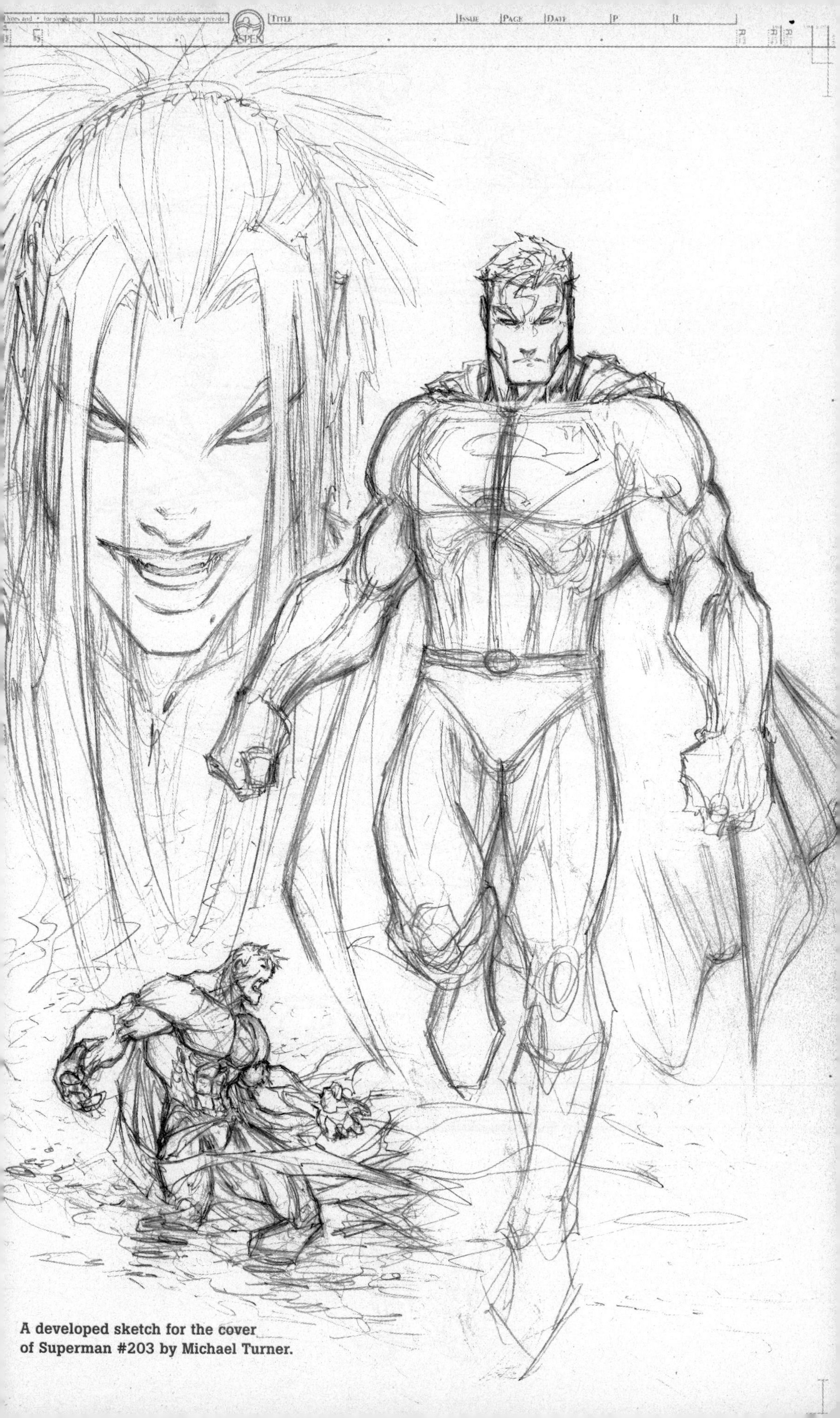

A developed sketch for the cover
of Superman #203 by Michael Turner.

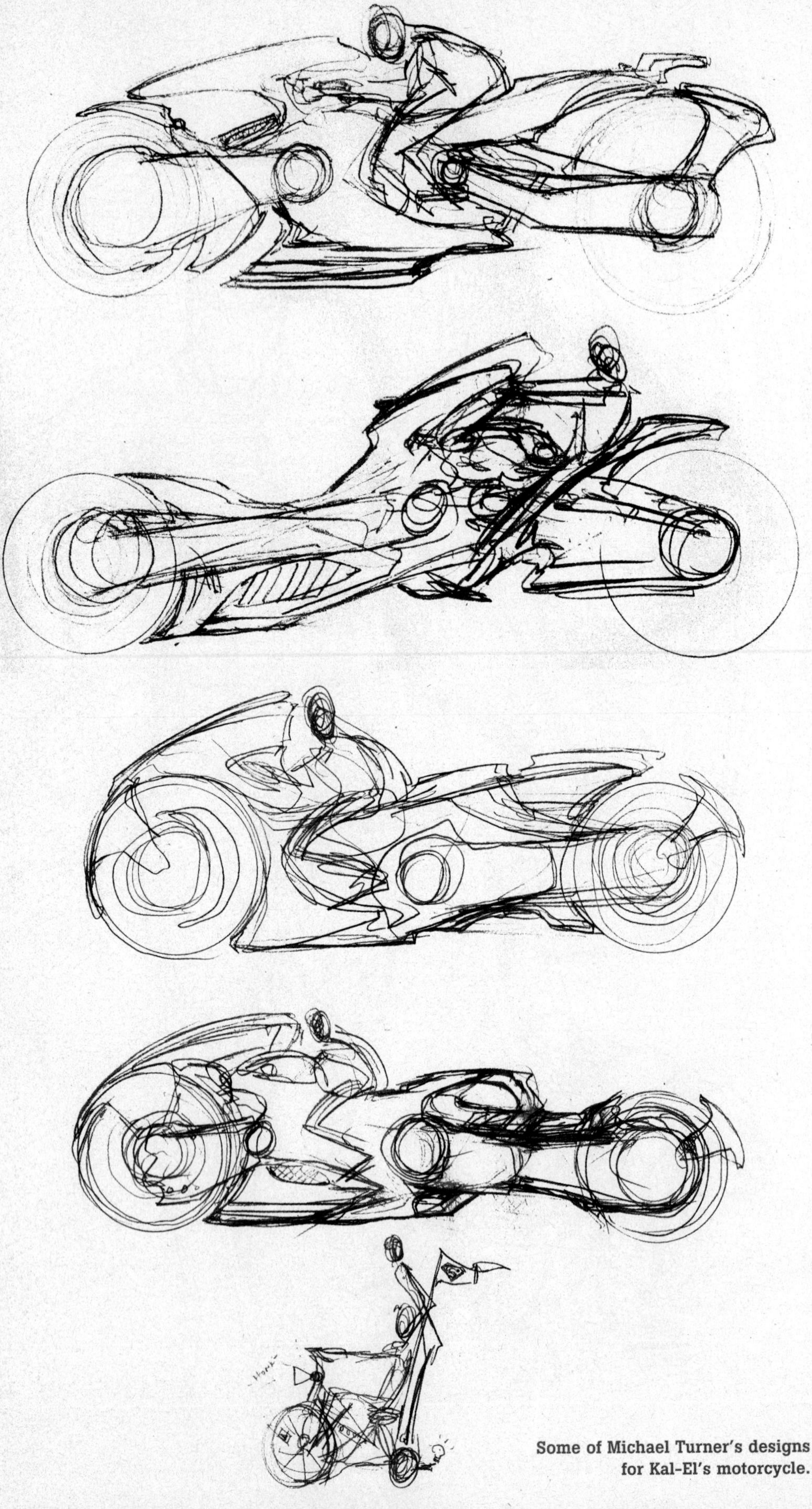

Some of Michael Turner's designs
for Kal-El's motorcycle.

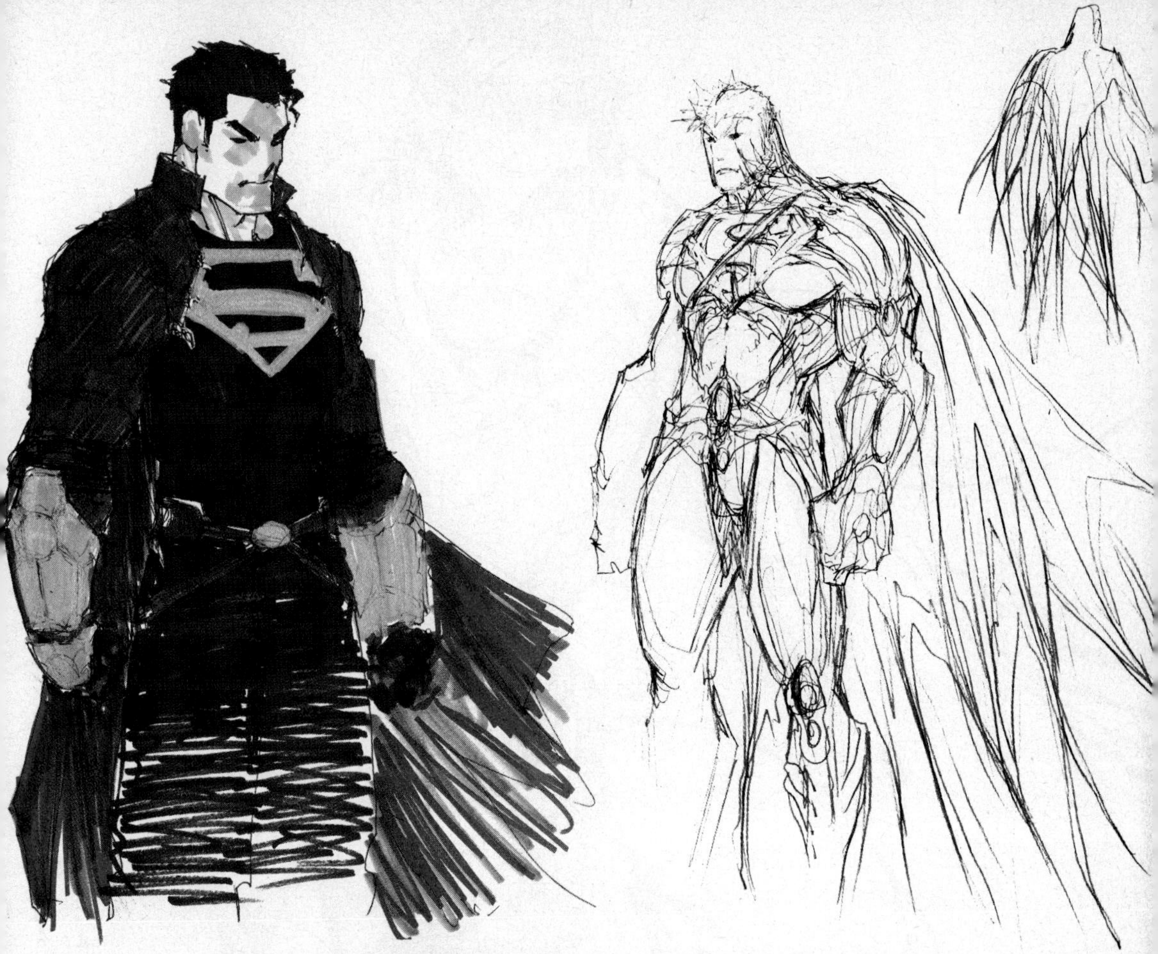

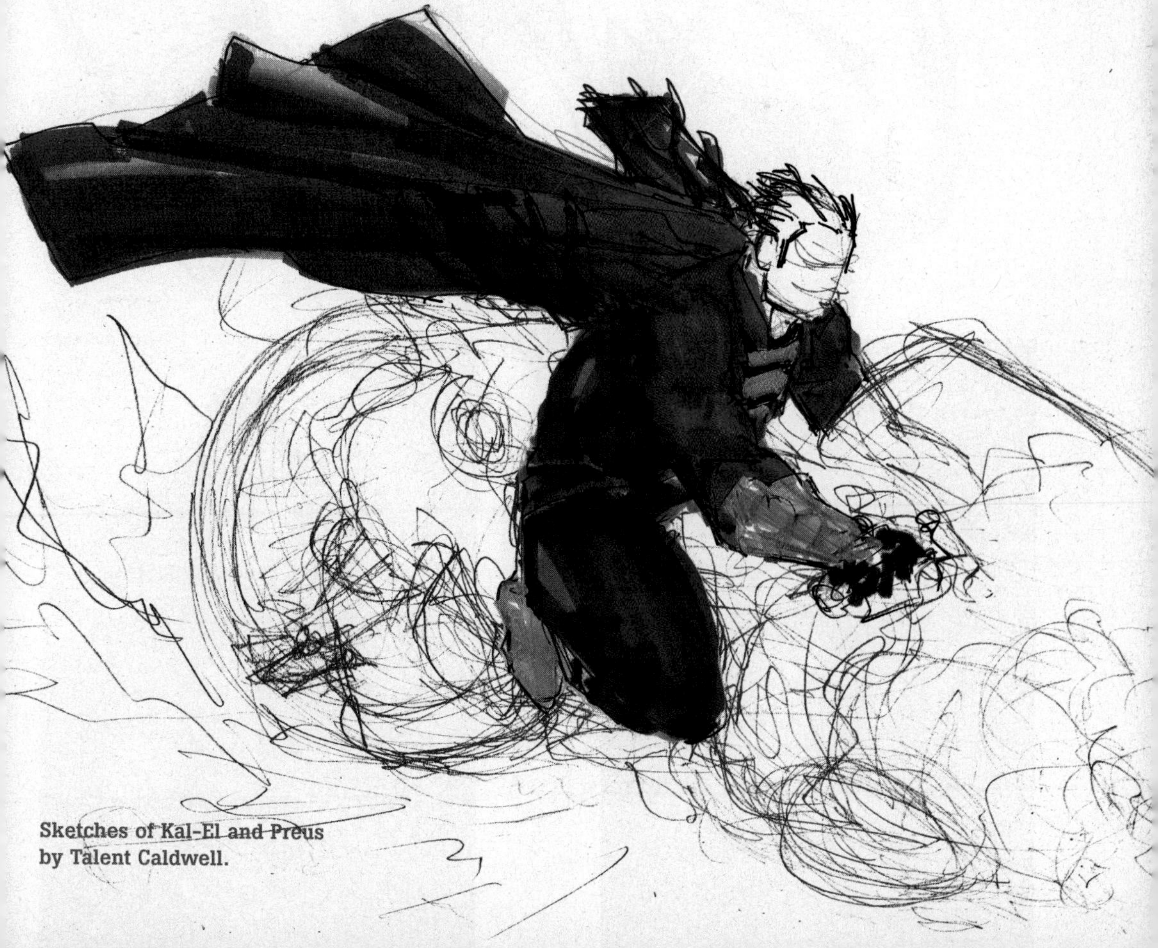

Sketches of Kal-El and Preus
by Talent Caldwell.

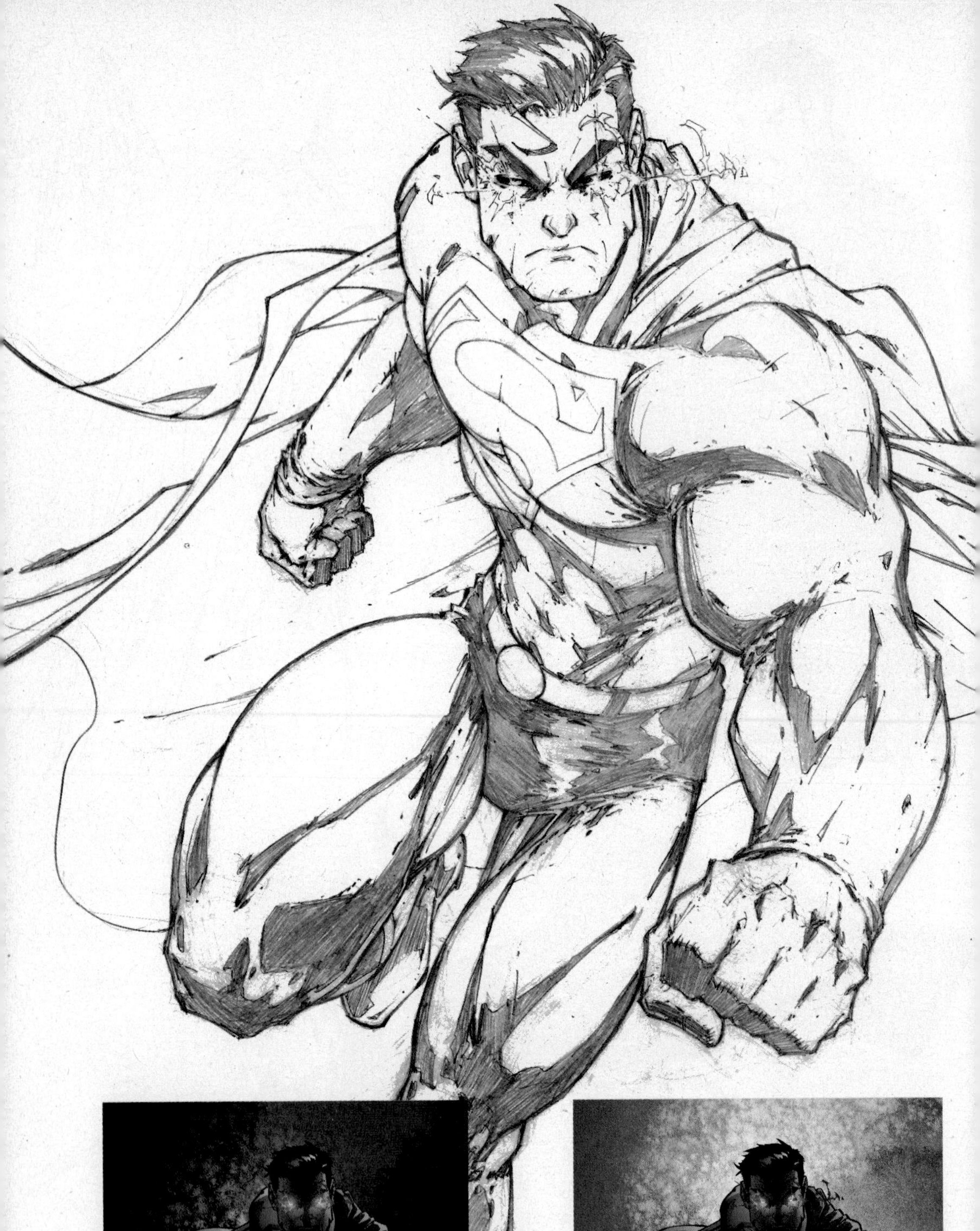

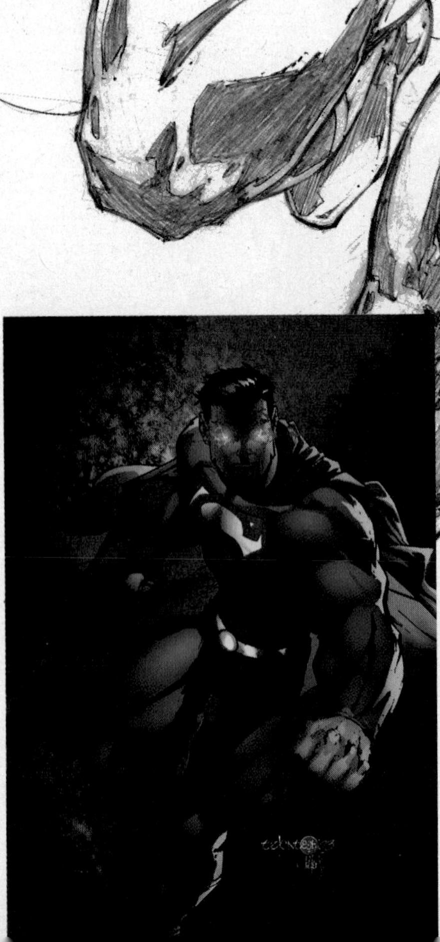

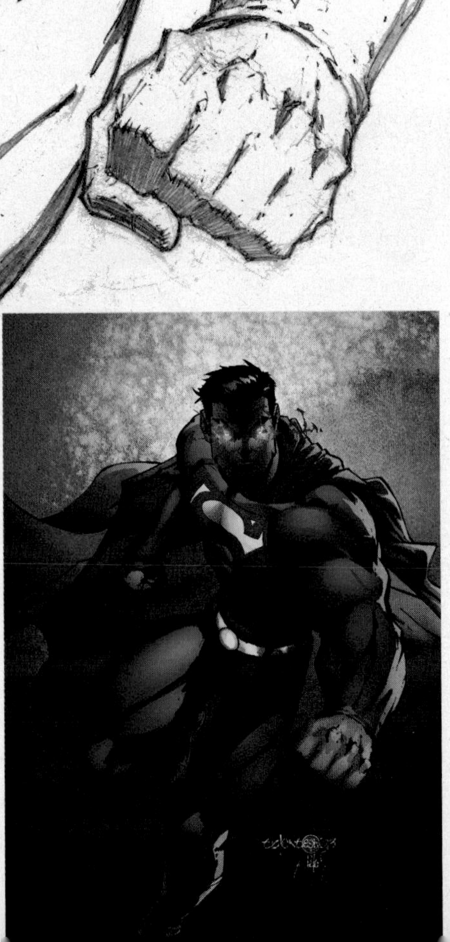

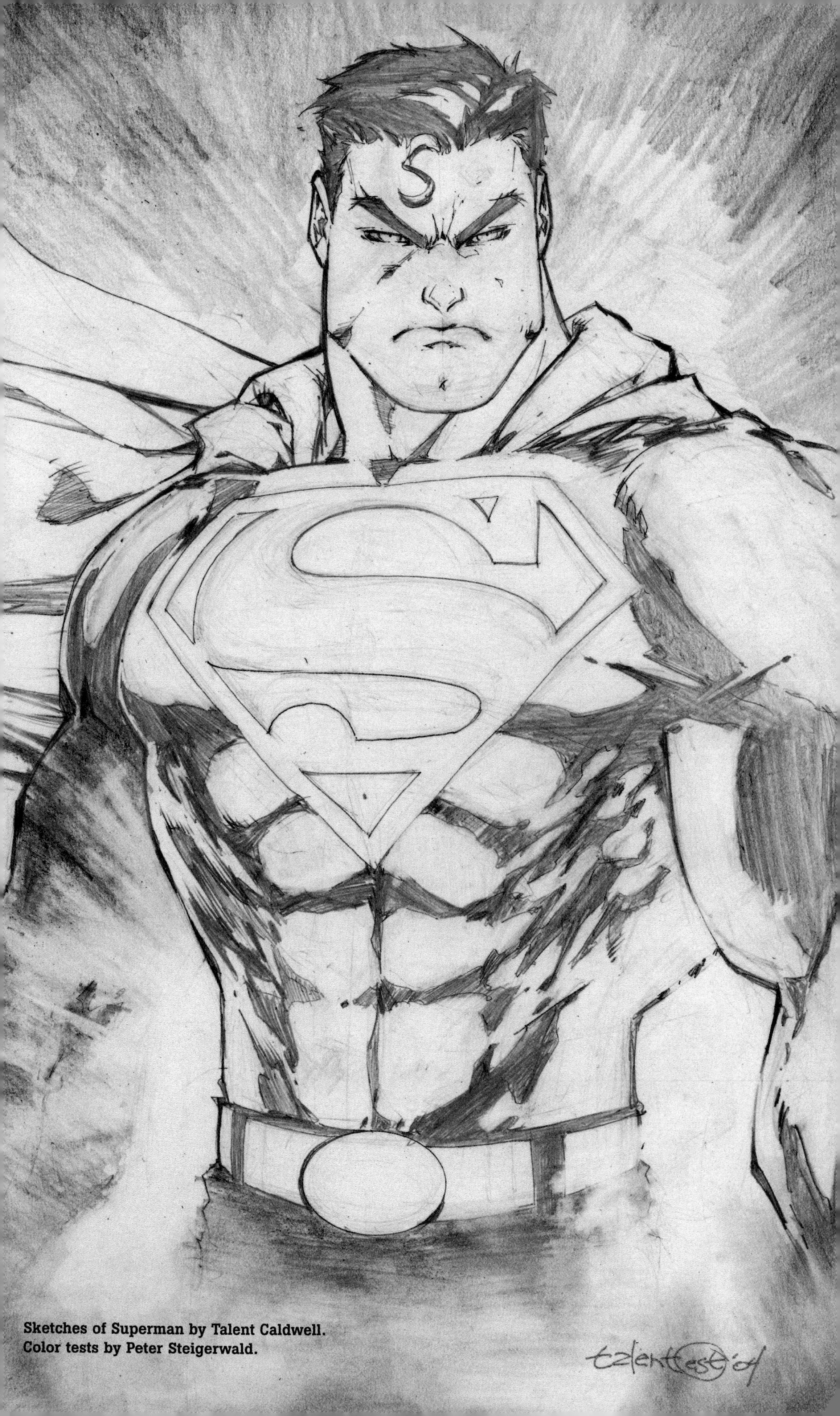

Sketches of Superman by Talent Caldwell.
Color tests by Peter Steigerwald.

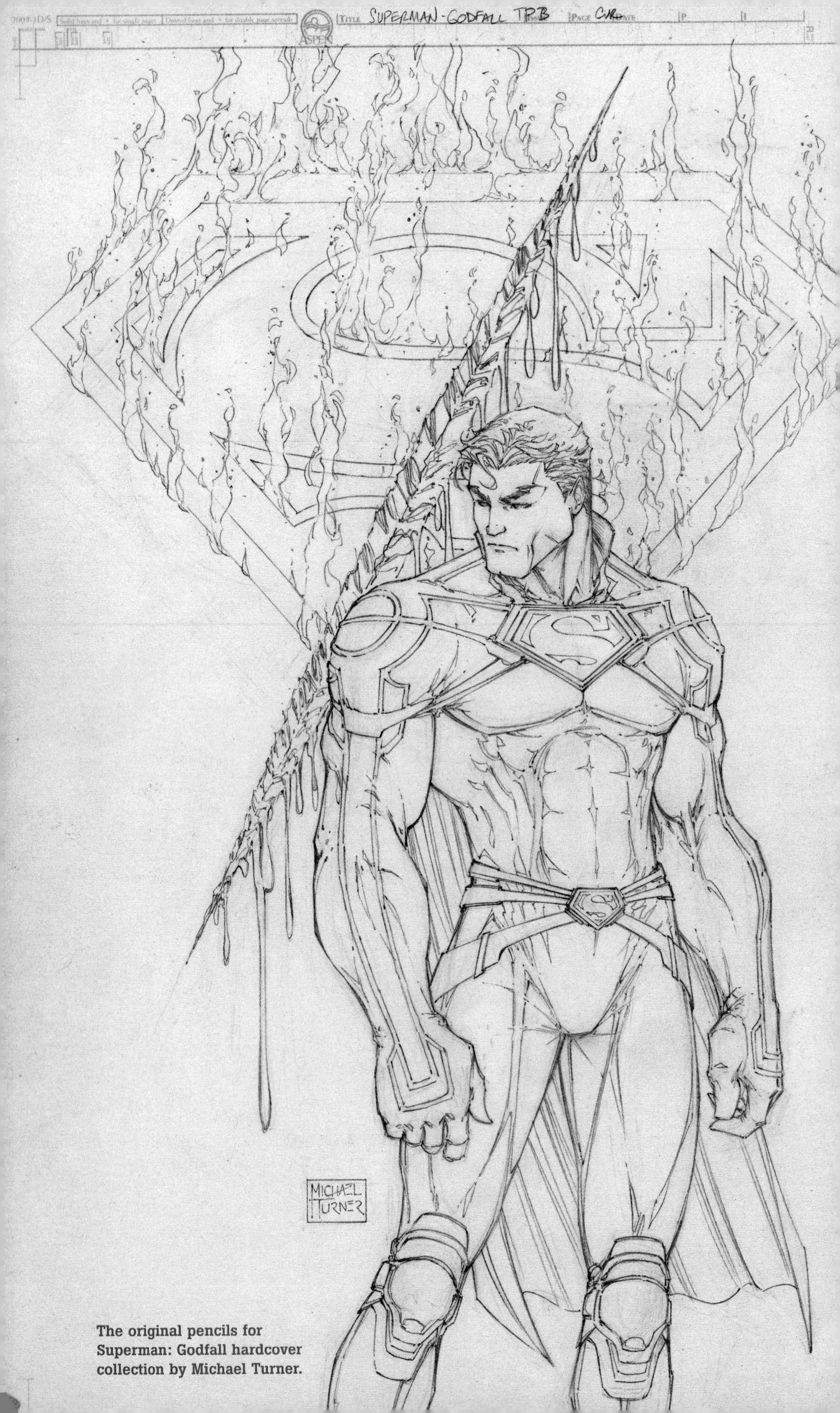
TITLE SUPERMAN-GODFALL TPB
PAGE CVR
MICHAEL TURNER

The original pencils for Superman: Godfall hardcover collection by Michael Turner.

GODFALL BACKLIST

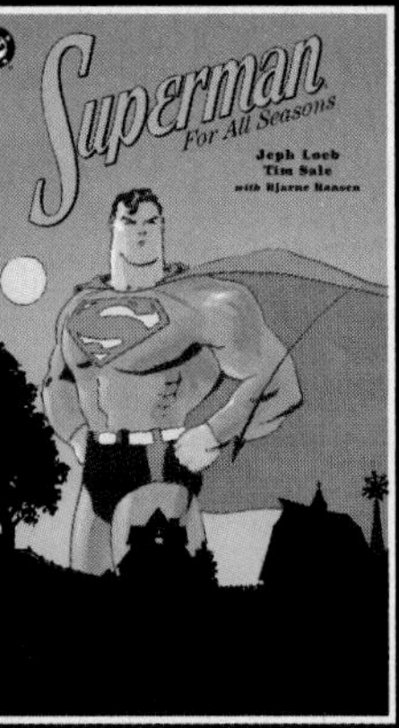
Superman
For All Seasons
Jeph Loeb
Tim Sale
with Bjarne Hansen

SUPERMAN FOR ALL SEASONS
JEPH LOEB/TIM SALE

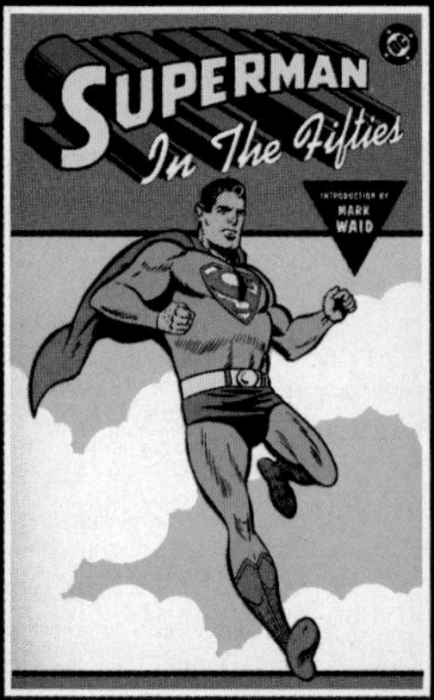
SUPERMAN
In The Fifties
INTRODUCTION BY MARK WAID

SUPERMAN IN THE FIFTIES
VARIOUS

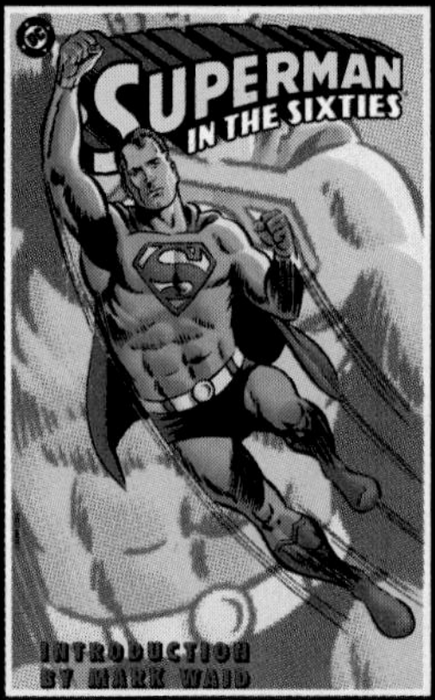
SUPERMAN
IN THE SIXTIES
INTRODUCTION BY MARK WAID

SUPERMAN IN THE SIXTIES
VARIOUS

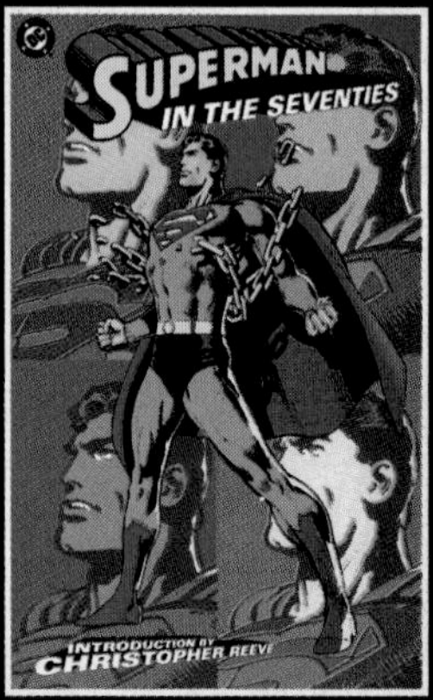
SUPERMAN
IN THE SEVENTIES
INTRODUCTION BY CHRISTOPHER REEVE

SUPERMAN IN THE SEVENTIES
VARIOUS

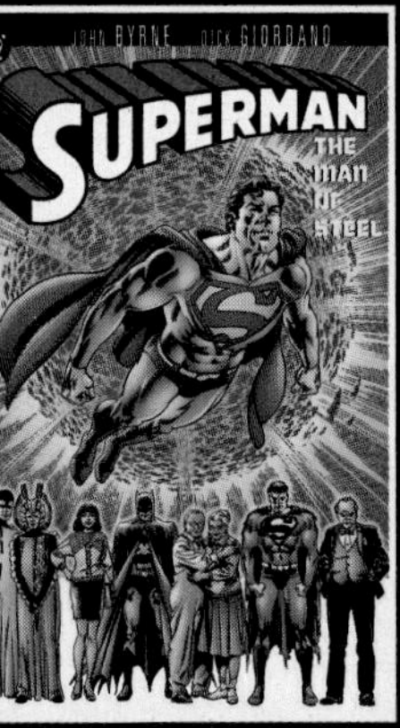
JOHN BYRNE DICK GIORDANO
SUPERMAN
THE MAN OF STEEL

SUPERMAN: MAN OF STEEL
VOLUME 1
JOHN BYRNE/DICK GIORDANO

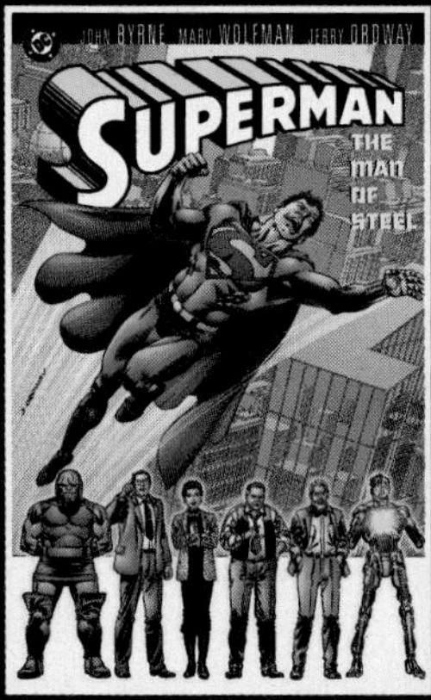
JOHN BYRNE MARV WOLFMAN JERRY ORDWAY
SUPERMAN
THE MAN OF STEEL

SUPERMAN: MAN OF STEEL
VOLUME 2
JOHN BYRNE/MARV WOLFMAN/
JERRY ORDWAY

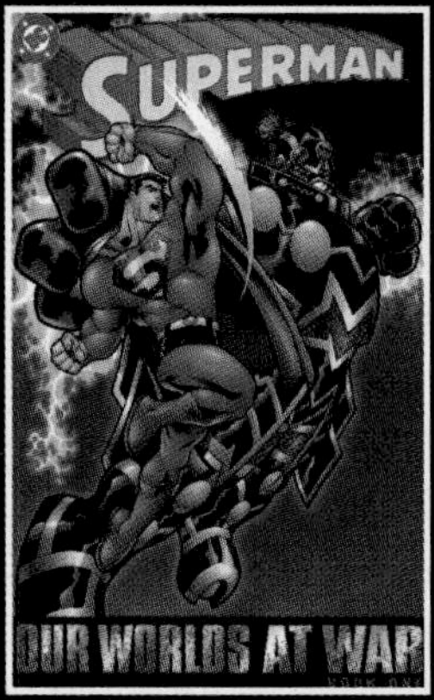
SUPERMAN
OUR WORLDS AT WAR

SUPERMAN: OUR WORLDS AT WAR
VOLUME 1
VARIOUS

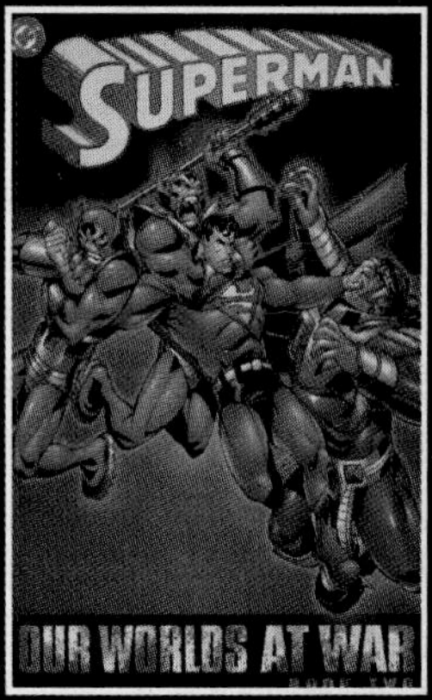
SUPERMAN
OUR WORLDS AT WAR
BOOK TWO

SUPERMAN: OUR WORLDS AT WAR
VOLUME 2
VARIOUS

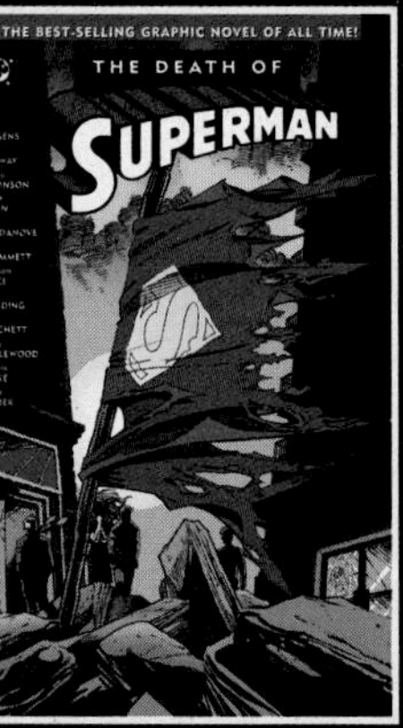
THE BEST-SELLING GRAPHIC NOVEL OF ALL TIME!
THE DEATH OF
SUPERMAN

DEATH OF SUPERMAN
VARIOUS

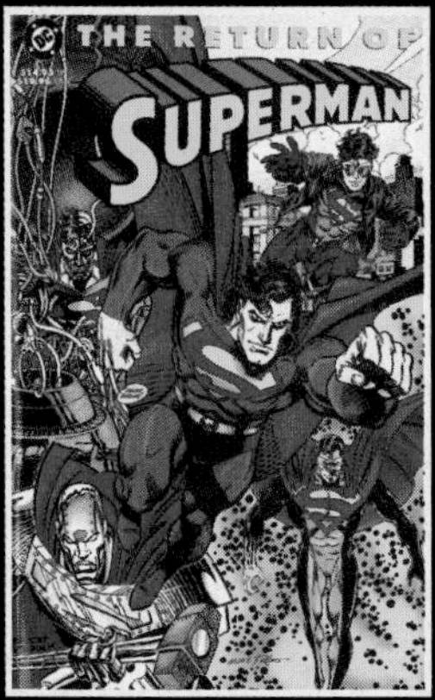
THE RETURN OF
SUPERMAN

RETURN OF SUPERMAN
VARIOUS

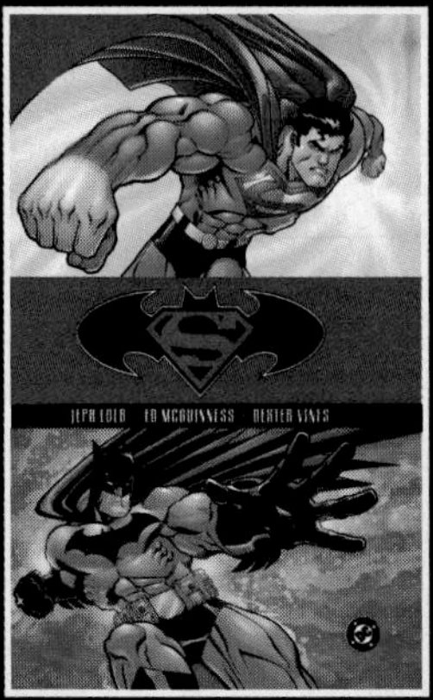
JEPH LOEB ED MCGUINNESS DEXTER VINES

SUPERMAN/BATMAN:
PUBLIC ENEMIES
JEPH LOEB/ED MCGUINNESS

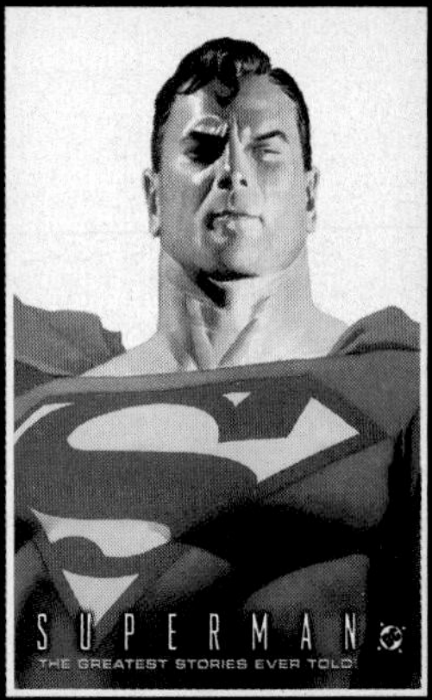
SUPERMAN
THE GREATEST STORIES EVER TOLD!

SUPERMAN: THE GREATEST
STORIES EVER TOLD!
VARIOUS

FOR READERS OF ALL AGES

JUSTICE LEAGUE: LIBERTY & JUSTICE
P. Dini/A. Ross

JUSTICE LEAGUE: SECRET ORIGINS
P. Dini/A. Ross

SUPERMAN: ADVENTURES OF THE MAN OF STEEL
P. Dini/S. McCloud/R. Burchett/B. Blevins

SUPERMAN ADVENTURES: UP, UP AND AWAY
M. Millar/various

SUPERMAN ADVENTURES: Vol. 2 NEVER-ENDING BATTLE
M. Millar/various

SUPERMAN: PEACE ON EARTH
P. Dini/A. Ross

GRAPHIC NOVELS

BIZARRO COMICS
Various writers and artists

IT'S A BIRD...
S. Seagle/T. Kristiansen

SON OF SUPERMAN
H. Chaykin/D. Tischman/
J.H. Williams III/M. Gray

SUPERMAN: END OF THE CENTURY
S. Immonen/J. Marzan Jr.

COLLECTIONS

THE KENTS
J. Ostrander/T. Truman/T. Mandrake/M. Bair

KINGDOM COME
M. Waid/A. Ross

LEGENDS OF THE WORLD'S FINEST
W. Simonson/D. Brereton

SMALLVILLE Vol. 1
Various writers and artists

STEEL: THE FORGING OF A HERO
Various writers and artists

SUPER FRIENDS
Various writers and artists

SUPER FRIENDS: TRUTH, JUSTICE AND PEACE
Various writers and artists

SUPERGIRL
P. David/G. Frank/T. Dodson/
C. Smith/K. Story

SUPERGIRL: MANY HAPPY RETURNS
P. David/E. Benes/various

SUPERMAN & BATMAN: GENERATIONS
J. Byrne

SUPERMAN & BATMAN: GENERATIONS 2
J. Byrne

SUPERMAN & BATMAN: WORLD'S FINEST
D. Gibbons/S. Rude/K. Kesel

SUPERMAN: THE DARK SIDE
J.F. Moore/K. Dwyer/H. Barta

SUPERMAN: THE DEATH OF CLARK KENT
Various writers and artists

SUPERMAN/DOOMSDAY: HUNTER/PREY
Dan Jurgens/Brett Breeding

SUPERMAN: THE DOOMSDAY WARS
Dan Jurgens/Norm Rapmund

SUPERMAN: EXILE
Various writers and artists

SUPERMAN/GEN13
Various writers and artists

SUPERMAN: NO LIMITS!
Various writers and artists

SUPERMAN: PANIC IN THE SKY
Various writers and artists

SUPERMAN: PRESIDENT LEX
Various writers and artists

SUPERMAN: RED SON
M. Millar/D. Johnson/K. Plunkett

SUPERMAN: RETURN TO KRYPTON
Various writers and artists

SUPERMAN: TALES OF THE BIZARRO WORLD
Siegel/Forte/Boring/Swan

SUPERMAN: THE TRIAL OF SUPERMAN
Various writers and artists

SUPERMAN: THEY SAVED LUTHOR'S BRAIN
R. Stern/J. Byrne/B. McLeod/
J. Guice/K. Dwyer/various

SUPERMAN: 'TIL DEATH DO US PART
Various writers and artists

SUPERMAN VS. PREDATOR
D. Michelinie/A. Maleev

SUPERMAN VS. THE REVENGE SQUAD
Various writers and artists

SUPERMAN: THE WEDDING AND BEYOND
Various writers and artists

SUPERMAN: WHATEVER HAPPENED TO THE MAN OF TOMORROW?
A. Moore/C. Swan/G. Pérez/
K. Schaffenberger

SUPERMAN: THE DAILIES
J. Siegel/J. Shuster

SUPERMAN: THE SUNDAY CLASSICS
J. Siegel/J. Shuster

WORLD WITHOUT A SUPERMAN
Various writers and artists

ARCHIVE EDITIONS

SUPERGIRL ARCHIVES Vol. 1
(ACTION COMICS 252-268, SUPERMAN 123)
Siegel/Binder/Mooney/Plastino

SUPERGIRL ARCHIVES Vol. 2
(ACTION COMICS 269-285)

SUPERMAN ARCHIVES Vol. 1
(SUPERMAN 1-4)

SUPERMAN ARCHIVES Vol. 2
(SUPERMAN 5-8)

SUPERMAN ARCHIVES Vol. 3
(SUPERMAN 9-12)

SUPERMAN ARCHIVES Vol. 4
(SUPERMAN 13-16)

SUPERMAN ARCHIVES Vol. 5
(SUPERMAN 17-20)

SUPERMAN ARCHIVES Vol. 6
(SUPERMAN 21-24)
All by Jerry Siegel/Joe Shuster

SUPERMAN: THE ACTION COMICS ARCHIVES Vol. 1
(ACTION COMICS 1, 7-20)

SUPERMAN: THE ACTION COMICS ARCHIVES Vol. 2
(ACTION COMICS 21-36)

SUPERMAN: THE ACTION COMICS ARCHIVES Vol. 3
(ACTION COMICS 37-52)
All by Jerry Siegel/Joe Shuster

SUPERMAN: MAN OF TOMORROW ARCHIVES Vol. 1
(SUPERMAN 122-126,
ACTION COMICS 241-247)

SUPERMAN IN WORLD'S FINEST COMICS ARCHIVES Vol. 1
(WORLD'S FAIR COMICS 1940,
WORLD'S BEST COMICS 1,
WORLD'S FINEST COMICS 2 -15)

WORLD'S FINEST COMICS ARCHIVES Vol. 1
(SUPERMAN 76, WORLD'S FINEST 71-85)

WORLD'S FINEST COMICS ARCHIVES Vol. 2
(WORLD'S FINEST 86-101)
All by B. Finger/E. Hamilton/
C. Swan/various